Conflict of Interests

Cornell Studies in Industrial and Labor Relations Number 29

Conflict

of

Interests

Organized Labor and the Civil Rights Movement in the South, 1954–1968

ALAN DRAPER

ILR Press
Ithaca, New York

Library of Congress Cataloging-in-Publication Data

Draper, Alan.
Conflict of interests: organized labor and the civil rights
movement in the South, 1954–1968 / Alan Draper.
p.   cm.—(Cornell studies in industrial and labor relations
; no. 29)
Includes bibliographical references (p.   ) and index.
ISBN 0-87546-315-0 (cloth: acid-free paper).—ISBN
0-87546-316-9 (pbk.: acid-free paper)
1. Civil rights movements—Southern States—History—20th century.
2. Southern States—Race relations.   3. Afro-Americans—Civil
rights—Southern States.   4. Trade-unions—Southern States—
History—20th century.   5. AFL-CIO.   I. Title.   II. Series.
E185.615.D715   1994
305.8′00975—dc20   93-46081

Copies may be ordered from bookstores or directly from

ILR Press
School of Industrial and Labor Relations
Cornell University
Ithaca, NY 14853-3901

Printed on acid-free paper in the United States of America
5   4   3   2   1

Contents

Acknowledgments

THIS PROJECT BEGAN years ago in the basement of Philip Weightman's home in Washington, D.C. I was then researching my dissertation and had the good fortune to meet Mr. Weightman, who served as the AFL-CIO's Committee on Political Education minorities director in the 1960s. While we examined letters, mementos, and other treasures, Mr. Weightman educated me about labor's role in the civil rights movement. His adventures as labor's emissary to black voter registration groups and his description of the other ways labor promoted black enfranchisement fascinated me. At that time, however, I needed to complete my degree and could not give his reminiscences the undivided attention they deserved. Now, released from the burden of a dissertation, I have returned to the intriguing issues Mr. Weightman introduced me to.

I have traveled widely and received many kindnesses since I left Mr. Weightman's home. I would like to thank the American Philosophical Society, the National Endowment for the Humanities, and St. Lawrence University for the financial support they provided. Their generosity made it possible for me to visit the Alabama State AFL-CIO in Birmingham, Alabama; the Arkansas State AFL-CIO in Little Rock, Arkansas; the Special Collections Department of the Atlanta University Library in Atlanta, Georgia; the Birmingham Public Library in Birmingham, Alabama; the Special Collections Department in Firestone Library at Princeton University, Princeton, New Jersey; the Labor-Management Documentation Center at the New York State School of Industrial and Labor Relations at Cornell University, Ithaca, New York; the Manuscripts Division of the Library of Congress in Washington, D.C.; the Louisiana State AFL-CIO in Baton Rouge, Louisiana; the Special Collections Department of Loyola University Library, New Orleans, Louisiana; the George Meany Memorial Archives in Silver Spring, Maryland; the Southern Historical Collection at the University of North Carolina in Chapel Hill, North Carolina; the Southern Labor Archives at Georgia State University in Atlanta, Georgia; the Special Collections Department of Zenobia Coleman Library at Tougaloo College, Tougaloo, Mississippi; the Special Collections Department at the University of Texas at Arlington Library, Arlington, Texas; and the Robert F. Wagner Labor Archives at New York University in New York City, New York. I thank each depository for permission to cite from collections I used in the course of my research. Robert Dinwiddie, acting director of the Southern Labor Archives, deserves special praise. He was an indispensable and knowledgeable guide to the fine collection on southern labor history at Georgia State. He made my many trips to Atlanta both enjoyable and productive.

The results of my archival research appeared first in scholarly journals. I would like to thank the publishers of *The Historian, Labor History, Labor's Heritage, Labor Studies Journal, Southeastern Political Review,* and the University of Alabama Press for permission to use this material. Previously published chapters have been revised substantially and new material added to them in preparation for this book.

One of the pleasures of studying contemporary history is the chance to interrogate those you are writing about. Luckily, my subjects indulged my visits, responded to my letters, and answered my phone calls. I deeply appreciate the patience and consideration they showed me. During the past few years I called on Bill Becker, Julian Carper, Sibal Taylor Holt, Keir Jorgensen, E. T. Kehrer, James Kilby, Ed King, Tom Knight, Fannie Neal, Carolyn Phillips, Mae Helen Ramsay, David Ramsey, Victor K. Ray, John Salter, Elizabeth Segal, Donald Slaiman, Dennis Smith, Brewster Snow, A. C. Trammell, and Barney Weeks. Emory Via merits special thanks for the thoroughness with which he responded to my questions and for being a wonderful host.

It was a pleasure to meet not only those who made history, but those who practice it professionally. This book offered me the chance to cross disciplinary boundaries from political science to history. Neil R. McMillen and Robert H. Zieger offered the right mix of advice, criticism and encouragement. They bear no responsibility for what follows and I only hope this book meets the high standards their own work has set.

I have also benefited from the generosity of many people at my home institution, St. Lawrence University. Laurie Olmstead in word processing patiently revised and revised and revised yet again. Sheila Murphy, our department secretary, did all the work while I masqueraded as Chair of the Government Department. My colleagues in the Government Department, particularly Fred Exoo, Ansil Ramsay, and Ahmed Samatar, tolerated my sense of humor and my meager attempts at leadership. While colleagues in the Government Department offered a stimulating intellectual environment, the friendship of Professors Richard Guarasci and Robert Schwartz provided a home. Their contributions not only mark this book, but the book of life I write each day.

I also owe a debt to my friends from New York and Wisconsin. Now that I no longer stalk them on the basketball court, I submitted them to an even worse punishment of listening to me talk about my book as it developed. Jeff Burstein, Larry Engelstein, Wally Malakoff, and Don Palmer suffered this cruel torture with grace and charity. I hope someday to return the favor.

My parents, Robert and Clarice, and my brother, Douglas, have become what family members become as one gets older—my closest friends.

My greatest debt is to my wife, Jacqueline, and my children, Sam and Rachel. Without them this book certainly would have been finished sooner, but the process would not have been nearly as exciting or as much fun. This book is dedicated to them, for their smiles and their laughter.

Conflict of Interests

Introduction
Labor and the Civil Rights Movement

> In its grand outlines the politics of the South revolves around the
> Negro. . . . Whatever phase of the southern political process one
> seeks to understand, sooner or later the trail of inquiry leads to
> the Negro.
>
> —V. O. Key, *Southern Politics in State and Nation*

I N THIS BOOK I examine the role organized labor played in the civil
rights movement. I analyze how those responsible for political action
within the labor movement, such as the American Federation of
Labor and Congress of Industrial Organizations (AFL-CIO) and its state
council officials, responded to the struggle for black political equality.
Surprisingly, this intersection of black and labor history has received little
attention from scholars. The seminal work of F. Ray Marshall continues to
tower over the field not only because of its considerable merits but because
the field is so thin.[1] When labor's role is mentioned at all, it is usually
criticized for not doing more to support the struggle for black equality.
Michael Honey contends that blacks gained "civil rights support in the
South not from the unions, but from their own institutions . . . the Southern Conference and the Highlander Folk School."[2] Herbert Hill argues
that the AFL-CIO fumbled a "great opportunity to make a new beginning
in the South" when it failed to work alongside "black or white civil rights
activists who might have provided the idealism, the energy, and the
commitment to the building of an interracial, southern union movement."[3]

Foremost among the AFL-CIO's sins of omission, according to its
critics, was its failure to endorse the 1963 March on Washington for Jobs
and Freedom. Critics perceived labor's absence from the march as a sign of
the AFL-CIO's indifference to the struggle for black equality. Countless
civic organizations sent money, organized bus trips, and recruited pro-

testers for the march, but the AFL-CIO was not among them. The AFL-CIO
then added insult to injury when it closed its headquarters in Washington
on the day of the march, making its facilities unavailable to tired and
thirsty protesters. The AFL-CIO Executive Council explained its absence
somewhat defensively, contending that it supported the march's aims but
demurred from the tactic of public protest to achieve them.[4]

While critics dismiss the AFL-CIO's objection as mere pretense, an
excuse for labor's conservatism or, worse, its racism, there is evidence that
labor's qualms were genuine. George Meany, along with others who
sympathized with the march's objectives, honestly feared the march would
go awry and set back civil rights legislation then pending in Congress.
Years later, when Jervis Anderson was preparing his biography of A. Philip
Randolph, who directed the march, he asked Meany to explain the AFL-
CIO's demurral. Meany reiterated in his interview with Anderson the
same objection to the march that he first articulated in 1963. Meany told
Randolph's biographer: "The civil rights legislation had not yet been
enacted, and while we did not object to any of our affiliates participating,
we were worried that the march might touch off a situation which might
set us back legislatively. I was fearful that there would be disorder, that
people would get hurt, and that it would build up resentment in Congress."[5] Nor was Meany the only one to harbor such fears at the time.
Questions raised by the AFL-CIO about the wisdom and appropriateness
of the march as a tactic were aired within the civil rights community itself.
Civil rights leaders, including National Association for the Advancement
of Colored People (NAACP) president Roy Wilkins and Urban League
executive director Whitney Young, Jr., expressed the same doubts that
Meany did.[6]

Not only was Meany concerned that the march would hurt legislative
progress in Congress, but he was reluctant to associate labor with tactics
that might damage the image of middle-class respectability he sought for it.
More than most labor officials, Meany wanted to prove that labor was a
responsible, worthy contributor to American society. For instance, Meany
tried to demonstrate the gentility of the organization he led by once
bragging to a reporter that he "never went on a strike in my life, never ran a
strike, never ordered anyone else to go on strike, and never had anything to
do with a picket line."[7] This desire for respectability led Meany to disavow
such political tactics as street demonstrations that might associate labor
with such crude and vulgar activities. Consequently, under his leadership,
the AFL-CIO did not endorse the 1963 March on Washington or any other
public protest. Meany expressed the same skepticism regarding demonstra-

tions in 1968, when the AFL-CIO failed to endorse the Southern Christian Leadership Conference's (SCLC) Poor People's Campaign, as he had in 1963.[8] Meany's blanket refusal ever to see a tactical advantage in street protests reveals much about the insecure, obsequious personality of the American labor movement during his tenure.

The point is not to apologize for or defend the AFL-CIO's failure of nerve in this regard but to explain its sources. These are grounded far more in Meany's attempt to demonstrate labor's responsibility by separating itself from the march and its potential for violence than in any divergence of aims between the AFL-CIO and the march's sponsors. A. Philip Randolph portrayed differences between the AFL-CIO and the march in just this light. In December 1963, Randolph told a radio interviewer: "I think Mr. Meany conscientiously thought that to bring hundreds of thousands of people to Washington we were certain to have trouble; he honestly felt that way about it. And this was, I believe, the basic reason for his opposition to the AFL-CIO going on record in support of the March."[9] Perhaps Randolph could afford to be magnanimous toward Meany in the glow of the march's success. Still, this is a far cry from the view of such critics as Philip Foner, who charged that the AFL-CIO "condemned" the march.[10] This is simply a canard.

Even if the accusation of critics is unfounded, a conflict over tactics should not be dismissed as irrelevant. Disagreement about the march revealed differences between labor and the civil rights movement over the pace of racial change. It also exposed an even more revealing fundamental difference. Labor was never able to appreciate the moral energy that animated the civil rights movement. Although allied politically with the civil rights movement, labor never grasped its essence as a social movement. In this respect, the march revealed much about labor itself. The civil rights movement resembled labor's own past as a social movement that could engender sacrifice and solidarity and express a moral vision. But now this was only a dim memory that labor could not or would not recall. Rather than recognize a sense of militancy and idealism in the march, labor perceived it as a threat to its own search for respectability. It regarded the march more as a hindrance that would disturb its lobbying efforts in Congress than as an event that could build the community necessary to sustain a social movement.

Moreover, the labor movement's economism, its privileging of workplace over other issues, left labor unprepared to respond to the challenges the civil rights movement posed. The problem with economism was not that its vision precluded an argument for civil rights. As we shall see, some of labor's most active and courageous supporters of civil rights for blacks were from the most reactionary AFL-CIO unions, those most dedicated to economism. Economism, as well as communism, was elastic enough to accommodate a variety of racial practices.[11] The problem with economism was that it systematically undermined the relevance of black civil rights to unions. The privileging of workplace issues under economism tended to diminish the issue of black citizenship and relegate it to a nether world of platitudinous insignificance. Consequently, when labor educators presented arguments for integration, their reasons were as likely to be dismissed by members as irrelevant as they were to be rejected as racial heresy.

Labor's relationship to the civil rights movement is a tale of two movements that shared political goals but had different priorities, timetables, and cultures. It is also a story of stunning hypocrisy. At its first meeting in 1956, the AFL-CIO Committee on Civil Rights sanctimoniously threatened to stop cooperating with the National Conference of Christians and Jews unless it desegregated its local chapters.[12] The committee must have had a perverse view of its jurisdiction because it took no action against AFL-CIO–affiliated unions that engaged in the same discriminatory practices it found so offensive in others. Some affiliated unions still barred blacks from membership, maintained segregated locals, and tolerated separate seniority lists. It is also a tale of willful ignorance. In 1963, AFL-CIO secretary-treasurer William Schnitzler asked Paul Christopher, AFL-CIO Region VIII director, for a list of positive achievements in the area of civil rights in his district. After providing some examples, Christopher could not resist concluding his letter to Schnitzler with a needle: "You did not ask for a report on those organizations and firms where we still have a long way to go."[13]

But it is also a chronicle of political courage. Many union members in the South disagreed with AFL-CIO racial policy. Like other southerners, they believed in Jim Crow and supported segregated schools. Many were Klansmen or Citizens' Council members, and they voted for Alabama governor George Wallace and other politicians who promised to defend segregation. The civil rights movement was so unpopular with the white southern rank and file that it could jeopardize the careers of those who supported it. Moreover, membership in southern unions was voluntary because every state in the South, with the exception of Louisiana, had a right-to-work law. Thus local unions could be hurt by resignations over civil rights policy which they considered tangential to their collective bargaining objectives. Despite these costs, labor made significant contributions to the struggle for black equality which have not received the attention they deserve. Rather, scholars have belittled and dismissed the assistance labor provided. Not only does this view deny the substantial contributions labor made to the struggle for civil rights, but it fails to appreciate the price labor paid for its support.

This book is about labor's relationship to the civil rights movement, not its civil rights record. I will not review union efforts, such as they were, to remove racial bars to membership, to open up apprenticeship programs to blacks, to eliminate separate seniority lists, and to permit blacks to bid for jobs from which they had been excluded. These issues have received extensive treatment elsewhere, and there is no reason to duplicate those efforts here.[14] I recognize that the distinction between labor unions' efforts to eliminate their own discriminatory practices and those of society at large is somewhat artificial. Credibility in one arena depended on performance in the other. Regardless of their interdependence, it is important to distinguish between these two tracks. Civil rights groups certainly did. The NAACP vigorously criticized discriminatory practices within unions at the same time it cooperated with the AFL-CIO in the Leadership Conference on Civil Rights, in black voter registration drives, and in lobbying Congress for civil rights bills.[15] More radical civil rights groups, such as the Congress of Racial Equality (CORE) and the Student Non-violent Coordinating Committee (SNCC), were also not above cooperating with labor politically despite its lack of clean credentials.[16]

The burden of responding to the civil rights movement within labor did not fall on either the affiliated unions or AFL-CIO headquarters in Washington. For the most part, affiliated unions intoned ritual support for civil rights but tried to avoid controversy over an issue they viewed as peripheral to collective bargaining. Some AFL-CIO–affiliated unions, however, did respond more enthusiastically to the civil rights movement than others, but a full account of their response is left to future researchers.

Another story that should be pursued is the response of southern black trade unionists who are surprisingly and ironically absent from the present account. Perhaps black unionists did not perceive their unions as a legitimate or relevant conduit for their civil rights demands. The civil rights activity of black union members might have been drawn off and expressed by organizations other than their unions. It is also possible that black local union leaders provided little leadership on this issue because, like their white counterparts, they considered civil rights peripheral to their workplace mission. Finally, these officials may also have feared that a militant civil rights position could provide ambitious opponents with an alternative base from which to challenge their power.

The focus throughout this book is on AFL-CIO state councils in the South and their response to the civil rights movement. Because of their location in the South, these state councils were vulnerable to the first and most severe aftershocks to civil rights. Members and local union affiliates in the South pressured their state councils to define labor's position on segregation and on the measures state legislatures and southern politicians took to defend it. Southern state councils had to respond when legislatures in their states proposed measures to circumvent the Supreme Court's *Brown v. Board of Education* decision, they had to contend with local politicians who ran on pledges of defiance, and they had to counter racist appeals that threatened to undermine relations with their own members. They had more at stake in the struggle for black equality than any other part of the labor movement. Consequently, their response to the dilemmas and opportunities an emergent civil rights movement posed to them is the major theme of this book.

I have devoted more attention to some areas of the South than others because civil rights activity was uneven across the region. Most attention is focused on Arkansas and Virginia, where the strategy of massive resistance to desegregation first developed, and on the Deep South states of Alabama and Mississippi, where civil rights encountered its most unyielding and violent response. Organized labor in these states was drawn reluctantly but inexorably into the storm that erupted over civil rights for blacks there.

The South and American Politics

The South has been the subject of a rich and massive social science literature. Nevertheless, the many books, monographs, and articles about the South have had little impact on our views of American politics. Scholars have celebrated the United States as a liberal nation but have done so only by deliberately ignoring the South's illiberalism.[17] The South's defense of slavery and then its denial of civil and voting rights to blacks mocked liberal principles of equal and inalienable rights. The South, as Ira Katznelson argues, was an illiberal society within a liberal nation.[18]

If America's fealty to liberalism made it exceptional among nations, then the South was the exception within the exception, the enigma within the enigma. Foreigners, it appears, are more willing than Americans to acknowledge the South's illiberalism and not dismiss it as a mere inconvenience. Rather than place the United States first among those nations that achieved universal suffrage, Swedish sociologist Goran Therborn placed it among the laggards because of the legal disenfranchisement of blacks in the South until 1965.[19]

As southerners are quick to point out, the South is the only part of the United States ever to suffer the indignity of defeat in war and occupation by an invading army. The South's slave mode of production and late commercial development, its narrow electorate and one-party politics, its culture of white supremacy and religious fundamentalism set the region apart. Despite a recent conformance to national practices, the South remains apart: more conservative, more religious, and less wealthy than the rest of the country.[20]

The South is not an aberration that can be dismissed. Quite the contrary, America's destiny has been shaped by its most atypical region. The South's impact on American politics has been out of proportion to its economic power or demographic size. The South is the tail that has wagged the dog of American politics.[21] The South held the Democratic party hostage to civil rights planks that did not threaten white supremacy, it dominated Congress through the committee chairs its representatives held, and its congressmen formed a powerful conservative coalition with Republicans that stunted the growth of the American welfare state.[22] Although the South's grip on the Democratic party and Congress has waned recently, it still remains a potent force that displays more political unity than any other region.

THE NEW SOUTHERN LABOR HISTORY

Much as the South and its concerns have driven American politics, so the South has been driven by its preoccupation with race. "In its grand outlines," V. O. Key writes, "the politics of the South revolves around the Negro. . . . Whatever phase of the southern political process one seeks to understand, sooner or later the trail of inquiry leads to the Negro."[23] Just as American political scientists have described the United States as if the South did not exist, so have some labor historians been guilty of describing the South as if the race issue were not paramount. These historians are exponents of what one of them describes grandiloquently as the "new southern labor history."[24] They concede that the racial culture of the South was a powerful deterrent to organizing but not nearly so powerful that it could not be overcome by a racially principled, committed, vision- ary labor leadership. According to the new southern labor history, the failure of unions to organize in the South rests not on the low-wage, competitive, small-firm structure of southern industry so convincingly presented by F. Ray Marshall, or on the political, religious, racial, and ideological resources available to anti-union employers that Barbara Griffith describes in telling detail.[25] Rather, the responsibility for failure rests with the unions themselves. When these historians turn their attention to the 1930s and 1940s, they see missed opportunities for interracial unionism, equivocation—or worse—capitulation to white racism, organizing strategies that played to labor's weakness among whites instead of its strength among blacks, and a purge of Communists that deprived unions of their bravest, most committed activists. Michael Honey, a practitioner of the new southern labor history, writes: "Had the CIO used a different approach, one which helped to advance the cause of black civil rights as well as unionization, it might have produced a significantly different result. At the very least it would have left an inspiring memory."[26]

Organizing the South was difficult, dangerous work. Marshall and Griffith recount the obstacles unions encountered there, yet the obstacles to interracial unionism were still greater. The examples provided by the new southern labor history show that interracial unionism was possible only under certain demographic and workplace conditions. First, interracial unionism had a chance of success only in industries or firms in which blacks constituted at least half the work force. George Mitchell, who worked with the CIO in the South during the 1930s, noted the demographic conditions that contributed to interracial unionism. "It is plain from the Birmingham experience," Mitchell wrote, "that the pressure which induces White workers to join with the Negroes is economic competition. Mixed or joint unionism has been used almost exclusively in occupations where the two races do similar work and where the Negroes are actually or potentially a large part of the work force. . . . Whatever of interracial good will is generated in the movement does not spread rapidly or with sufficient force to bring White working people who can organize effectively without the Negroes to include in their unions small Negro minorities."[27] A second, more unusual condition that contributed to interracial unionism existed where blacks played a critical role in the production process. The pace of production in slaughterhouses, for instance, was controlled by blacks who worked on the killing floor.[28] Whites were more likely to ally with blacks under these two conditions because they could serve their workplace interests in no other manner. Where blacks were a minority of the work force or were peripheral to the production process, however, southern whites preferred Jim Crow locals, and the intervention of the international union was usually required to override this majority, local union preference.

Given the limiting conditions under which interracial organizing succeeded, the new southern labor historians have built their case on mar-
ginal unions. Consequently, the lessons these historians derive from their
examples are not relevant either to the AFL, which enjoyed a far greater
membership in the South than the CIO, or to unorganized production
workers in predominantly white firms and industries. Thus the historical
significance of their examples is dwarfed by the size of the organized and
unorganized work force to which they do not apply.

The new southern labor history also criticizes the unions for employing
a mistaken strategy that played to its weakness among southern whites
instead of its strength among southern blacks. Although it is true that
blacks were far more receptive to union appeals than whites, it was
imprudent for organizers to build a base of support among blacks first in
plants where they were a minority. The racial culture they encountered
forced organizers in these firms to display white activists at the head of an
organizing drive in order to attract white support. Such was the case of an
organizing drive at Firestone in Memphis recounted by Michael Honey. In
1939 the Rubber Workers recruited blacks to lead the campaign at Firestone because they responded more eagerly than whites to union appeals.
But this organizing drive failed when whites refused to support it because
they feared the racial consequences of unionism promoted by black
leaders. Two years later and much wiser, the Rubber Workers returned to
Firestone and succeeded because they recruited whites to lead the organizing campaign. Blacks were no less enthusiastic about the union, but the
presence of whites at the head of the new organizing drive did much to
allay the racial fears of previously skeptical whites.[29] The new southern
labor history condemns unions for playing to their weaker hand among
whites, yet unions found doing so unavoidable at Firestone and at other
plants with predominantly white work forces in the South.

A related criticism leveled by the new southern labor history is that
labor made a strategic mistake when it failed to "confront the black
question fully."[30] But this did not prove nearly as fatal as these historians
suggest.[31] Equivocation did not save labor organizations from being condemned as "nigger unions" by whites, but it did not cost them black
support either. Blacks were fervent unionists because of the workplace
benefits they hoped to derive from unions, not because they valued the
rhetorical, pious claims unions made against discrimination. Bruce Nelson
noted that black workers on the Mobile and New Orleans docks supported
the Marine and Shipbuilding Workers of America despite its practice of
racial separatism because they believed the union could improve their

working conditions. When Nelson turns his attention to the struggle for
the loyalty of black longshoremen in the South, he acknowledges, "insofar
as the ILWU [International Longshoremen's and Warehousemen's Union]
represented an attractive alternative to the ILA [International Longshoremen's Association] in New Orleans it was less because they had formed an
interracial union than because they promised an aggressive battle to
improve working conditions on the waterfront."[32]

Even unions that went beyond piety to demonstrate a real commitment
to racial equality, such as the United Packinghouse Workers of America
(UPWA), attracted black workers primarily on a workplace, not a racial,
basis. This is clear from John Hope Franklin's 1950 survey of the UPWA,
which revealed that a disappointing number of southern black UPWA
members did not know that the union opposed discrimination and could
not identify the union's antidiscrimination policies or accurately interpret
them.[33] Even Michael Honey admits that "despite the limits of interracial
organizing in the southern CIO, in the 1930s many blacks accepted these
limits in order to get organized and to gain benefits and allies."[34] If this is
true, then CIO organizers made an astute decision to take black support for
granted and equivocate on race in order to attract whites.

An example of a local that confronted the black question fully is Food and
Tobacco Local 22 in Winston-Salem. Communist party militants played a
prominent role in this local, which, in addition to fulfilling its workplace
responsibilities, also mobilized the local black community politically and
publicly criticized Jim Crow. But the local had a fatal weakness that can be
traced to its identification with black demands. Blacks made up little more
than half the 10,300 member work force at Reynolds Tobacco Company.
Black workers supported the union completely, but only 50 to 150 of the
5,000 whites employed at Reynolds ever joined Local 22. When the local
called a strike in 1947, whites did not hesitate to cross the picket line. New
southern labor historians attribute the local's defeat to anticommunism, but
its principled position on racial matters was probably more costly. Its refusal
to compromise on race meant that the local would reflect the racial divide
within the work force at Reynolds rather than overcome it.[35] In any event,
the demise of Local 22 provides little support for the idea that labor failed to
organize the South because it was not liberal enough on race.

Finally, the greatest weakness of the new southern labor history is its
failure to appreciate the paralyzing dilemma that confronted organizers
and labor leaders who recognized the costs of segregation but were constrained by a membership and region that were determined to defend it.[36]
The new southern labor history may dismiss this constraint, but union

leaders ignored it at their peril. By their failure to appreciate the depth of and commitment to white supremacy, the new southern labor historians ultimately blame the victim.

Although they may be blinded by romanticism, the new southern labor historians do appreciate the pivotal role of the South in American political development.[37] The South's influence in Congress and the Democratic party permitted it to act as a brake on the New Deal and on reform efforts that followed. Southern Democracy, with its one-party system, its restricted electorate, its preoccupation with race, and its issueless campaigns combined to produce a conservative politics that extended into national political life. The greatest threat to this "politics of disorganization," as V. O. Key described it, came from the labor movement. Key believed, as do the new southern labor historians, that labor would act as the vanguard in the realignment of southern politics.[38] But when labor failed to organize the South in the 1930s and 1940s, hopes for an end to the rotten borough system of the South ended as well. With labor's defeat, the politics of the South did not turn, and neither did the politics of the country.

Perhaps this interpretation is overdrawn, the syllogism too neat. It certainly underestimates the ability of unions to accommodate themselves to southern Democracy. But it does indicate what is at stake in the issues these historians raise.

The AFL-CIO was keenly aware of the South's place in national politics. Labor leaders recalled that southern Democratic congressmen defected from their party in 1947 to pass the Taft-Hartley Act and in 1959 they voted with Republicans to pass Landrum-Griffin. In addition, the power of the South to impede reform within the Democratic party and its contribution to the conservative coalition in Congress were sources of bitterness and frustration to them. But they were most troubled by the South's role within the larger organization of American politics. Labor leaders had always envied the British party system and wished American politics could be restructured on that model with ideologically polarized, class-based, disciplined political parties. The American party system did not approach this model, they believed, because of the South. AFL-CIO leaders felt the South belonged in the Republican party and that the region prevented the Democratic party from realizing its true identity as similar to the British Labour party. The South's presence in the Democratic party made American political parties ideologically incoherent, irresponsible, and irrational.[39]

This was the context in which those responsible for political action within unions came to appreciate the civil rights movement. They expected the civil rights movement to resolve the southern political problem for labor. Blacks would do the political work that southern workers the unions had failed to organize in the 1930s and 1940s should have done. Black enfranchisement would initiate the realignment of southern politics that labor leaders desired. Conservative, upper-class whites would defect to invigorate the southern Republican party, while blacks joined with working-class whites to liberalize the Democratic party. The South would become a competitive, two-party region and no longer succumb to one-party rule; political campaigns would raise issues and no longer descend into demagoguery; political organization would be based on class and no longer depend on transitory, personalized factions; and politics would revolve around economic issues and no longer be absorbed by race. With a southern wing that reflected rather than opposed Democratic policies, the American party system would begin to resemble the party system in Britain. Black enfranchisement would "nationalize" the South at the same time that it "rationalized" national politics. Samuel Lubell observed in 1956 that "the crucial factor which will determine how quickly or slowly a two-party system develops is the changing status of the Negro, who has always been the basis of the one-party South."[40] This fact escaped no one in the labor movement who was dismayed by the South, and it decisively shaped labor's response to an emergent civil rights movement.

OUTLINE OF THE BOOK

Although this book may not be last word on labor and the civil rights movement, I am confident that in many ways it is the first. In 1969 Numan V. Bartley forecast that the response of southern institutions, such as unions, to the civil rights movement would "likely provide academicians with the subject matter for a great many books."[41] A generation later, Bartley's prediction remains unfulfilled with regard to organized labor's record. Perhaps labor's response to the civil rights movement has not received the attention Bartley anticipated because historians have been diverted by the conflict over job discrimination that arose between Roy Wilkins of the NAACP and George Meany of the AFL-CIO. Yet it is surprising that this conflict should so absorb historians because it never deflected Wilkins and Meany from what each considered the more important task at hand: black enfranchisement in the South. Whatever objections Wilkins had to discriminatory practices by unions and whatever resentment Meany felt about blacks' criticisms of it, these did not jeopardize the political goals they held in common.

What worried Meany more than the bad publicity his dispute with the NAACP generated was the conflict that escalated over civil rights in his own organization. This included not only pressure from black members who defended NAACP charges of discrimination by unions but also criticism from southern white unionists who opposed AFL-CIO support for black political equality. This latter conflict was particularly troubling because it jeopardized the vitality of southern unions and threatened the partisan realignment in the South that black enfranchisement was supposed to augur.

But the seriousness with which AFL-CIO and state council officials viewed the threat of a renegade South was not accompanied by an equally serious analysis of their members' antagonism to civil rights. Labor leaders believed that conservative anti-labor groups cynically used race as a ruse, a subterfuge, to undermine their authority and the loyalty of southern members to their union. These officials dismissed the rank and file's response to civil rights as irrational or credulous because their organizational responsibilities sensitized them to the political benefits and opportunities the civil rights movement offered labor. Their organizational position, their responsibility for political action, permitted them to appreciate how the civil rights movement could undermine southern Democracy, create the basis for a responsible party system on the British model, threaten anti-labor legislators who were otherwise beyond labor's reach, and promote liberal policies labor favored.

But other members of the southern labor movement who did not have political responsibilities and did not share the unique organizational perspective of state council or AFL-CIO officials saw the civil rights movement through a quite different lens. The civil rights movement, in their eyes, did not offer deliverance from an oppressive political system that undercut labor's political influence regionally and nationally. Rather, civil rights threatened the class privileges southern whites enjoyed at work and the caste privileges they enjoyed outside of it. There was nothing delusory or insignificant to white workers about the benefits they enjoyed over blacks in the Jim Crow South: better jobs, higher wages, better schools for their children, more government services for their neighborhoods, more social respect, more political rights, and an assumption of justice that was denied blacks. Consequently, white union members in the South had a very different view of how the civil rights movement would affect their interests than that held by the unions' political leaders. These competing visions of the interests of white workers, one articulated by union political leaders, the other by its rank and file, one desperate to create a class-based party system that included blacks, the other determined to preserve a caste-based party system that excluded them, created an explosive tension within the southern labor movement. How this tension was expressed and resolved is the story of this book.

The first chapter examines labor's response to the *Brown* decision and the rift it created between union leaders and their members in the South. Union members, like other southerners, opposed school desegregation, and union leaders had to take this into account when they framed their response to *Brown*. The first chapter presents a panoramic view of the South. The second focuses on the response of the labor movement in Arkansas and Virginia, where the most school closings to prevent desegregation occurred. The third chapter describes the Sisyphean efforts of labor educators to convince southern members to support AFL-CIO civil rights policy. Educational programs were needed to repair the rift *Brown* created between southern members and the AFL-CIO and to ensure that members did not fall prey to the conservative arguments of segregationists. This chapter also examines labor's efforts to desegregate its own events and facilities in the South. Conference resolutions did not signify to delegates where labor stood on civil rights as much as conference arrangements did. The fourth chapter begins my examination of labor's strategy to undermine southern Democracy by encouraging black enfranchisement. It analyzes labor's attempt to realign the party system in Texas and Arkansas by forging coalitions with minorities. Chapter 5 describes how the Alabama AFL-CIO opposed Governor George Wallace and competed with him for the hearts and minds of its members. The final chapter covers the career of Mississippi AFL-CIO president Claude Ramsay, who worked tirelessly for black equality, the national Democratic party, and labor unions in a state that reviled all three.

The story recounted here is not a pretty one. The rank and file included its share of racists, and the leaders—except for those with political responsibilities—equivocated on civil rights for blacks. But this book should put to rest myths that labor was indifferent to the struggle for black equality when, in fact, that issue formed the cornerstone of its political strategy. It should also confirm the central place of race in our politics and reveal the organizational pressures that framed union responses to it. At the same time that the civil rights movement created new, exciting political possibilities for labor in the form of partisan realignment, it also posed a threat to labor's organizational maintenance objectives by creating conflict between the leadership and its rank and file in the South. This book reveals how labor managed both the risks and the rewards that the civil rights movement posed to it.

1

Labor and the Brown Decision

We are not attempting to tell them that we want the schools
segregated, integrated, or any other 'grated.' We just want schools
for our children to attend.

— Victor Bussie, Louisiana AFL-CIO president

T HE LONG MARCH THROUGH the courts was finally over. On May 17,
1954, Chief Justice Earl Warren of the Supreme Court read its
unanimous opinion in the case of *Brown v. Board of Education*. His
delivery was as punctual, spare, and direct as the opinion he wrote. He told
the assembled spectators and reporters that the Court had asked itself in
Brown if racial segregation in public schools deprived children of equal
opportunity. The chief justice looked up from his text to indicate the
gravity of the question and then gave the Court's response: "We believe
that it does." His final remarks left no doubt where the Court stood. "We
conclude that in the field of public education the doctrine of 'separate but
equal' has no place. Separate educational facilities are inherently unequal.
Therefore we hold that the plaintiffs . . . have been . . . deprived of the
equal protection of the laws guaranteed by the Fourteenth Amendment."[1]

The *Brown* decision tore down the pernicious doctrine of separate but
equal that had deprived blacks of economic opportunities, relegated them
to inferior schools, and institutionalized the ideology of black inferiority. It
reopened a chapter of American history that ended shamefully when
whites in the South simply replaced the bonds of slavery with the chains of
penury and disfranchisement to deprive blacks of the fruits of emancipa-
tion.[2] The Court's verdict on *Brown* was decisive because its implications
went beyond mere school segregation to outlaw all forms of state-sponsored
segregation: in beaches, buses, parks, hospitals, and wherever else legally

mandated segregation occurred. *Brown* was a more massive assault that was armed with a more powerful weapon, the authority of the Supreme Court, than any previous challenge to Jim Crow. The second Reconstruction had begun.

The demands for civil rights that *Brown* encouraged led to organized resistance by whites to defend the threatened color line. Jim Crow had never been so threatened as it was by *Brown*, and the South responded with a militant defense of its racial order. Citizens' Councils and other white supremacist groups emerged to defend the color line and take back whatever slack existed in it. A new reign of terror designed to intimidate blacks and remind them of their subordination swept through the South after *Brown*. Blacks who advocated desegregation were evicted by landlords, denied credit by merchants, fired by employers, and physically assaulted. NAACP chapters in the South were hounded relentlessly, and eleven thousand blacks were purged from the voting lists in Louisiana alone.[3]

New demands for racial conformity applied as much to whites as they did to blacks. As segregationist sentiment hardened, white dissenters were ostracized and intimidated. Institutions that countenanced integration were threatened. In 1955, for example, the Packinghouse Workers union planned to hold an integrated conference at the Walahuge Hotel in Atlanta but had to find an alternate site when the hotel canceled because it feared economic reprisals.[4] Any violation of segregation would now be met with stern measures, with no room for compromise or ambiguity. Roy V. Harris, president of the Citizens' Councils of America, threw down the gauntlet before an audience in Florida: "If you're a white man, then it's time to stand up with us, or black your face and get on the other side."[5]

The response of such southern institutions as schools, churches, and governments to this period of intense racial scrutiny and challenge has been well chronicled.[6] Yet, surprisingly, the response of organized labor in the South to the challenge of black equality has been overlooked.[7] The demands massive resistance and the civil rights movement placed on organized labor and the unions' response to those challenges have received little attention. This omission is noteworthy because of the light this history can shed on the troubled relationship between unions and blacks.

Union reactions to *Brown* are also significant because they reveal the organizational pressures an emergent civil rights movement posed to union leaders. The AFL-CIO and some southern union leaders welcomed *Brown* as a harbinger of changes that eventually would topple southern Democracy and the South's conservatism.[8] But local union officers, business agents, and state council officials were constrained in their support of black equality by their accountability to a rank and file that did not share their views. Union leaders feared that support for black civil rights would cost them votes the next time they ran for office. They feared not only that support for *Brown* would jeopardize their careers but that it would threaten their unions as well. Membership in southern unions was voluntary because of the presence of right-to-work laws in every state but Louisiana. Union leaders feared that if they supported *Brown*, members might resign in protest, which would hurt the union financially and undermine workplace solidarity. Aware that their members had strong and contrary opinions on the issue, union leaders wondered whether it was prudent to weaken their union over a matter that leaders themselves considered tangential. Union leaders, especially those in the South, had to balance their opposition to massive resistance with concerns about their political future and organizational maintenance objectives. They had to weigh opposing massive resistance against the political and organizational costs this would incur. Until historians perceive union leaders responding to an organizational context and take southern racism as seriously as union leaders had to in the wake of *Brown*, the response of labor to the civil rights movement, or even its failure to organize the South, will remain shrouded in myth.

UNIONS AND THE CITIZENS' COUNCILS

Both the AFL and CIO applauded *Brown* when they were separate organizations and reaffirmed their support when they agreed to merge. The AFL-CIO unity convention in December 1955 proclaimed that labor "wholeheartedly supports the decisions of the Supreme Court in outlawing segregation in the public schools." Thurgood Marshall, who successfully litigated *Brown* before the Supreme Court, spoke at the convention to request labor's help in the difficult task of bringing the South into compliance. Marshall told the union delegates: "If we are to be successful in this task we will need more than ever before the support of organizations such as those here represented who are in a position to transform resolutions into action programs at the local level."[9]

On February 9, 1956, the newly created AFL-CIO Committee on Civil Rights convened for the first time. H. L. Mitchell, president of the National Agricultural Workers Union, warned the committee that the growth of Citizens' Councils in the South posed a clear and present danger to the labor movement.[10] Mitchell charged that Citizens' Councils leaders were often business people who participated in anti-labor organizations, intervened in organizing campaigns to prevent interracial unionism, and intimidated union officials who supported integration. Mitchell told the Committee on Civil Rights that the Citizens' Councils were "ostensibly aimed at 'keeping the Negro in his place' through use of economic boycotts and intimidation. On the basis of our recent investigation we are convinced that it is also directed at the trade union movement. . . . Unless a program initiated by the AFL-CIO and the national and International Unions is developed to expose the White Citizens Councils, future organizing campaigns planned by AFL-CIO may as well be stopped at the Mason-Dixon line." Mitchell's report led the AFL-CIO Executive Council to issue a blistering attack on the Citizens' Councils.[11] Meany delivered the AFL-CIO statement in which he condemned the Citizens' Councils as a "new Ku Klux Klan without hoods," compared them to the Nazis, and described them as "anti-union and anti-democratic."[12]

Meany's remarks were reported widely throughout the South. Newspaper headlines, often accompanied by editorials, excoriated the AFL-CIO for its statement on the Citizens' Councils and attacked AFL-CIO leaders as "champions of integration and enemies of the Southern way of life."[13] The coverage Meany's statement received brought AFL-CIO headquarters a deluge of mail from angry southern members. Letters ranged from those who felt Meany and the AFL-CIO Executive Council did not understand the South to those who were outraged by its condemnation.[14] Jack Gager, trustee of Papermakers Local 203 in Moss Point, Mississippi, patiently tried to explain to Meany how damaging it was for the AFL-CIO to support integration in the South. He warned:

> People now are beginning to believe, that our aim is desegregation and we are faced with the problem of trying to convince them better but it is trying one. How are we to convince people who are born in the tradition such as we have here that we are not advocating, Integration, when the leaders of our great organization make [such] statements . . . to the press? . . . President Walter Reuther's of U.A.W. [sic] says turn out the hate mongers, well if we were to turn out all the people down here who want segregation we would not have enough of us left to carry on our union's business much less help others to organize. . . . Again, I would like to point out that while I can agree with the men who make the policy of our great organization there are a greater number of people who do not. . . . I believe that we have a big enough job of organizing down here as it is without having to fight a segregation battle too."[15]

Other letters were not so reasoned and sympathetic. A. B. Blackwelder, Sr., of Columbia, South Carolina, wrote: "You seem to forget where you are in your tirade against the people of the South. . . . If outside trouble makers and adgitators [sic] had not come in and stirred up ill feelings there would not have been all this ado among our people. . . . You are wrong when you say the citizen's councils are working against labor unions. . . . Your organization is in a good way to lose the support of some of our people down here if you continue your present attitude." The writer then echoed a view held by other former AFL members in the South when he held the recent merger responsible for the Executive Council's statement. "We never had any sympathy with many of the CIO policies and it looks like the old AFL is now adopting some of their plans," Blackwelder told Meany.[16] Local 654 of the Papermakers in Rome, Georgia, urged the AFL-CIO Executive Council to direct its ire at groups that were truly subversive, such as the NAACP, instead of the Ku Klux Klan (KKK).[17] Another local union, Machinists Lodge 271 in Birmingham, Alabama, advised Meany that outsiders "who know little or nothing about the real situation" should not interfere but instead let southern unionists solve their own problems.[18] After declaring emphatically that "we are for segregated schools," Iron City Lodge 60 of the Brotherhood of Railway Carmen from Birmingham, asked rhetorically, "Do you realize how many thousands of the Hoodless Ku Klux are members of the affiliate labor organizations of the AFL-CIO?" It then warned that if the AFL-CIO planned to purge itself of Citizens' Council members it had better make haste because "the White Citizens' Councils may purge themselves of the AFL-CIO."[19]

Meany responded to each letter and reiterated that the Citizens' Councils were a Trojan horse designed to undermine the labor movement. They were dominated by anti-union employers who hid behind race hate to camouflage their real aim of weakening labor unions. But he also tried to take the bite out of the *Brown* decision. Meany reminded his correspondents that the Supreme Court had given the South time to adjust to desegregation and had turned enforcement over to local courts. Finally, Meany wrapped himself in the flag and urged union members to obey the law as good citizens.[20]

But events in Chattanooga, Tennessee, before the merger should have warned the AFL-CIO to expect a sharper response than simply angry letters. In July 1955, the Chattanooga school board announced that it intended to comply with the *Brown* decision. The AFL Chattanooga central labor council was the only civic organization in the city to commend the school board for its decision. But the central labor council's resolution elicited an outcry from local unions, which protested that it did not reflect their sentiments and charged the council with "supporting organizations and sociological theories . . . dedicated to removing the last vestiges of our southern heritage." Typographers Local 89, Electrical Workers Local 311, and locals from the Carpenters and Printing Pressmen unions passed resolutions that denounced the central labor council and pledged their support for segregated schools.[21] A special meeting of the labor council to consider rescinding its resolution attracted the largest turnout of delegates in twenty years. The council leadership defended its position as "moderate" and "middle-of-the-road," but local union delegates were unappeased and unimpressed. Pressure to retract the resolution was so intense and overwhelming that the council finally capitulated. It explained in defeat that "because of the highly controversial nature of the issues raised by the Supreme Court's decision on segregation in the public schools, issues which cut across our ranks, tending to divide us, it is hereby declared to be the policy of the Chattanooga central labor union henceforth to refrain from involving itself on either side of the issue. We urge all AFL unions likewise to refrain, leaving the matter to the individual."[22] This surrender note, however, failed to placate local unions, which now sought to punish the central labor council and remind it who was master. Two local unions disaffiliated formally and others did not bother to give notice but simply stopped forwarding their per capita dues.

The volume of mail the AFL-CIO received in response to the Executive Council's statement on the Citizens' Councils and the depth of feeling the letters expressed did not go unnoticed.[23] In July 1956, the AFL-CIO Committee on Civil Rights reported with characteristic understatement that the "tone of the correspondence indicated that many people in the South were still subject to considerable tension from the Supreme Court decision on school integration." It recommended that the AFL-CIO take a lower profile on the issue and refrain from public declarations of its views. Such pronouncements only seemed to inflame emotions, create division, and undermine the authority of the AFL-CIO and the loyalty of southern members to their unions. In light of the antagonism and resentment that AFL-CIO public statements created, the Committee on Civil Rights recommended a tactical retreat. It suggested that the AFL-CIO discreetly remove itself from the controversy and work through its affiliated unions, its field representatives, and groups outside of labor to track and monitor the activities of the Citizens' Councils within unions.[24]

It was clear from early reports that the Citizens' Councils made their greatest inroads among union members in Alabama. Part of the reason for their early success was the threat civil rights challenges posed to the color line in Alabama. The Montgomery bus boycott, petitions from local

NAACP chapters to desegregate the schools, and riots over Autherine J. Lucy's attempt to break the color line at the University of Alabama had created an electric atmosphere throughout the state. In addition, the success the Citizens' Councils enjoyed among organized workers in Alabama can be traced to the composition of the state's unionized work force. Industrial unions constituted a larger proportion of the membership in Alabama than elsewhere in the South. Members of these unions held views on *Brown* more at variance with the publicly stated position of their internationals than any other part of the unionized work force. Consequently, members from industrial unions felt more betrayed, bitter, and resentful over what they perceived as improper meddling by their unions in local affairs. For instance, union members at Continental Can Company in Fairfield warned Meany: "If you continue to favor integration . . . we will band together with other locals in the South and fight for what we believe to be our rights." Members of the United Steel Workers of America (USWA) at the Tennessee Coal and Iron division of U.S. Steel in Birmingham threatened that "if we have to choose between staying in the union or see our segregated way of life being destroyed we will pull out and form our own union."[25] According to one Citizens' Council's estimate, three-quarters of all council members in the Birmingham area held union cards. In one very active chapter on the city's west side, 90 percent of the council members were union members.[26]

In addition to joining the Citizens' Councils, union members in Alabama voted their preference for white supremacy. A 1955 "private school" amendment to the state constitution that was intended to circumvent *Brown* carried every labor district except Gadsden, according to AFL-CIO Committee on Political Education (COPE) area director Daniel Powell. Two years later, in 1957, Eugene "Bull" Connor used openly racist appeals to achieve insurmountable pluralities from white working-class districts when he defeated the incumbent commissioner of public safety in Birmingham. Trade unionists also voted with their feet.[27] Union members from nearby steel, paper, and rubber plants stormed the University of Alabama campus to defend the color line when Autherine J. Lucy tried to matriculate. The *New York Times* reported from Tuscaloosa that Meany's and Walter Reuther's statements in support of Lucy's effort to register at the university "set organized labor back twenty years in this area." One local labor leader told the *Times,* "These men believe in segregation and they believe that the Northern leaders who have never been in the South have no right to intervene."[28] Following the Lucy incident, more union members in Tuscaloosa attended a meeting of the West Alabama White

Citizens' Council than showed up for a COPE dinner that was scheduled for the same night. Samuel M. Englehart, Jr., who led the Citizens' Councils in Alabama, recalled that "the labor boys played a big part in the segregation fight. The business people would give lip service, but the labor people would get out and work."[29]

In March 1956, Mitchell reported from Alabama to Boris Shiskin, director of the AFL-CIO Civil Rights Department, "There is substantial disaffection among nearly all of the trade unions both here in Birmingham and in Montgomery and it is being exploited to the fullest extent by the leaders of the White Citizens Council movement." A follow-up letter five days later was more detailed and pessimistic: "Organizers attached to the AFL-CIO and the national and international unions told me 'off the record' that they have never seen the membership of the local unions so stirred over any issue as they have been by the racial crisis in the South. The union members eagerly follow the Dixiecrat demagogues . . . and have joined the White Citizens Councils by the thousands." Mitchell reported that in Fairfield, Tarrant City, and Bessemer, steelworkers "are the base of organization for the White Citizen Councils." The situation in Montgomery was even worse than in Birmingham, Mitchell disclosed. The bus drivers union in Montgomery would accept a settlement of the bus boycott only on the previous terms of rigid segregation. The bus boycott so outraged a Communications Workers of America (CWA) local in the city that it passed a resolution stating that blacks "should be *forced* to ride the buses" and then for good measure voted to recommend that the CWA disaffiliate from the AFL-CIO. A staff representative from the CWA visited the local following its vote and was physically removed from the union hall when he tried to explain labor's civil rights policy. An Oil, Chemical and Atomic Workers (OCAW) local of twelve hundred members in Montgomery added to the spirit of rebellion in the capital city when it too voted to break away from the AFL-CIO. Mitchell finished his report from Alabama by noting that he had heard talk about an independent union movement organized on segregated lines. He warned that if such an alternative arose it would be attractive to many white members.[30]

Mitchell's fears were realized when an independent union emerged at the Hayes Aircraft plant in Birmingham. The plant had over thirty-two hundred workers and was organized by the United Auto Workers (UAW). Recent friction with the international had resulted in so many resignations from the local that only a bare majority of the plant's workers still paid their union dues. Elmer Brock, a Citizens' Councils organizer and member of the Painters union, knew of the local's vulnerability and began a membership drive to enlist disgruntled workers into a competing union, Southern Aircraft Workers, Inc. On May 27, 1956, the secessionist group elected its officers and prepared to contest the UAW for bargaining rights at the plant.[31] A UAW official recalled the rebel movement at Hayes years later in an interview with Stanley Greenberg:

> When they really started integrating the schools, we began to have some trouble. At the Hayes International local, some members wanted to picket the schools, and wanted me to come out against integration. They wanted me to picket the schools. They put up pickets around Ramsey and Phillips High. I told them, "I'm not going down," and they told me that "we are going to take care of you around election time." I was reelected, but it had its toll. I didn't win by much and there were a lot of hard feelings among the membership. The Ku Klux Klan was active in the membership, and when I served on the biracial committee, the Ku Kluxers were ready to tear the council down.[32]

Brock then attempted to raid Local 589 of the Iron Workers, which represented five hundred workers at Butler Manufacturing in Birmingham. Rebels there formed a competing union called Southern Fabricating and Steel Workers, Inc.[33]

Efforts were planned to broaden the dual union movement beyond Birmingham. Brock issued a "Manifesto of Southern Labor" that charged AFL-CIO leaders with "aiding and abetting the complete integration" of whites and blacks over "the objections of both." A rally to "defend the cherished ideals of our Southland" at the Birmingham Municipal Auditorium gave birth to the Southern Federation of Labor (SFL).[34] The SFL was only one of several independent unions that were formed to preserve segregation. The Southern States Conference of Union People in Tennessee was organized as an alternative to the "race mixing in unions and elsewhere" advocated by the AFL-CIO; the United Southern Employees Association was active among textile workers in the Piedmont; and Southern Crafts, Inc., sought to organize railroad workers.[35]

But the dual union movement died in infancy. The rally in Birmingham attracted only five hundred enthusiasts. Other independent unions dedicated to segregation ignored the rally and failed to affiliate with the Southern Federation of Labor. In addition, two weeks before the inaugural convention of the SFL, Brock was defeated at Butler. The Iron Workers retained bargaining rights to their plant by a two-to-one margin after a speedy campaign and election by the National Labor Relations Board (NLRB). The election at Butler was intended to give the new SFL a psychological boost but instead became its epitaph. The defeat at Butler dampened the spirit of the rebels at Hayes Aircraft, and no representation election was ever held there.[36]

The dual union movement faced enormous obstacles. First, rebel groups that seceded forfeited access to a local union's assets and property because these were often held in the name of the international union. Second, secession jeopardized economic gains southern workers had won and threatened a return to the North-South wage differential. Third, rebel unions faced the daunting task of winning representation rights over the opposition of both employers and entrenched unions.[37] Fourth, dual unionism required southern union members to be consistent in their ideological commitments, to show ideological constraint, and to reject ambiguity. But as Bartley suggests, "by relying upon the Councils to protect their caste position and the unions for their class position," southern unionists could reconcile their support for segregation with their union membership.[38] By applying their values selectively, union members in the South could avoid the anguish of having to choose between loyalty to their race and loyalty to their union that militant segregationists tried to impose on them. Finally, southern unionists felt a great deal of loyalty to their local unions and were thus willing to absolve them from sins committed elsewhere in the labor movement. Local unions in the South often reflected the defiance of their communities, which dimmed the enthusiasm of members to disrupt or challenge them.

Though the dual union movement failed miserably, it cannot be dismissed. The Iron Workers at Butler did not attempt to defend AFL-CIO racial policy when they were challenged but fought fire with fire. When Brock accused the AFL-CIO of donating money to the NAACP, an Iron Workers representative denied the charge and assured his members that "so far as I know there is no breach of the Segregationist principles of the South occurring anywhere in organized labor."[39] Clearly, the sentiments that gave rise to the secessionist movement wounded unions and placed them on the defensive. One observer noted that the "dissipation of energies over the race issue and fear of it" had brought the labor movement in the South "to a point of near immobility." Contributions to AFL-CIO COPE for political work dried up, relations between local unions and their internationals were embittered, and resignations left local unions weaker and more vulnerable.[40]

The eye of the storm was in Alabama, but the entire South felt its effects. Through the summer and fall of 1956 the AFL-CIO kept a low profile as the Committee on Civil Rights had recommended. Paralyzed by the strength of the front that was passing through its ranks, the AFL-CIO nervously tracked its progress and the damage it left in its wake. The AFL-CIO retreated from public battle and increasingly relied on intelligence reports from its affiliates on the enemy's approach. For instance, Meany requested that the Textile Workers Union of America (TWUA) survey its southern locals to gauge their reaction to a resolution passed at the union's 1956 convention that denounced the Citizens' Councils and supported the desegregation of public schools. The TWUA reported that local union leaders retreated when members confronted them about the resolution. Local union officials assured their members that they had voted against the resolution at the TWUA convention and explained that members were free to disregard it.[41] In one textile mill, the entire membership from one section of the plant, including stewards and the local union president, stopped paying dues in protest over the convention resolution.[42]

THE JEWISH LABOR COMMITTEE SURVEY

In addition to its affiliates such as TWUA, the AFL-CIO also relied on help from outside organizations. One group that was active in the race relations field was the Fund for the Republic. The trade union consultant for the fund, Benjamin Segal, had an abiding interest in civil rights and was active in desegregating public facilities in Washington, D.C. Segal was also familiar with the special problems race posed to unions in the South from his work there in the 1940s for TWUA. Thus Segal moved swiftly to involve the fund in an area where the "need was greatest and the least was being done": the impact of racial conflict on trade unions in the South.[43] For instance, it was Segal who recruited H. L. Mitchell and commissioned his report on the Citizens' Councils that later became the basis for the AFL-CIO's condemnation of them.[44]

The fund also paid for George S. Mitchell, executive director of the Southern Regional Council (SRC), to lead workshops on civil rights at union education meetings.[45] But in October 1956, Mitchell told Segal that he could no longer carry the torch. The need for labor education on civil rights was so great that his attempt to satisfy it prevented him from fulfilling his other responsibilities at SRC. He recommended that Emory Via, executive secretary of the Atlanta Labor Education Association, replace him.[46] With the approval of the AFL and CIO education directors, Via was hired as labor consultant to the SRC for a nine-month trial period.[47] The fund agreed to finance Via's salary, with SRC responsible for his overhead and travel expenses. When his trial period expired, Via's employment was extended with his salary and expenses now financed by

Segal's Trade Union Program on Civil Liberties and Rights, which was supported by the fund and union contributions.[48]

Via's first task at SRC was to participate in a study directed by the Jewish Labor Committee (JLC).[49] Emanuel Muravchik, national field director of the JLC, had obtained a grant from the Fund for the Republic to survey the impact of AFL-CIO support of civil rights on southern local unions.[50] Researchers were to query local union officials and international representatives in the South about whether the racial issue had been raised within their local unions, the context in which it appeared, whether it affected local union activity, and the attitudes of their members on segregation. Morton P. Elder of the SRC was to serve as field coordinator.

Via's jurisdiction was Georgia, and his reports were not encouraging. One of the locals Via surveyed was UAW Local 34, which represented General Motors workers in Atlanta. This local had a history of conflict with its international over race that dated back to when it was first chartered. "When the Atlanta GM plant was organized," a UAW official told Lloyd Bailer, "the white workers not only refused to admit Negroes into the union but attempted to secure their discharge. A compromise was effected wherein they were left in possession of their jobs but banned from the union." Only later was the UAW able to force the local to accept blacks as members.[51] The *Brown* decision brought the local's racist past back to the surface. UAW Local 34 first gained notoriety in April 1956, when Representative James C. Davis of Atlanta told the U.S. House of Representatives that twelve hundred autoworkers in his district had signed a petition protesting UAW contributions to the NAACP.[52] The local drew the attention of UAW officials in Detroit when they received reports that UAW and AFL-CIO racial policy was condemned freely at union meetings with the encouragement of the local leadership. Via found that as the authority of the UAW and AFL-CIO collapsed inside the local, respect for the Ku Klux Klan and Citizens' Councils replaced it.[53] Approximately fourteen hundred members of UAW Local 34 joined the Georgia KKK following *Brown*, as did fifteen hundred members of UAW Local 887 and twenty-five hundred members of UAW Local 874, which were also located in Atlanta.[54] But only Local 34 could boast that it included Eldon Edwards, the Grand Dragon of the KKK in Georgia, as one of its members. Elder's note that "every white supremacist movement has been firmly supported by its active rank and file" confirmed Via's evaluation that UAW Local 34 would not deviate from its racist past in its response to *Brown*.[55]

When Via tried to investigate CWA Local 3204 in Atlanta, union officials initially were unwilling to cooperate. The international union leadership was so wary of the issue that it had instructed its staff not to speak with anyone about racial matters inside the union. Local union officials first obtained top-level clearance from the CWA and then spoke with Via only because they felt he could be trusted.[56] The suspicion and caution that Via encountered—to the point of official censorship in the CWA—was experienced by other JLC researchers. Elder found that wherever he went he encountered "the deadly serious demand for anonymity." Union officials were so much thrown on the defensive by the views of their members that Elder described his informants as "looking over their shoulders" and telling him "they would flatly deny being interviewed if identified."[57]

In Tennessee, conflict over AFL-CIO racial policy disrupted a special CIO state council convention called to consider merger with its AFL counterpart. Debate over AFL-CIO civil rights policy was so acrimonious that CIO state council president Leonard Evans ruled discussion of the issue out of order and required delegates to confine their remarks to the prospective merger.[58] In Nashville, local union leaders from the TWUA and Machinists told Elder that their members flocked to the Tennessee Society to Maintain Segregation led by A. A. Canada, a member of the Printing Pressmen.[59] This was true also of Steelworkers locals in Chattanooga who experienced disturbances of a more serious nature. When blacks attempted to speak at union meetings, whites demanded that they sit down. To the dismay of the union, which was allied with Estes Kefauver's wing of the statewide Democratic party, whites took out their frustrations by voting the States' Rights ticket while blacks retaliated by voting Republican.[60]

In Memphis, UAW Local 988, which represented eight hundred white and six hundred black workers at an International Harvester plant, was in turmoil over the desegregation issue. The local union leadership maintained segregated drinking fountains and toilets in its union hall and publicly criticized the AFL-CIO's condemnation of the Citizens' Councils. Over 80 percent of all whites in the local and half the local's officers belonged to the Citizens' Councils.[61] The local's vice-president served as labor chair for the Democrats for States' Rights, a Citizens' Councils front, and the local contributed $100 to a Citizens' Council rally in Memphis.

An indication of the lengths to which this local would go to defend white supremacy occurred when a white delegate died shortly before the 1955 UAW convention. The local union executive board then reduced the number of delegates it would send to the convention from three to two, to

prevent a black alternate from replacing him. The black appealed successfully to the international to have his credentials restored only to have
the local bring charges against him for poor performance as chair of the by-
laws committee. This sparked a protest from over one hundred black union
members who disrupted his hearing, claiming the local's judicial panel was
prejudicial. Order was not restored until police arrived and arrested two
demonstrators for disorderly conduct.[62] Racial tension within the local
reached such a point that the international in Detroit sent in a trouble-
shooter, Vice-President Herschel Davis, to conciliate and bring the local
into compliance with union policy. When Davis spoke at a local union
meeting he was heckled and drowned out by shouts of "Go on back
North."[63] According to Davis, the local was "no longer holding meetings
for union business" but instead was meeting "to fight integration."[64] Turmoil at International Harvester spilled over into a Firestone plant organized by the Rubber Workers. Elder was utterly defeated by what he saw in
Memphis. He wrote, "Whatever the answer, Memphis seems in dire and
hasty need of it."[65]

The situation in the Carolinas was as discouraging as it was in Tennessee.[66] The textile industry was a major employer in these states and
adhered to a whites-only employment policy. Consequently, many members in the textile centers were firm segregationists. The only unionists
more outspoken in defense of segregation than the textile workers were
from the building trades. In Columbia, South Carolina, a Carpenters local
rented its union hall to the Ku Klux Klan for its meetings and had a Klan
charter hanging in its local union office. In every southern state, including
the Carolinas, building trades unions were the vanguard of segregationist
sentiment within the labor movement and were staunch Citizens' Councils advocates.[67]

In Mississippi, the birthplace of the Citizens' Councils, union organizing
temporarily came to a standstill as a result of AFL-CIO statements in
support of integration. Union leaders were no longer invited to civic
functions, and efforts to qualify their members to vote were resisted. According to Elder, AFL-CIO support for integration had cost unions in Mississippi
"at least ten years of progress." Unions returned to their former status as
pariahs in the Magnolia State as a result of the mounting racial unrest.[68]

The unrest *Brown* created within unions reached as far west as Texas.
Civil rights dominated the 1957 merger convention of the Texas AFL and
CIO state councils. The day before the convention was to consider a civil
rights measure, the resolutions committee hearing on the proposal lasted
more than five hours. A representative from OCAW Local 4-228 in Port

Neches warned that if the convention told "the members they got to go for integration of the schools—they'll break away from you!" Another OCAW delegate argued that "the courts should decide on school integration" and recommended that the convention "keep down discussion by soft-pedaling it in our organization." These appeals were countered by Joe Patton from the National Maritime Union, who argued that "if we believe in something dammit let's stand up . . . for it." Patton accused OCAW Local 4-23 of discrimination when it prevented members from its black counterpart, OCAW Local 4-254, from participating in the dedication of a new union hall. The hearing ended appropriately when committee members returned from their recess for dinner only to find that their minutes book had been stolen.[69]

Debate on a civil rights resolution at the convention was just as acrimonious as that in the committee. Even though the resolution simply reiterated the statement on *Brown* articulated at the 1955 AFL-CIO merger convention, opponents tried to postpone consideration of the measure to the next convention. The resolution finally passed, but its sponsors were so placed on the defensive by the debate that they felt it necessary to remind delegates that "nowhere in this report do we mandate any local union or any local member to abide by it."[70]

But nowhere were reports as bleak as those from Alabama. Four of the seven members of the Montgomery County Citizens' Council executive board carried union cards.[71] As a result of the Montgomery bus boycott, Street Railway Local 765 had become a Citizens' Council stronghold. Elder found that opposition to AFL-CIO policy on school desegregation and to purported labor contributions to the NAACP was expressed in the bus barns, at local union meetings, and at meetings of the local's executive board. Proposals to disaffiliate and join the Southern Federation of Labor were aired freely. Membership in Local 765 had declined by half. Elder reported: "This local has a heavy membership in the WCC and many of its members became bitter over the bus boycott. As the boycott continued its success, more and more local union members were laid off and the entire group became more violent in their opposition to all racial subjects, seeking to present their opinions whenever and wherever possible."[72] Members from the Carpenters local in Montgomery showed their support for the aggrieved bus drivers when they built a gallows in downtown Montgomery from which the NAACP was hung in effigy. To ensure that the public awarded credit where it was due, the gallows was inscribed, "Built by Organized Labor."[73] Even more embarrassing, the Carpenters hall, which local unions in Montgomery used for their meetings, had become a rallying place for the Klan and its crosses were displayed openly in the hall. When a staff representative from the Retail, Wholesale and Department Store Union confided to Elder that his "people are staunch segregationists and would leave the union if school integration was to become a yes or no question," his remarks applied as well to the entire labor movement in Montgomery as it did to the locals he serviced.[74]

Steel Workers locals around Birmingham were also vulnerable to Citizens' Council influence. An SRC report noted that white steelworkers in the Birmingham suburbs of Fairfield, Bessemer, and Tarrant City "supplied the core strength of the Councils of that area."[75] Elder found considerable agitation over racial matters among the twenty-five hundred officers and members of United Steel Workers local union "A." He reported: "This local union was considerably worked up over the Lucy case at University of Alabama and also protested vigorously . . . President Meany's remarks on civil rights. This movement was led and supported by L.U. officers. . . . The situation here is quite explosive and would certainly respond to capable leadership by white supremacists."[76] Dangerous levels of segregationist sentiment were also reported within steel and rubber locals around Tuscaloosa, among paper and shipping workers in Mobile, and from the railroad brotherhoods in junctions like Selma.

The JLC survey covered 110 locals from 32 different international unions. It confirmed that union members were willing volunteers in the army to defend white supremacy. At the press conference to release the JLC report, Muravchik acknowledged that "the overwhelming majority of white union members" in the South disagreed with labor's advocacy of public school desegregation and there was "considerable support for the White Citizens' Councils among union members."[77]

Almost all the southern labor leaders interviewed by the JLC researchers acknowledged that the race issue was more important in their unions now than it had been before the Supreme Court decision. Two-thirds of the locals surveyed reported that "most" white members were opposed to school integration. Not one local reported "few" white members opposed. One-third of the locals reported that "many" or "most" of their white members had strong feelings against the AFL-CIO for its stand against school segregation, although the members' loyalty to local unions remained strong. Fifty of the 110 local unions surveyed were reported to have experienced "trouble" over racial issues. AFL-CIO support for school desegregation was the most frequently cited source of conflict, followed by union contributions to the NAACP and economic competition with blacks.

According to Muravchik's analysis, local unions in the border South were as likely to report trouble as those in the Deep South, integrated locals were as likely to experience turmoil as those that were lily-white, and industrial unions were as likely to be disrupted as craft locals. The survey, however, did note that "troubled" unions included members who belonged to white supremacist groups or had local union leaders who took the initiative to heighten racial tension. In addition, unions located in areas of significant civil rights activity were more likely to oppose *Brown* openly than those in areas where the color line was unchallenged. Local unions were part of an intense countermobilization that occurred in areas such as Montgomery and Birmingham that were the scene of recent civil rights activity. But these distinctions miss the survey's point: enough locals from enough different unions in enough different places actively opposed *Brown* to distribute the embarrassment within the labor movement fairly evenly.

Even more depressing than the breadth of reaction to *Brown* the survey found was the lack of positive suggestions to cope with that reaction. "Successful" handling of the problems *Brown* caused was measured by the ability of labor leaders to rule them out of order or find some other way to sidetrack them because "no other short run method of handling these situations has been found." One ray of hope the survey uncovered was the degree to which "higher segments of the labor leadership," state council officers and international representatives, supported the AFL-CIO position. This group advocated gradualism but was at a loss to suggest strategies the AFL-CIO might pursue to assist the process. Muravchik's summary of the survey's findings was short yet descriptive. "Is there disaster? No. Trouble? Considerable. Possibilities of trouble? Widespread."[78]

EQUIVOCATION AND THE DEFENSE OF PUBLIC SCHOOLS

Local union leaders and international union representatives assigned to the South were immobilized by their members' racist attitudes which some of them shared and inspired. Some held elective office and did not want to offend potential supporters by taking an unpopular position in favor of school desegregation. Caught between AFL-CIO and international union resolutions applauding *Brown*, and their members' deep and obvious disagreement with it, some local union officers sought refuge in declarations of neutrality. When Steel Workers Local 5431 in Knoxville denied use of its meeting hall for a pro-segregation rally, local union president William J.

Johnson reassured his members that this refusal was because the hall had already been leased and did not indicate that the local was taking a stand "in the segregation issue, one side or the other."[79] OCAW Local 4-228 in Texas acknowledged that "the subject of integration of the races in public schools of Texas is a subject on which there is a difference of opinion . . . among some of our membership. . . . If this subject is allowed to become a major issue within the local union, it may result in dissension which would seriously affect the welfare of the local union." Aware of the danger *Brown* posed, the local union resolved to take a position of "complete neutrality on this subject of integration . . . and that we not go on record either for or against integration in the public schools."[80]

At best, democratic accountability produced an ignoble silence from southern labor leaders. Although Birmingham unions seethed with defiance over racial policy, the minute books for the Birmingham Industrial Unions Council and the Birmingham Federation of Labor reveal that between 1956 and 1961 no resolutions regarding the issue were ever introduced and the matter was rarely discussed in either body.[81] At worst, accountability led labor officials to pander to their members' meanest instincts. Some did not find this a difficult task because they shared the same racist attitudes as their members. Others wished the civil rights movement would die out and relieve them of the pressure it created. They nostalgically longed for a return to how things were before the *Brown* decision. Where this view was expressed, it was often accompanied by the desire that southern unionists be left alone to solve their own problems. Interference from the AFL-CIO, international unions, or northern liberals only made matters worse. The first sentiment was an implicit defense of white supremacy; the second was a thin excuse to do nothing to change it.[82]

Union leaders were mindful of their members' racist attitudes for a second reason. All of the states in the South had right-to-work laws except Louisiana. Closed shops were illegal. Union leaders feared that members would resign from the local if it took an unpopular civil rights position. This would weaken the local financially and undermine its ability to present a solid front against employers. Thus support for school desegregation not only jeopardized trade union careers, but it threatened institutional resources as well.

After a year as labor consultant for the SRC that required him to participate in labor education programs, travel extensively, and speak with innumerable trade unionists, Via summarized the reaction to *Brown* that he encountered within southern unions:

From 1954 through 1956 a great portion of the labor movement in the
South had backed away from actively considering constructive solutions to
racial problems. In many quarters the best that could be expected was a
careful defensiveness. . . . The union leader's main concern was with
maintaining organizational strength with as little disruption as possible; in
the main this is a concern that should not be harshly criticized. . . . But it
was an outlook which so predominated Southern thinking that it began to
exclude positive considerations. . . . It can now be seen that this tack did
considerable harm. [But] it would be a mistake to raise this criticism of
union leadership efforts without immediately recognizing the real and often overpowering pressures under which they were operating. . . . Opinion
in community after community, and usually the state governmental policy, was leveled against any objective consideration of Southern racial
problems, much less any inclination to engage in constructive action.[83]

Via's tendency to make a criticism and then retract it, to qualify each
remark, is evidence of the hopes he held and his awareness of the discouraging realities that foreclosed them. Others were also aware of the indeci-
sion and paralysis that gripped the labor movement following *Brown* and,
like Via, were not sure how long it could withstand the pressure. In 1957,
Father Louis J. Twomey, S.J., chair of the industrial relations program at
Loyola University in New Orleans, noted that he was encountering "increasing difficulties with unions over the race problem. As far as I can
judge, union men are split wide open over this problem."[84] A year later, as
the courts began to review Louisiana's segregated public school system,
Twomey became even more distressed by the response he encountered
from unions. He told F. Ray Marshall, then engaged in research for his
book on union racial practices: "One of the most disquieting developments
in the South since the Supreme Court decision outlawing segregated
public schools is the reaction among union men. A seeming majority of
the rank and file place higher priority on their loyalty to the White
Citizens Councils than on their loyalty to their unions."[85]

As state governments sought ways to circumvent the Court's decision and
state legislatures passed acts of interposition and debated closing public
schools, the burden of responding to *Brown* fell increasingly to AFL-CIO
state councils in the South. They responded with caution and evasion in an
attempt to pacify local unions upon which they depended financially.
Whereas internationals could place rebel locals under trusteeship, local
unions had the power to punish wayward state councils by disaffiliating. All
too aware of their dependence on local unions, southern state councils
redefined the issue in a way that drained it of the racial implications local

unions found so objectionable. State councils argued that the issue was not to save public schools from judges who would integrate them but to defend public schools from advocates of massive resistance who would close them instead. On this basis in 1954 AFL and CIO state councils in Georgia opposed a "private school" amendment and in Mississippi opposed an amendment permitting the state legislature to abolish public schools.[86] As Louisiana AFL-CIO president Victor Bussie told delegates to the 1961 state council convention: "It is not a question of whether you want the schools segregated or integrated. We have been very careful in the halls of the legislature to stay away from that question. . . . But I say to you that it is our responsibility to see that our children have this opportunity for an education." Bussie then warned that private schools would be unable to handle the crush of students if public schools were closed, that right-to-work supporters were behind the attempt to close public schools, that the race issue was a diversion meant to disguise the anti-union intentions of its promoters, that school closings jeopardized the ability of the United States to compete with the Russians in the space race, and that schools rescued children from sweatshops. In his concluding remarks Bussie urged the delegates to "go back and tell our members what it is all about. . . . [We are] not attempting to tell them that we want the schools segregated, integrated, or any other 'grated.' We just want schools for our children to attend."[87] But even this cautious restatement of the issue was enough to bring the wrath of the membership down upon the state councils. Local unions disaffiliated, membership decreased, revenue declined, and state council officers were embarrassed publicly when local union leaders repudiated their position.

Despite their caution and indirection, their attempt to redefine the arena of conflict away from what they perceived as the troublesome if not regrettable *Brown* decision to the even more troublesome if not dangerous resistance it provoked, state council leaders demonstrated more courage by defending public schools than the leaders of most other organizations, and they paid dearly for doing so. White union members took a back seat to no one in defending white supremacy and, given the institutional incentives, it took no small amount of rectitude from state council officers to resist the temptation to join them.[88] A reporter familiar with the trial of unions in the South noted: "It is often thought that the enlightened rank and file is always at war with a leadership immersed in moral and intellectual darkness. In reality, the opposite is more often true. Political sophistication and broad-mindedness are more common among union officials than among union members, and more common among officials at the top than at the local level."[89]

Not only were state councils in the South far more supportive of *Brown* than their constituents, but they responded more constructively than AFL-CIO affiliated unions. If state councils responded with indirection and caution to the opposition from below, this still compares favorably to the willful ignorance and indifference displayed by affiliated unions. Ruben Farr recalls USWA president David McDonald telling the staff, " 'You people from the southern states, I don't want to make a statement on this race issue that would hurt our union down there. The papers are after me every day, putting pressure on me to make a statement. I'm staying away from it as far as I can.' "[90] The outstanding exception to this typical response of evasion and avoidance was supplied by the Packinghouse Workers. At a district conference in Atlanta, UPWA president Ralph Helstein attacked Governor Marvin Griffin's call for tuition grants to private schools as an alternative to integrated public schools, defended the educational value of school desegregation for both white and black children, and pledged that his union would "fight to end all segregation and discrimination in whatever forms they appear."[91] OCAW president O. A. Knight ventured bravely into his southern district, which seethed with Citizens' Councils and Klan activity, to admonish his members to respect each other and obey the law. Other affiliates that took a similar stand included the TWUA, which tried to calm its members' fears regarding school desegregation, and the Pulp, Sulphite and Paper Mill Workers, which warned its members that the "real threat" was not school desegregation but the dismantling of "one of the basic principles of democracy—the free, public school system."[92] Otherwise, Via's comment in 1958 that "internationals are failing to a greater degree than state bodies to face what needs to be done" rings true.[93] Another disappointed labor educator thought the default he observed among affiliated unions resulted because "national unions feel they do not understand the South and wish to avoid upsets among their affiliates."[94]

Institutional concerns explain why state council officers did not do more to oppose school segregation. But these leaders should be credited for going as far as they did in support of *Brown*—much farther certainly than their members were willing to go or affiliated unions had the courage to when all the incentives lay in the other direction. Many state council officials approached the edge of the politically possible because they were ideologically sympathetic to black demands for civil rights. But their response was influenced even more by the frightening mobilization of conservative sentiment that massive resistance conjured up. State council leaders were far more concerned about the mischief the popular conservatism inspired by massive resistance would do to them than the harm it would do to blacks. They feared that massive resistance was creating a political atmosphere conducive to the passage of new, restrictive labor legislation. Opposition to *Brown*, they believed, was a clever subterfuge created by labor's opponents to promote a conservative, anti-labor political agenda. Mitchell's confidential report in 1956, which revealed that labor's political opponents were in the vanguard of the massive resistance movement, confirmed these suspicions. State council leaders opposed massive resistance because of what they believed was its hidden agenda, more restrictive labor legislation.

CONCLUSION

It would be easy to assert that union leaders should have provided more leadership to the desegregation forces, that they should have defended civil rights for blacks in principle rather than avoid the issue, that they should have condemned segregated schools as odious whether they were public or private. But it would be impertinent to judge the southern union leadership according to a history we would have preferred. To do so is to neglect the formidable institutional costs and democratic pressure from the rank and file with which they had to contend. Political courage must be measured against the constraints and opportunities available. Otherwise, judgments about responses to *Brown* lapse into an empty moralism. J. Harvie Wilkinson III exhibited sensitivity to the heightened racial tension of the period when he proposed that "political courage in the late 1950s meant standing for open schools . . . or admitting that *Brown*, however hateful, was still the law."[95] State council officers at the top of the union hierarchy in the South were more likely to pass this test than local union leaders at the bottom.

Another way to judge the responses of union leaders is to compare them to those of their contemporaries. If union leaders equivocated in response to *Brown* or, at their best, met Wilkinson's standard for political courage, this was no worse than the response from southern religious or business leaders at their best. Because the church in the South enjoyed more prestige than unions and more community leadership was expected of it, it can be argued that the church's failure to resist racial extremists contributed far more to their success than the less egregious defaults by unions. Nor does the business community fare any better than the church in comparison to unions. Its peak organizations, state and local Chambers of Commerce and National Association of Manufacturers chapters, were less willing to confront the defenders of white supremacy than were state councils.[96] Thesè comparisons are essential to evaluate union behavior. They not only provide criteria by which to evaluate union responses, but are reminders of how powerful and ubiquitous racism was by how unde-manding those standards are.

It is also noteworthy that the unions' response to *Brown* would have disappointed realignment theorists like V. O. Key, who believed that unions would serve as midwives to the New South. Unions, which appear as peripheral actors in the body of Key's *Southern Politics in State and Nation*, suddenly emerge in his conclusion as knights who would rescue southern virtue from the sordid racial history that imprisoned it.[97] If the labor movement did not fulfill this promise, it is because Key imagined the labor movement to be different than it was rather than for its own failures. Key, a progressive, who composed *Southern Politics* in the 1940s when industrial unionism appeared to be ascendant, envisioned a labor move-ment that was the CIO at its best: biracial, tinged with social idealism, centralized, and dynamic. But these qualities have always been in short supply within the American labor movement, even in the CIO that served as his model. Whatever merits his description of unions might have had nationally, it was completely inappropriate for the South, where CIO influence was especially weak and the building trades supplied the bulk of members. In addition, the decentralized structure of American labor allowed local unions to conform to, not oppose, local racial practices. They were not just unions that simply happened to be located in the South, they were *southern* unions. Given the circumstances with which they had to contend, these unions did not perform badly, they were just miscast for the role Key assigned them to play.

Finally, a review of how unions responded to *Brown* demonstrates that racism posed a formidable dilemma to union leaders. It would be banal even to mention racism as a factor leaders had to consider if the new southern labor historians had not dismissed it from their evaluation of union strategy. Even those who acknowledge the power of racism but condemn union leaders for capitulating to it need to be reminded of the institutional context in which southern union leaders operated. They were accountable to a rank and file who believed in white supremacy, and they feared that support for civil rights would threaten their organizations by driving away current and prospective members. This is especially true for the period after *Brown* when southerners rallied to defend the threatened color line, racial demagogues found large and supportive audiences, and there was an acute sensitivity about and ruthless defense of the southern racial order. Union statements condemning segregation that might have been overlooked and tolerated in the past when the color line was secure now provoked angry cries of betrayal and resentment from southern union members when the color line was in peril. According to Numan V. Bartley and Hugh D. Graham, "liberally minded political analysts underrated the intensity of white opposition to the *Brown* decision" because they never took white supremacy seriously enough.[98] Southern contemporaries of *Brown* certainly were never guilty of this. Their determination to save the color line belies the soft edges historians would later place around their resistance. Perhaps another, less decisive moment than *Brown* might have permitted a more direct, less equivocal response from labor. But the racially charged atmosphere in which union leaders had to address their members following *Brown* all but foreclosed this alternative. If under these circumstances union leaders proceeded cautiously in supporting *Brown*, it was because they had much to be cautious about.

2

Meeting the Challenge of Massive Resistance in Virginia and Arkansas

The only thing that can keep the race issue from tearing our labor movement apart is that strong leaders can cow their members into silence on the subject. . . . I can assure you that the situation is delicate.

—Victor Ray, editor of the *Arkansas Union Labor Bulletin*

FOLLOWING THE *BROWN* decision most unions in the South tried to avoid the issue by claiming that it was peripheral to their collective bargaining objectives. The AFL-CIO also retreated after its initial remarks in support of *Brown* drew such ire from union members in the South. Southern state councils, however, could not escape the tumult surrounding *Brown*. The issue was thrust upon them when their state legislatures convened in special session to devise ways to prevent school desegregation. State councils were under intense pressure from local union affiliates and their members to define labor's position on segregated schools and on the measures state legislatures took to defend them. This pressure was greatest in Virginia and Arkansas, where the largest number of schools were closed to prevent desegregation. School closings gave the issue an urgency in these states that aroused reactions from the labor movements within them.

This chapter examines the challenges that *Brown* posed to the Virginia state council and the Arkansas AFL-CIO, and how they responded to them. These case studies provide the fine detail that deepens the panorama presented in Chapter 1. State council officials in Virginia and Arkansas opposed massive resistance because they feared the popular conservatism it inspired would be used to restrict union activities. But state council leaders had to be circumspect in their criticism of massive resistance because they were accountable to a rank and file who supported segregated schools and sympathized with the resisters. Consequently, these leaders tried to defend *Brown* in a way that would least offend their constituents. Aware of their dependence on local unions and of the sentiments within them, union leaders tried to redefine the issue from one of school desegregation to one of preserving free public education. The Arkansas and Virginia state councils never put forward a principled defense of integration, but rather tried to deflect and deny the racial dimension of *Brown* in an attempt to reconcile their members to the decision. The issue, state council leaders maintained, was keeping public schools open for all children, not closing them to blacks. State councils posed as defenders of public schools even if this required school desegregation. But this cautious approach did not satisfy a white membership that was implacably hostile to school desegregation.

VIRGINIA

No state moved quicker or further to circumvent the Supreme Court's *Brown* decision than Virginia. In August 1954, Governor Thomas B. Stanley appointed a Select Committee on Public Education, chaired by state senator Garland Gray, to devise a plan that would bypass *Brown*. The committee's report, known as the Gray plan, made three recommendations. First, it proposed modifying the state's compulsory school attendance law so that no child was required to attend an integrated school. Second, it required local school boards to develop and administer pupil assignment plans according to nonracial criteria. Finally, it recommended that the state make tuition grants available to children who did not want to attend integrated public schools so that they could attend segregated private schools.[1] But the Virginia state constitution, which prohibited the payment of public funds to private schools, would first have to be amended to accommodate the plan's tuition grants proposal. This required a referendum to call a special constitutional convention to consider such an amendment.

On December 15, 1955, the yet unmerged AFL and CIO Virginia state councils issued a joint statement that condemned the Gray plan and opposed the call for a constitutional convention. They asked Virginians to join them in protecting "your public free school system." The councils complained that the Gray plan did not clarify whether the state intended to support two systems of education, one public and one private.[2] They also criticized the Gray plan, not because it was designed to circumvent integration, but because not everyone could take advantage of the segregated private school alternative that the plan endorsed. The plan was unfair because low- and middle-income parents could not afford to send their children to segregated private schools even with the assistance of tuition grants from the state.[3] But these arguments were more than some local unions could bear. Some local unions publicly disavowed the state leadership for its position,[4] and locals from the Aluminum Workers and Papermakers disaffiliated in reaction to it.[5]

The AFL and CIO state councils received $5,000 from the AFL-CIO for use in the referendum campaign and joined the Virginia Committee on the Preservation of Public Schools to oppose convening a constitutional convention.[6] This committee, however, was so defensive about desegregation that its slogan, "Don't Vote for Private Schools for the Rich, Integrated Schools for the Poor," conceded the race issue to its opponents. Local union members were not moved. Joseph F. Heath, AFL-CIO regional director responsible for Virginia, wrote to AFL-CIO Civil Rights Department director Boris Shiskin in Washington, "By and large I think that the [Local] Central Bodies laid down on the job," and expressed disappointment with the labor effort he saw.[7] The referendum to call a constitutional convention carried the state by a two-to-one margin.

No sooner were the votes in than the Gray plan became moot. The Gray plan's "local option" provision, under which local school boards drew up pupil assignment plans, still left open the possibility for school desegregation. On January 14, 1956, the Arlington school board, under court order to desegregate, announced that it would begin a phased desegregation of its schools. This crack in the wall of segregation, however, only increased the determination of state officials to build a higher and stronger wall. The Gray plan was designed only to prevent enforced integration. Now public officials rushed to come up with proposals that would prevent the integration of public schools under any circumstances. Virginia congressman William Tuck reflected this hardening of segregationist sentiment when he said of the Arlington school district, "If they won't go along with us, I say make 'em!"[8]

Virginia embraced massive resistance. In place of the Gray plan, Governor Stanley introduced his own legislative package. He proposed to remove pupil placement from local school boards and give this task to a state agency, to close any school system that was forced to integrate under court order, and to withhold state funds from school districts that integrated. The local option window under the Gray plan was now closed and across it were written the words: Massive Resistance.

Harold Boyd, president of the newly merged Virginia AFL-CIO, testified on the governor's proposals at a special session of the state legislature.

He opposed the massive resistance package because it would "result in the destruction of our free public school system," interfere with local self-government, deprive public education of the funding it needed, and contribute to juvenile delinquency by removing compulsory school attendance laws. Boyd charged that the governor's proposals were even more unworkable than the Gray plan they replaced, and he criticized legislators who had been the most ardent supporters of the Gray plan for abandoning it.[9]

The 1957 Virginia AFL-CIO convention reaffirmed the position that Boyd articulated in front of the state legislature. The issue, argued the state council leadership, was not whether public schools should desegregate but the future of public education in Virginia. The convention resolved "to strongly oppose any and all attempts which could weaken or ultimately destroy our free public school system."[10] The state council publicized this view the following year when it published *Will Virginia's Children Have Schools?* for distribution to its statewide membership. The leaflet, drawn from an article that had appeared in *I.U.D. Digest*, traced the sordid history of massive resistance and warned members of its dire consequences.[11]

But if the state legislature could be condemned for repudiating positions it previously embraced, so could the Virginia state council. When public officials adopted the strategy of massive resistance, the state council moved to occupy the ground recently vacated. It became an advocate of the local option provision of the Gray plan that it had criticized previously. This shift became evident when Virginia COPE endorsed Dr. Louise Wensel in her bid to unseat Senator Harry Byrd in the 1958 general election. Wensel campaigned on the local option alternative to massive resistance, and Virginia COPE threw its resources behind her unsuccessful challenge. Massive resistance had shifted the center of the debate to the right, and the state council moved with it. But to the dismay of the council, the membership was moving even faster. This increasing gap between the leadership and rank and file did not escape the notice of Senator Byrd, who acknowledged during his campaign that, "for the first time, I am getting some active support from the labor people," despite the state council's formal endorsement of his opponent.[12]

Jewish Labor Committee representative Jacob Schlitt toured the state in 1958 and reported that "the majority of trade unionists would be in favor of a private segregated school system . . . as opposed to integrated public schools. This, despite the fact that the state labor leadership has spoken out . . . in favor of preserving a free public school system in Virginia. It is unfortunately true that Boyd *et al* are miles ahead of their membership and in fact are also way in front of the leadership of most of the other organizations in Virginia. On the other hand, the local leadership is . . . in agreement with their membership . . . or if not in complete agreement they apparently maintain the position that labor has nothing to do with the school issue." In Richmond, representatives from the International Ladies' Garment Workers' Union, the Amalgamated Clothing Workers Union, and the Retail Clerks told Schlitt they were "very pessimistic about any improvement in the school integration issue." In Norfolk, a delegate to the city's labor council proposed a motion for the next state convention requiring the state council to oppose closing public schools to prevent desegregation. Schlitt reported that the delegate's request died for lack of a second. Schlitt described the building trades in the Norfolk-Newport News area as "quite conservative" and "opposed to school integration."[13] But no trade unionists were more committed to the strategy of massive resistance than the textile workers of Front Royal, Virginia.

No public high school in Front Royal would admit blacks so they had to attend school outside the county. Faced with a court order to admit twenty-two black students to the high school and end this indignity, the local school board refused and closed the high school instead. Warren County High School became the first school in Virginia to close as part of the massive resistance strategy.

Warren County was also the home of the American Viscose Corporation, the largest private employer in the area. American Viscose was organized by Textile Workers Local 371, which represented 1800 members, 150 of whom were black. When the high school closed to forestall integration, a segregated private school was organized. Local 371 spearheaded the drive to solicit funds and organized a checkoff of its members that raised $1,600 per week to build a new, segregated private school. In the interim, a segregated private school used the local union hall as the site of its senior dance and as its home court for basketball games.[14] A move to expel from the local black members who were involved in the desegregation suit was dropped only when it was explained that the blacks had not violated any union regulations.[15] Black members complained of harassment and charged that stewards failed to process their grievances.[16] Finally, the local committed $8,000 from its treasury toward the purchase of bonds for the construction of the private school and an additional $500 for an annual scholarship. Senator Byrd was elated and surprised by the local's enthusiastic support for massive resistance. He wrote Governor Lindsay Almond, Jr., "This is the first time I have ever known labor unions to make such a contribution when, in fact, the central organizations have endorsed integration."[17]

The local's generous support of massive resistance received wide press coverage and was a source of acute embarrassment to the labor movement. The TWUA charged that the local's proposed expenditures violated the union's constitution and were contrary to previous union convention resolutions that advocated compliance with *Brown.* The local was then placed under trusteeship, its assets frozen, and its elected leaders removed from office. Segregationists leaped immediately to the defense of the embattled local. Senator J. Strom Thurmond of South Carolina denounced TWUA officers as labor bosses and demanded a congressional investigation. Local 371 defended its actions as consistent with the union's constitution and appealed the order placing it under trusteeship. When the TWUA Executive Council ruled against it, the local took its case to the floor of the 1960 TWUA convention. It argued that every local had the right to invest its funds in any project that a majority of its members felt was in the best interest of the local and the community. But delegates to the convention felt otherwise and the local's appeal was rejected.[18]

State councils, however, did not have the luxury available to international unions of placing rebel locals under trusteeship. Quite the opposite power relationship existed: local unions could disaffiliate and punish state councils by depriving them of income on which they depended. State council officers in Virginia were all too aware of their dependence on local unions and were evasive when confronted with the school desegregation issue. They participated in the desegregation battle but claimed to be fighting a different war for public schooling. Boyd admitted to the Governor's Education Commission in 1959 that "we have not dealt with this problem on the basis of segregation versus integration, but on the basis of the maintenance and preservation of our free public school system."[19] Mindful of its financial dependence on local unions and of their segregationist sentiment, the state council demonstrated considerable imagination in advancing arguments that defended public schools while simultaneously avoiding the racial issue. For example, in his officer's report to the 1959 Virginia AFL-CIO convention, Boyd warned that the business climate in Virginia—in which all workers had a stake—would suffer if public schools were closed. He told the delegates: "New industry would not locate here. Jobs would have been lost . . . The banks and small business companies would have suffered or be forced to close. Our whole economy could have been destroyed if public schools were destroyed."[20] The state council also argued that abolishing public schools would be a form of disarmament in the face of the international Communist conspiracy;[21] that members should not be deceived by "smooth and beguiling words on the race issue" because they were spoken by people whose real aim was to destroy unions;[22] that union members had an obligation to obey the law; that members had to guard against the southern weakness for lost causes and should capitulate to the inevitable;[23] that the private school alternative to public education was impractical and unworkable; and, finally, that repeal of the compulsory school attendance law would contribute to juvenile delinquency and turn Virginia into a Dickensian workshop of exploited child labor.[24]

The desegregation controversy within the Virginia labor movement surfaced publicly when the Virginia AFL-CIO held its 1959 convention in Richmond. In his opening remarks to the delegates, Boyd defended his public statements in favor of public schools. These were not his personal opinions, he said, but reflected the will of previous conventions and of the state council executive board for which he spoke. He then voiced regret that following his statements some local unions told the press, "The AFL-CIO does not speak for us." Such displays of disunity only undermined his ability to serve Virginia's workers and encouraged labor's enemies. Boyd wondered if local union leaders who made such statements were not guilty of the very crime for which he stood accused: substituting their own judgment for that of their members. Finally, he admitted that the state council had lost members since its last convention in 1958. The secretary-treasurer's report confirmed that this decline was caused by disaffiliations arising from the state council's opposition to massive resistance.[25]

When delegates returned from their lunch recess, Resolution 5, requesting local unions to support free public schools, was called. Delegates anticipated conflict over the resolution and were not disappointed. William A. Lillard, a member of the state council executive board and president of TWUA Local 371 in Front Royal, rose to speak against the resolution. He announced that he came to the convention instructed by his local union "to oppose anything that has to do with free integrated public schools." Immediately, Ralph Cline, another TWUA representative, took issue with Lillard. He expounded on the virtues of education and proclaimed his complete support for the resolution. Aware of the issue's divisiveness and fearing open conflict on the convention floor, an Electrical Workers delegate, W. R. Grizzard, motioned "that this matter of integration or segregation" be tabled and sent back to committee. Upset that the mask had been removed from the resolution, Boyd corrected Grizzard: "There is no mention of integration or segregation in this. The sole question is this: Shall we work for free public schools or shall we not." But Grizzard was not interested in playing charades and replied, "I am aware of the fact, Brother Boyd, that it does not specifically mention integration or segregation, but I think that most of us who are here as delegates can read between the lines." Grizzard's motion to table elicited responses from the floor. A delegate from the Motor Coach Employees warned that to table the resolution would only continue the turmoil and confusion within the labor movement over the issue. A representative from the Bakery Workers also rose to oppose the motion to table. He put the mask back on the resolution that Grizzard had unceremoniously torn off. He added: "I do not think that it is up to us in this convention to talk about whether it is going to be integration or segregation. All we are interested in is a public school system." Lillard replied that the sword of Damocles hung over all of them. "We were one of the first that were close [sic]. You think some of you, that it can't happen to you. It will. It will." Boyd interrupted and asked Lillard to confine his remarks to the motion on the floor or he would be forced to rule him out of order. Lillard replied that he was speaking to the resolution and complained, "Every time I open my mouth I am out of order or drowned out by the applause of somebody that wants this thing killed." Cline from the Textile Workers then moved to close debate and vote on the motion to table. Finally, the motion to recommit was defeated and the original motion to support free public education carried.[26]

In his book on massive resistance in Virginia, Robbins L. Gates accurately placed labor in Group Three along his integration continuum. He described Group Three members as "public school savers [who] believed that integration could be kept very limited by operation of a pupil assignment plan, and objected to tuition grants" because they would siphon funds away from public schools. Gates distinguished Group Three members from the moderate segregationists in Group Two but also from the advocates of integration in Group Four. Group Four members, such as the NAACP, believed that integration was long overdue and applauded the Supreme Court decision.[27] The state council never went as far as membership in Group Four because of the organizational and political pressures it faced. Such a stand would have antagonized local unions and would have jeopardized the political careers of the state council leaders. Following a discussion with Boyd and Julian Carper, Schlitt said the leadership of the Virginia AFL-CIO "is not going to stick its neck out further than it has to."[28] In fact, the state council leadership did stick its neck out but was not anxious to have it cut off. The leaders hoped to survive, not be martyrs.

But as was true throughout the controversy, the state council soon accommodated itself to positions it had previously rejected. When Governor Almond proposed an alternative to massive resistance that included tuition grants, the state council supported it. The governor's proposal was based on the "freedom of choice" doctrine, which held that the state should ensure that integrated schools were available for those choosing them and that tuition grants for private schools were available for those who wanted to attend segregated schools. According to Boyd, the state council endorsed the freedom of choice option because it supported measures that would "bestow the highest degree of individual choice."[29] The advantage of this approach for the state council was that it not only offered a pragmatic alternative to massive resistance but that it protected the council from accusations that it favored either integration or segregation. Freedom of choice treated integration and segregation as if they were on the same moral plane. The moral bankruptcy of the freedom of choice prescription, however, soon became evident in the state council's reaction to the desegregation controversy in Prince Edward County.

In 1959 the school board in Prince Edward County closed its schools rather than comply with a court order to integrate. A segregated private school was organized that white children attended with the aid of tuition grants from the state. But in 1964, the Supreme Court enjoined the county from using tuition grants for private schools as long as public schools remained closed.[30] In addition, the Court ordered Prince Edward County officials to reopen the public schools on a desegregated basis. Then the federal courts intervened again and dealt another blow to massive resistance. In a case pertaining to Surry County, the courts ruled that tuition grants could not be used for children who attended segregated private schools even if public schools were available.

Prince Edward County was the last outpost of massive resistance and the most defiant. After the county closed its schools, resolutions at state labor conventions condemned the tragedy occurring there.[31] But the Surry decision made the state council uncomfortable because it conflicted with the freedom of choice approach. Surry, the council's newsletter stated, "endangers the so-called 'freedom of choice' system that is supported by many people who fought massive resistance." The article continues in the third person to present a hypothetical argument that there is an equivalence between "forced integration" and "forced segregation" and that "one is just as destructive of personal liberty as the other." Obviously uncomfortable with the conclusions of its own doctrine, to the point of relying on the anonymous third person to avoid claiming these conclusions as its own, the state council disposed of the issue by concluding that the decision, regrettable as it was, must have rested on solid constitutional grounds.[32]

At no point in the controversy did the state council ever put forward a principled defense of school integration: that blacks should be free to attend the same schools as whites, that separate was unequal as the Supreme Court had said, or that blacks were entitled to the same rights and privileges as other citizens. Nor did any other predominantly white organization take this position in a state where massive resistance was popular and the Byrd machine reigned. Even those with a stake in maintaining public schools, such as the Virginia Education Association (VEA) and the Congress of Parents and Teachers, were not as critical of massive resistance as the state council. The VEA did not criticize massive resistance laws when they were first considered by the state legislature, and a motion to support massive resistance was only defeated on a tie vote, 517 to 517, at the Congress of Parents and Teachers. Business groups also bowed before the power of the resisters and did not publicly oppose massive resistance until after it was clear that this strategy was doomed. The power of the massive resistance movement was so great that even when Governor Almond broke ranks with it, his proposal for tuition grants still required parliamentary maneuvers to get through the legislature. It is against this context and these comparisons that the response of the Virginia AFL-CIO to *Brown* should be judged.

The state council did not gain much by retreating to support tuition grants or by equivocating on the principle of integration. Even its timorous, cautious statements in defense of public schools brought the wrath of the membership down upon it. Local unions disaffiliated, membership declined, and labor leaders lost credibility in a state that was dedicated to massive resistance. Yet from the very start and to its credit, the state council leadership withstood these blows and fought to preserve public schools even if this required integration. There was even thought to be some tactical virtue in its equivocation on the principle of school desegregation. State council leaders believed, with undue optimism as it turned out, that retreat would permit them to discuss the issue with their members without being dismissed as integrationists. Instead of pious pronouncements that elicited hostile rejections, the state council tried to approach its members with arguments that avoided the racial issue at stake in an attempt to reconcile them to school desegregation. They misjudged their members, but they cannot be faulted for trying to build bridges, not burn them in pious proclamations. The state council's response to massive resistance was not pretty, but it demonstrated more courage than most organizations in Virginia displayed at the time, and it paid dearly for doing so.

ARKANSAS

Unions in Arkansas did not experience the turmoil those in other states did in response to *Brown*. In 1954 the Arkansas CIO was the first and only AFL or CIO state council in the entire South to hold an integrated dance as part of its convention entertainment. Morton Elder toured the state for the Southern Regional Council in 1956 and found only a few isolated local unions in southern Arkansas that had succumbed to the Citizens' Councils virus. The bulk of the statewide membership, located around Little Rock and Fort Smith, was uninfected. Here Elder found no evidence of racial strife, and he commented, "The leaders of the newly merged AFL-CIO state Council seem to be doing a very good job on political action and education."[33] The Little Rock school crisis of 1957, however, shattered the calm detachment Elder had found just a year earlier. Before that crisis, nowhere in the South was the labor movement less affected by *Brown* than in Arkansas. After it, the labor movement in Arkansas was more paralyzed by the passions *Brown* unleashed than anywhere else in the entire South.

Elder had good cause to congratulate the labor leaders in Arkansas for the job they were doing. At the merger convention of the AFL and CIO state councils in 1956, former Arkansas governor Sidney McMath set the tone when he warned those present to beware of a Trojan horse in their midst. Eisenhower Democrats and States' Rights party supporters proposed "to save the white man from the Negro—again" to disguise their true intentions. Race was the issue used by these fifth columnists, he cautioned, but the destruction of unions was their real objective. Attacks on blacks and appeals to prejudice were just the beginning of a broad hate campaign that would target Catholics, Jews, and union members next. He urged the delegates to reject false solutions pedaled by false prophets and to respect the law.[34]

The false solutions McMath alluded to were scheduled to appear on the ballot in November.[35] Two interposition measures that challenged the federal government's authority, as well as a pupil assignment proposal modeled after the Gray plan, were before the voters. On August 25, 1956, the Arkansas state council executive board met to consider what recommendations on these measures it would forward to the Arkansas COPE convention scheduled to meet the following day. Henry Woods, McMath's law partner, advised the board to oppose the measures. Woods argued that

52

Conflict of Interests

interposition was a flawed legal doctrine and that the proposed amend-ment to the state constitution would be ruled unconstitutional if adopted by the voters. In addition, the state council should defend the authority of the federal government against arguments, like those found in interposi-tion, that would weaken it. Woods believed that unions had received far better treatment from the federal government than from the states.[36] The board concurred, and the following day the COPE convention voted to oppose the interposition measures and the pupil assignment plan. The delegates then endorsed Governor Orval Faubus for a second term even though he had come out in favor of the referendum initiatives the conven-tion had just rejected. In November the three referendum proposals triumphed easily and Faubus was reelected. Wayne Glenn, executive secretary of the Arkansas state council, conceded to AFL-CIO COPE director James McDevitt, "We knew the three segregation measures would pass, but we took a firm position against them all."[37]

But the mettle of the state council was still to be tested. Following these defeats, its political fortunes declined still further as a result of the Little Rock school crisis.

Public officials in the South reacted in different ways to *Brown*. In Virginia, politicians rushed to devise proposals that would circumvent the decision. In Little Rock, the day after the Court announced its decision on *Brown*, the school board requested the superintendent of schools to draw up a plan to bring the school district into compliance. A month later, Superintendent Virgil T. Blossom presented his desegregation proposal called the "Little Rock Phase Plan." This called for the desegregation of Little Rock Central High School in September 1957 as the first step in a plan of staggered school desegregation. However, the day before the 1957 school year was to start, Governor Faubus called out the National Guard, which proceeded to bar nine black students from entering Central High School. Federal district court judge Ronald N. Davies then enjoined the governor and the National Guard from interfering with the phased inte-gration of Little Rock's schools. After the governor removed the National Guard, a mob of a thousand whites went on a rampage outside the school as the nine black students used a side door to enter Central High School. Claiming that "mob rule cannot be allowed to override the decisions of the courts," President Dwight Eisenhower ordered the 101st Airborne Division into Little Rock and placed the National Guard under federal orders.[38] On September 24, three weeks into the school year, the nine black students entered Central High School through the front door under military escort. The school remained open under military guard for the remainder of the school year. When in 1958 the Supreme Court upheld the district court's integration order, Governor Faubus closed every public high school in Little Rock. The only high school activity that survived the governor's order was the football season.

The AFL-CIO in Washington reacted swiftly to events in Little Rock.[39] On September 12, in the middle of the school crisis, AFL-CIO president George Meany publicly condemned Faubus's use of the National Guard to challenge federal authority, and he applauded Judge Davies's decision to proceed with school integration. The crisis in Little Rock, according to Meany, required President Eisenhower to federalize the National Guard and "sustain the authority of the Federal government." Such action was necessary to "defend the Union against treasonable assaults from within," and to defend the country from Communists abroad who would use the incident to besmirch its reputation.[40] Two weeks later the AFL-CIO Executive Council issued a statement censuring the mob that rioted outside the school and supporting President Eisenhower's decision to call in the troops.[41]

The Arkansas state council also entered the fray. A week before schools were scheduled to open in Little Rock, Governor Faubus testified in Pulaski County Chancery Court that violence could be expected if school desegregation was not delayed. Arkansas AFL-CIO president Odell Smith criticized the governor's remarks as irresponsible and dismissed his unsubstantiated reports of expected violence. Smith did acknowledge that "there is a wide difference of opinion in this community, and . . . many working people question the wisdom of integration at this time." But he urged "all citizens and especially working people to peaceably accept the decisions of the courts, to comply with their orders, and the rules and regulations of our duly elected school board members."[42]

But unlike the AFL-CIO in Washington, the Arkansas state council did not enjoy the luxury of being a thousand miles from the conflict or of being safe from its repercussions. As the school crisis escalated, troops patrolled Central High School, and angry parents demonstrated outside the school, the state council lapsed into silence. It did not respond to an appeal for a citywide day of prayer that church and civic leaders organized to reduce tension, and it did not issue a statement on the Central High School crisis. When Benjamin Segal, trade union consultant for the Fund for the Republic, asked Arkansas AFL-CIO Secretary-Treasurer Bill Williams for his views, Williams tried to put the best face on the council's paralysis, arguing that blacks were making quiet progress in the Arkansas labor movement before the school crisis. A black served on the state council executive board, union meetings were integrated, and blacks were invited and urged to attend all labor education programs. If the state council were to act in the current atmosphere of raw emotion and polarization, Williams pleaded, it would jeopardize the progress that had already taken place. Williams cited the state council's cancellation of a labor education program scheduled for southern Arkansas, where Citizens' Council activity was rife, as an example of its prudence. "It was felt," Williams explained, "with this feeling prevailing, we could not afford to risk that which has taken years to build." Williams concluded, "The present situation is so charged with emotion that I believe we will all agree that it is very difficult to go about solving the problem intelligently right now."[43]

Not everyone agreed with Williams. AFL-CIO COPE area director Daniel Powell believed that the state council exaggerated the danger it faced and suffered from a failure of nerve. He wrote to McDevitt at AFL-CIO headquarters in Washington: "The excessive racial tension which has been created by the Little Rock school situation has tended to temporarily paralyze the state and city labor leadership [from] participating . . . in any program or activity into which the racial issue might likely be injected. . . . While racial tension in Arkansas is probably higher than in any other southern state except Alabama, in my opinion, our Arkansas labor leadership has magnified this tension in their [own] minds."[44]

As the shock of the events at Central High School wore off, the state council awakened from its lethargy. The issue of how to respond was first broached at its January 1958 executive board meeting. Just before the meeting ended, Bill Kimberling from the UAW confessed that his international union had asked him to inquire why the state council had not taken a position on the Little Rock school crisis. He responded sheepishly that the board had not even met since the incident. He then expressed his own view that the school crisis was the result of outsiders coming in, not to prevent desegregation but to destroy unions, and he was disappointed that the board had not said so. Others, however, felt differently. One board member believed that the state council should express its views only on labor issues and should not issue statements on social questions outside its purview. Secretary Williams joined the discussion and acknowledged that he was being criticized severely in some quarters for "riding the fence on this issue." But he felt that "only education could solve the problem among the membership and that . . . couldn't be done overnight." Though board members had finally aired their views on the issue, they took no action.[45]

Meanwhile, Powell conspired with Odell Smith to prevent Governor Faubus from receiving COPE's endorsement in the 1958 Democratic gubernatorial primary. Powell told Smith that an endorsement of Faubus would be "extremely embarrassing to the National AFL-CIO . . . in view of the Governor's racial record." But Powell was also aware that it would be difficult to prevent labor from endorsing Faubus. The governor's spirited defense of segregation and his defiance of the law had only increased his popularity with the membership. Powell believed that if polled, 75 percent of the white rank and file and 65 percent of the local union and local central body leadership would vote for Faubus. Powell's experience at a weekend school in Little Rock at which local union leaders openly expressed racist views confirmed these impressions. Powell noted, "A year ago there appeared to be less racial tension in Little Rock than in any other city in my territory, but today the racial tension is higher here than even in Birmingham, Alabama."[46] To prevent an endorsement of Faubus, the state council raised the requirement to endorse from a simple majority to a three-quarters majority vote at convention. But Faubus was so popular that Powell was uncertain whether even a 75 percent majority rule could prevent endorsement. "Sad as it is," Powell informed McDevitt, "that is the situation."[47]

The COPE convention began on May 24. A resolution from the executive board was presented that chastised the governor for higher taxes, higher utility rates, and demagoguery. As a result of Faubus's "broken promises and his actions against the working people," the resolution read, "he has forfeited our support." Immediately, pro-Faubus supporters moved to table the resolution and block discussion of it. Arkansas AFL-CIO president Odell Smith ruled that there would be debate, and an appeal of his rule was defeated. Following spirited discussion that forced the convention to run late, the anti-Faubus resolution passed ninety-seven to twenty-four. While state council leaders were encouraged by the vote, it also confirmed that Faubus had enough support to resist a frontal attack on his racial record. State council leaders carefully omitted any criticism of the governor's racial policies from his list of sins because they knew how popular Faubus's defense of segregation was among their members. Nor could the leaders muster enough votes to endorse their selection, Chris Finkbeiner, against Faubus in the Democratic primary. The convention ended in a deadlock without issuing any recommendation or endorsement for governor.[48]

Though labor would have been badly split in the campaign even if Arkansas COPE could settle on a candidate, its failure to issue an endorsement gave unions even more opportunity than normal to take individual stands. The Electrical Workers state association endorsed Faubus on July 19.

The Camden Central Trades and Labor Council also endorsed Faubus. When informed by the AFL-CIO regional director that an endorsement in a gubernatorial race was a violation of its charter, the Camden council refused to rescind it. The State Council of Machinists would have endorsed Faubus if the general vice-president of the international had not been present to prevent it.[49]

The gubernatorial contest left the state council badly divided, as the fate of former governor Sidney McMath confirms. McMath's criticism of Faubus during the 1958 Democratic primary made him a point of contention among Faubus's supporters and opponents in the labor movement. Some local unions showed their displeasure with McMath and canceled his scheduled appearances at their local union meetings.[50] At the 1958 Arkansas AFL-CIO convention in November, a large group of delegates walked out as McMath began to speak. Faubus supporters then created pandemonium on the convention floor when they turned off the auditorium lights and the public address system went dead inexplicably during McMath's speech.[51] In June 1960, with a bare quorum present, the executive committee of the state council voted to discontinue the retainer to McMath's law firm. At its next meeting, with a fuller membership present, racial moderates rallied to McMath's side, reversed the previous vote, and restored the retainer.[52]

The 1958 state council convention at which the McMath incident occurred provided further evidence of the council's polarization and stalemate. Racial moderates took solace in the fact that every open segregationist who ran for a state council post and faced opposition was defeated. Although encouraged by these results, the moderates remained so wary of rank-and-file sentiment that they did not raise the racial issue at the convention. School desegregation would have been avoided entirely but for an attempt by the Faubusites to introduce a resolution that would have barred the Arkansas state council from taking a position on the question. A compromise was reached that required officers of the state council to consult with the executive board before issuing any statement on racial policy.[53]

Faubus, as expected, won the 1958 Democratic gubernatorial primary in a landslide. Victory in the Democratic primary was tantamount to election, and Faubus prepared to serve an unprecedented third term as governor. He immediately ordered that an election be held in Little Rock to determine if the voters supported school desegregation. With the high schools closed for the year and a referendum on desegregation before the voters, the state council finally entered the lists. Odell Smith stated, "The current school crisis presents us with two alternatives—choosing between expensive private schools or no schools at all." Either choice, according to Smith, imposed a hardship on workers. He then took the same tack the Virginia AFL-CIO had. The issue was not integration but the defense of free public education. The private school alternative that segregationists proposed as an alternative to court-ordered public school integration was too expensive for workers, warned Smith. Moreover, any attempt to ease this financial burden and fund private schools with public monies would be found unconstitutional. "It is my hope," the Arkansas labor president concluded, "that union members will support free public education by voting Saturday to keep our schools open."[54]

Smith's hopes were sorely disappointed. Seventy percent of Little Rock's voters favored segregated schools. Asked by AFL-CIO assistant director of education George Guernsey how union members voted in the election, Victor Ray, editor of the *Arkansas Union Labor Bulletin*, replied, "There are no accurate figures. However, I think I can give you an accurate report. Virtually every union member voted for segregated schools—which means they voted to close them. They voted the same way last July 29 when Faubus was elected." Ray then proceeded to share his discouragement and disappointment with Guernsey: "In the average union there were a few officers who opposed Faubus. Rank and file members were virtually unanimous for him. The same was true on the school-closing issue in Little Rock. This is a sad fact for some of us to face. But the truth is that the race issue is not less important to our union members—but more so. . . . The only thing that can keep the race issue from tearing our labor movement apart is that strong leaders can cow their members into silence on the subject. . . . I will appreciate any comments you may have on our handling of issues in Arkansas. I can assure you that the situation is delicate."[55]

More electoral fallout from the Central High School crisis ensued. In December 1958, elections to the Little Rock school board were held. Three ardent segregationists who favored keeping the high schools closed to prevent desegregation were elected along with three moderates who favored reopening the schools even if this meant token integration. At a meeting on May 5, 1959, the segregationists on the school board moved to dismiss forty-four teachers and principals. The three moderates promptly walked out to deny the meeting a quorum. In a rump session, the segregationists voted to dismiss the employees. Immediately, a Committee to Stop This Outrageous Purge (STOP) was formed, made up of elite business and civic groups in the city. STOP organized a petition drive to recall the segregationists on the school board. The Faubusites countered and organized the Committee to Retain Our Segregated Schools (CROSS), which mounted its own drive to recall the three moderates. Both committees circulated petitions, and all six members of the school board were subject to recall in a special election.[56]

Labor was badly divided in the recall election. Four building trades locals in Little Rock, along with the States' Rights Council, were the only organizations to endorse CROSS publicly. A labor group, which included the UAW and the USWA, organized informally to work on behalf of STOP.[57] Arkansas COPE director George Ellison informed James McDevitt at AFL-CIO headquarters that "labor has had people on both sides of these questions" and lamented that "the position of the AFL-CIO in Arkansas has never been made clear." Ellison believed the STOP campaign could be "the beginning of the end for Mr. Faubus" but acknowledged that "too many of our people are still afraid to take a position."[58] *The Arkansas Union Labor Bulletin* editorialized on behalf of STOP that the "dignity of working people" was insulted when the teachers were fired without a hearing or a list of specific charges. The issue was no longer integration or even the existence of public schools but the basic rights of employees. "Who will be next?" Ray wrote, "Where will the next 'purge list' be drawn?"[59] But neither the Arkansas state council nor the Little Rock central labor body could be persuaded to endorse the STOP slate. Powell believed that the state and city labor leaders refused to issue a statement because "they were afraid that it might defeat them for re-election or that it might cause some of the strong segregationist locals to disaffiliate."[60] Their organizational caution was prudent if not particularly courageous or principled. As a result of its editorial on behalf of STOP, the *Arkansas Union Labor Bulletin* lost thirty-five hundred of its ten thousand subscribers and Ray was censured by Typographical Local 92 and Pressmen's Local 59 in Little Rock.[61]

The results of the recall election were a mixed blessing for labor. The three segregationists were recalled and the moderates retained their seats. But the decisive factor in the election was the low turnout from white working-class wards that lined up solidly for CROSS.[62]

In his letter to George Guernsey that analyzed the Little Rock referendum on school desegregation, Victor Ray acknowledged that "the truth is that the Arkansas labor movement has had so much to trouble it during the past 11 months that it has been doing well to make any progress at all."[63] This depressing assessment accurately describes the impact that the Little Rock crisis had on the labor movement in Arkansas. The initial paralysis that gripped the labor movement is disturbingly similar to the passivity that Ernest Q. Campbell and Thomas F. Pettigrew found among religious leaders in Arkansas. Both labor leaders and clergy who supported desegregation were constrained because a majority of the constituents to whom they were accountable did not. In addition, labor leaders and clergy who followed national policy at great political risk felt abandoned when no sanctions befell those who disregarded it. Finally, many institutional incentives favored passivity. If for the clergy, defense of integration meant "lost members, lost financial support, and a lost opportunity to build the proposed north wing," the costs were just as severe for union officials. For state council leaders it meant fewer affiliated locals, less revenue, and a weaker, more divided house of labor. For both labor leaders and the clergy, these results jeopardized career ambitions they may have had and conflicted with their own standards of success, which required them to increase the membership, not see it fall; increase the budget, not see it decline; and unify the membership, not fracture it.[64]

These incentives may have been powerful but not overwhelming. The ideology of the people in charge made a difference. After the initial shock of Little Rock, Arkansas AFL-CIO president Odell Smith stood his ground. He firmly opposed Faubus and supported desegregation. Smith was also responsible for persuading his own union, the Teamsters, to endorse the STOP slate in the 1959 Little Rock school board recall election. The Teamsters' endorsement of the moderates is noteworthy because it was the only union to do so publicly. But when the Teamsters were expelled from the AFL-CIO, Smith had to give up the state council presidency. He was replaced by Wayne Glenn, who was occupied with matters within his union, the Pulp and Sulphite Workers, during his tenure. Glenn left the state council to become president of his union within a year. Only when Bill Williams resigned in 1959 and new officers were elected, George Ellison as president and Bill Becker as secretary-treasurer, did the state council finally have leaders who saw more rewards than risks in supporting civil rights. Under their direction, the Arkansas state council aggressively formed political coalitions with blacks and supported black demands for civil rights. Powell wrote: "Courageously, Ellison has carried out the AFL-CIO policy on racial non-discrimination and desegregation. As a result he has acquired the bitter enmity of the White Citizens Councils and the hostility of some of the building trades locals who have a substantial number of White Citizens Council members among their leadership and rank and file."[65]

But Ellison inherited a wounded, weakened state council. Following each new episode of the Little Rock school desegregation controversy,

from the drama at Central High School in 1957 to the recall election two
years later, more local unions disaffiliated.[66] Most of these defections came
from the building trades. Twenty-six Carpenters locals were affiliated with
the Arkansas AFL state federation on the eve of the AFL-CIO merger in
1955. Five years later, after all the racial turmoil, only seven Carpenters
locals remained. In 1955 the Arkansas AFL state federation included five
Plumbers locals. Five years later only one Plumbers local remained in good
standing. Disaffiliations left the state council so strapped for income that it
ran a deficit of $700 to $800 a month in 1960.[67] It survived financially only
because of subsidies it received from the AFL-CIO in Washington.

CONCLUSION

State council leaders in Virginia and Arkansas were far more supportive
of *Brown* than were their constituents. William Kornhauser argued that
union leaders are more racially tolerant than their members because they
are "more apt to stress the organization's strategic relations while local
members are more apt to emphasize status interests and racial sentiments
associated with them."[68] The "strategic relations" that so concerned southern labor leaders were the political repercussions of massive resistance.
State council leaders feared that massive resistance was a Trojan horse
designed to smuggle in new, restrictive labor legislation by labor's opponents. Their response to *Brown* was motivated far more by their fears
regarding the ulterior motives of resisters than by their sympathy with
black demands.

At no point did state council leaders in Virginia and Arkansas defend
the principle of integrated schools. Instead they tried to defuse the issue
and remove the emotional issue of race from it by supporting free public
education. This, they hoped, would mollify local unions and permit them
to discuss the issue with their members without being dismissed as integrationists. Their attempt to placate the rank and file, however, failed, and
the state councils in Virginia and Arkansas lost members, revenue, and
political influence. But before judging them as equivocators whose caution
earned them little reward, we must recall how vehement and visceral the
opposition to *Brown* was across the entire South. In 1958, AFL-CIO
COPE director James McDevitt told the COPE Administrative Committee, "In the South the racial issue is at a higher peak than at any time since
Reconstruction."[69] In Virginia and Arkansas particularly, where school
closings were not simply a threat but state policy, racial divisions were raw
and massive resistance was a powerful movement that enjoyed consider-

able political and social support. Under these circumstances, for labor leaders to defend *Brown* as the law, much less a good one, or to defend public schools, much less integrated ones, required political courage. Although these standards may not appear very demanding, they were stringent enough that in the fury surrounding *Brown* few civic organizations outside of labor could pass them.

3

Two Steps Forward
Labor Education and the Desegregation of
Union Conventions in the South

Our effort has been to get union members to think. . . . They may
discover that the Supreme Court is not always villainous, that the
Constitution and democracy have a certain compatibility, and that
Negro gains do not mean white losses. Simple lessons, but it is often
the first exposure to such an approach for many in a society where few
efforts are made to reach working whites.

—Emory Via, labor educator

T HE DULL, PREDICTABLE drone of the 1959 AFL-CIO convention was
interrupted suddenly by an unexpected outburst of temper and
emotion. Delegates were stunned when AFL-CIO president George
Meany lashed out at A. Philip Randolph, "Who in hell appointed you
as the guardian of the Negro members in America?" Meany's outburst
followed a speech by Randolph in which the black president of the
Sleeping Car Porters once again criticized the AFL-CIO for its failure to
prevent discriminatory practices within unions.[1] When Meany returned to
Washington, he was greeted by a flurry of letters from black trade unionists
who rushed to Randolph's defense and demanded that Meany apologize.
Civil rights organizations such as the NAACP also entered the fray.
According to Milton Webster, Randolph's lieutenant, the confrontation
at the convention was a blessing in disguise because it drew attention to
Randolph's indictment.[2] Randolph had made similar charges at countless
other conventions, and now Meany unwittingly gave them the publicity
they needed.

Chastened by the incident and by NAACP labor secretary Herbert
Hill's bristling condemnation of racial practices within trade unions, the
AFL-CIO approached the issue of discriminatory practices with a bit more
determination.[3] One area that came under review was the issue of segregated union conventions. Although a rope no longer ran down the aisle to
separate black from white delegates at union conventions in the South, Jim

Crow was still observed.[4] Black delegates slept in different hotels, took their meals apart from whites, and entertainment for delegates was strictly segregated. Departures from this norm such as the 1954 Arkansas CIO convention, which hosted a desegregated dance, and the 1956 Virginia AFL-CIO, which hosted a mixed banquet, were unusual. In general, union conventions in the South conformed to the doctrine of separate but equal. But as the civil rights movement gained momentum and labor's civil rights record came under withering fire, Jim Crow conventions could no longer be tolerated. Black demands to end this indignity and labor's need to bolster its sagging reputation on civil rights combined to bring a new energy to this problem.

Nor was labor completely passive in the face of the racism expressed by the rank and file. Reactions to *Brown* shocked AFL-CIO leaders, who feared its political repercussions. In 1956, H. L. Mitchell told AFL-CIO leaders that an educational program on race relations was urgently needed to curb some of the excesses he had observed. Mitchell recommended that the AFL-CIO establish a civil rights bureau in the South that could present arguments for desegregation and expose the duplicity of segregationists.[5] A letter that Alabama AFL-CIO president Barney Weeks received from a constituent indicates the extraordinary obstacles labor education on race relations would have to overcome. This letter was prompted by the bombing of an integrated high school in Clinton, Tennessee, which, just two years earlier, in 1956, had been the scene of riots so intense that the National Guard was called in when the school was first integrated. The writer suggested to Weeks that every local union in Alabama should contribute one brick per member to rebuild the razed school. Weeks, a courageous opponent of segregation, must have felt vindicated at first by this charitable suggestion, believing that at least some of his members saw through the treachery of the Citizens' Councils, and finally were beginning to realize that access to schools for their children was more important than denying it to blacks. At the end of the letter, however, the writer accused the NAACP of bombing the school because white people, who pay "for all of the schools for the Niggers," would not destroy property their taxes had financed.[6]

This chapter begins by examining the trials labor experienced in trying to desegregate its conventions in the South. Conference resolutions did not signify to delegates their state council's position on civil rights as much as conference arrangements did. There was no greater test of labor's integrity on civil rights than whether it desegregated its own events. The second half of the chapter describes the Sisyphean efforts of labor educators to convince southern members to accept national AFL-CIO policy on race. Educational programs were needed to repair the rift *Brown* created between southern trade unionists and the AFL-CIO, and to ensure that members did not fall prey to the conservative arguments of segregationists. But such education programs encountered formidable obstacles. Labor educators had to contend not only with a forbidding racial culture but with labor's own economism, its narrow focus on workplace issues. Labor educators found it difficult to establish the relevance of civil rights and expand the racial horizons of their students when union goals remained so limited and confined.

THE DESEGREGATION OF UNION CONVENTIONS

In 1886 the Knights of Labor, then at their peak, held their convention in Richmond, Virginia, capital of the old Confederacy. When the New York delegation arrived at the hotel where rooms had been reserved, a black member of the party, Frank Ferrell, was refused accommodations. Displaying its solidarity with Ferrell, the entire New York delegation left the hotel to board in black hotels and rooming houses. Grand Master Workman Terence Powderly, leader of the Knights, signaled his approval of this defiance of Jim Crow by selecting Ferrell to introduce him to the convention. Powderly mentioned the hotel incident in his opening statement and, turning to Ferrell on the stage behind him, said:

> When it became necessary to seek quarters for a delegation . . . it became evident that some [blacks] could not find a place in the hotels of this city, which is in accordance with long and established customs, and customs are not easily vanquished. Therefore, when one that happened to be of a dark skin, of a delegation of some sixty or seventy men, could not gain admission to the hotel where accommodations for the delegation had been arranged, rather than separate from that brother, they stood by the principles of our organization which recognizes no color or creed in the division of men. The majority of these men went with their colored brother. I made the selection of that man from that delegation to introduce me . . . so that it may go forth from here to the entire world that "we practice what we preach."[7]

Few unions that came after the Knights followed their example, and the Knights paid dearly for their defiance of the color line when southern members left the union in protest over its racial policy.[8]

Whether unions would practice what they preached was a volatile and open issue long after the Knights had disappeared. In 1950 the CIO banned segregation on premises it owned or leased. Ruben Farr, district director of USWA region 36 in Alabama, wrote CIO president Philip Murray to notify him that members in his jurisdiction were irate over this new policy. He noted that the decision jeopardized organizing drives already under way and that decertification petitions had begun to circulate in some plants.[9]

The issue of segregated union conventions and facilities received even greater attention with the rise of the civil rights movement following the AFL-CIO merger in 1955. Some AFL-CIO organizations pioneered in breaking down the walls of segregation. In 1959, West Virginia AFL-CIO president Miles Stanley threatened hotels in Charleston that if they did not accept black delegates he would hold the state labor convention in another city. Subsequently, when a black delegate from Local 863 of the Hotel and Restaurant Workers Union registered at the previously segregated Daniel Boone Hotel, he broke the color line not only at the hotel but for public accommodations in all of Charleston.[10] Similarly, when the George Vanderbilt Hotel in Asheville agreed to a request from the North Carolina AFL-CIO to accommodate black delegates, it was the first time, at least to COPE area director Daniel Powell's knowledge, that a hotel in North Carolina was desegregated.[11] State council conventions sometimes conformed to Jim Crow because no hotel in the entire state suitable for a convention would rent rooms to black delegates. For example, the Texas state council sponsored mixed dances and banquets at its 1959 convention but was unable "to secure unsegregated hotel facilities." This situation led Texas AFL-CIO president Jerry Holleman to suggest that the AFL-CIO contact a hotel chain and promise that unions would patronize its hotels in the South if it accepted blacks and threaten to pull all union conventions from its hotels nationwide if it refused.[12] Sometimes state councils were creative in avoiding the restraints of Jim Crow. When the Mississippi AFL-CIO held its 1960 convention in Vicksburg, state council president Claude Ramsay had lunch catered because he did not want black and white delegates separating to eat at segregated restaurants. But lunch had to be a buffet, without seating, or it would have violated local segregation laws.[13] Other state councils, however, remained unreconstructed and preferred to host segregated conventions even if integrated accommodations could be found.

The desegregation of labor conventions reveals the pressures the civil rights movement created for the AFL-CIO and southern state councils and how these organizations responded to them. On one hand, it was embarrassing and hypocritical for the AFL-CIO to condone segregated conventions when its official position supported integrated public accommodations and desegregated schools. This contradiction became an even greater public relations liability as the moral authority of the civil rights movement grew and discriminatory practices within unions were exposed. Finally, segregated conventions were an obstacle to the black-labor coalition that both the AFL-CIO and southern state councils were anxious to build.

On the other hand, the AFL-CIO, and especially southern state councils, could not overlook the racial views of their members. For instance, Wilbur Hobby almost lost his seat on the Durham central labor council after he introduced a resolution that black and white delegates to the state convention be given equal treatment.[14] AFL-CIO policy on *Brown* had provoked such an outcry from southern unionists that it threatened to undermine the authority of the AFL-CIO and the loyalty of southern members to their unions. State councils worried that a breach of Jim Crow might lead local unions to disaffiliate in protest over convention arrangements and that state council leaders would lose political support if they violated racial customs.

Thus the AFL-CIO and southern state councils were forced to walk a tightrope between demonstrating their support for civil rights by desegregating their events while not offending the racial etiquette of whites. As the civil rights movement gained momentum, the wire on which these organizations walked became thinner and thinner.

The pressure to desegregate state labor conventions arose first in Virginia. In 1957 the state council's convention was held in Roanoke. The Roanoke central labor council conformed with local ordinances by sponsoring separate dances for black and white delegates. In 1958, when the convention was held in Virginia Beach, black delegates complained that their accommodations were as much as forty miles from the convention center. A resolution was passed that fell short of requiring integrated conventions but demanded that future conventions "be held in cities and places where all delegates have proper and convenient facilities."[15]

The issue of desegregated facilities arose again in 1961. A. Philip Randolph sent a letter to Meany that bristled with anger and sarcasm over the segregated arrangements planned for the Virginia state council convention in August. According to the convention call, white delegates were to send their reservation forms to any of the segregated hotels listed, but black delegates were to forward their reservations to David Alston, a black member of the state council's executive board, who would find housing for them. The state council then compounded its felony when it noted with satisfaction that it had convinced the host of the convention, the Golden Triangle Hotel, "to serve luncheon to our Negro delegates in a 'private' dining room on the three days of the convention." Randolph wrote Meany that he doubted whether black delegates would truly enjoy "the dubious blessing" of their "segregated privacy." "But this is not all!" Randolph continued. "There must be merriment, but not without due obeisance and incantations to the god of white supremacy." He pointed out to Meany that "in the section captioned, Entertainment, the following is noted: 'The dance for the white delegates will be held in the Golden Triangle, Negro delegates will dance in the new and spacious air-conditioned hall of Longshoreman's Local 1248.' " Randolph was both searing and eloquent in his indictment of this exercise in Jim Crow:

> Verily, anyone who is seriously concerned about the progress of the cause of civil rights in the House of Labor must be shocked, bewildered and amazed at the air of bland innocence and Christian charity, with malice toward none, of these experienced, hard, responsible trade unionists who, after hearing the eloquent pleas of President Kennedy for the elimination of race bias; the public pronouncements of President Meany against color prejudice in unions; and witnessed the dramatic crusade of the Freedom Riders against jim-crow; the memorable U.S. Supreme Court decision against segregated public schools; the gallant and courageous uprising of Negro students against racial segregation in public stores; and the famous boycott of jim-crow buses in Montgomery under the leadership of Dr. Martin Luther King could deliberately send out a Call for a labor convention giving sanction and approval to racial segregation for its delegates.

Randolph next raised the issue of segregated labor conventions in the South at a meeting of the AFL-CIO Executive Council and referred specifically to the example of Virginia. Randolph recommended that Meany take steps immediately to rectify the deplorable situation there. Meany should inform the officers of the Virginia state council that the segregated arrangements for their convention were in violation of the AFL-CIO constitution; that the "racially discriminatory plan set forth in the Convention Call be scrapped, discarded, thrown out," or the state council would have its charter revoked; and that all central bodies be ordered immediately to end all forms of racial discrimination and segregation.[16]

AFL-CIO civil rights director Boris Shiskin defended the Virginia state council at the Executive Council meeting. At Meany's direction, he had investigated Randolph's charges and had spoken with Virginia AFL-CIO president Harold Boyd about them. Boyd told Shiskin that the convention call reflected the best arrangements that could be worked out given Virginia's racial climate. There simply was no hotel in the entire state that would accommodate black patrons and was also large enough to host the convention. A hotel in Williamsburg that had previously hosted a union education conference on an integrated basis was too small to host the state labor convention.[17] Shiskin assured Executive Council members that the Virginia state council had made good faith efforts to accommodate blacks at its convention and that it boasted a commendable civil rights record. The state council, Shiskin argued, had already given blood in support of black civil rights when it opposed the advocates of massive resistance. To punish the council for not integrating its convention when desegregated facilities were unavailable added insult to injury. Randolph's request for sanctions against central labor councils that hosted segregated conferences was rejected.[18]

But with the attention of the nation riveted on civil rights, Meany could not afford to ignore Randolph's charges. He invited Randolph, Milton Webster from the Sleeping Car Porters union, officers of the Virginia state council, and David Alston to his office in an attempt to resolve the conflict. Randolph left Meany's office only partially satisfied. Before the meeting the officers of the state council had convinced the management of the Golden Triangle Hotel to accept black union delegates as guests. But the delegation from Virginia was determined to hold separate dances for black and white delegates. To breach this barrier of the color line, they believed, would be too much for their white members to accept. Randolph then appealed to Alston to call off the separate dance for blacks and not give sanction to this form of segregated entertainment. He reminded Alston that organized labor "is not distinguished for its interest in giving dances" and asked his fellow member in the Negro-American Labor Council, "How can progress against racial segregation be justly claimed to have been made when segregation in social entertainment of the delegates still remains?" He explained that blacks had a special responsibility to act as the conscience of the labor movement and not countenance segregation in any form. Randolph asked Alston to cancel the scheduled dance: "Verily ours is a mighty and everlasting crusade for a new heaven and a new earth of consecration to righteousness and truth, and the intrinsic worth of every human being. And you may be assured that the little black boys and girls of Little Rock, Nashville, Birmingham, Montgomery, Tallahassee, and the Freedom Riders and sit-in students, who are bravely and gloriously fighting, suffering, sacrificing and struggling to annihilate the vicious color-caste culture of the South, will ever bless your memory. I know you will not fail them."[19] Randolph's blend of flattery and sermonizing had its intended effect. The day before the convention was to start, black delegates informed the Virginia AFL-CIO executive board that they had decided not to hold a separate event and wanted to attend the white dance.[20]

By the time the convention was called to order, both sides were exasperated despite their agreement on the principle of desegregated conventions. State council officers felt that blacks did not appreciate the efforts they had made and the political risks they ran when they convinced the Golden Triangle Hotel to be the first hotel to break the color line in Norfolk. Blacks felt that the state council was too quick to sacrifice a principle in order to appease prejudiced whites. A resolution that required the state council to hold future conventions in facilities that would accept delegates without regard to color was introduced. Its preamble mentioned the indignity black delegates felt when they had to be lodged in private homes rather than at the convention hotel, and it borrowed the rhetoric of the civil rights movement when it demanded rights for black delegates that were guaranteed by the Constitution. The resolution was approved unanimously.[21]

The Virginia state council convention the following year registered the progress that had been made but did not pass without incident. The Golden Triangle Hotel again hosted the convention and accepted reservations from both black and white delegates. This time entertainment was provided on an integrated basis. A floor show on the first night of the convention included black and white acts, and seating arrangements were open. The next night, black and white bands hired by the state council provided musical accompaniment for an integrated dance. But the convention was marred when hotel management would not let black delegates and their guests use the pool. Members of the Virginia state council executive board met immediately with management of the hotel to resolve this problem.[22]

In 1961, other state councils in the South came under pressure to change their traditionally segregated convention arrangements. Shiskin received an anonymous letter indicating that arrangements for the North Carolina AFL-CIO convention were being offered to delegates on a segregated basis. After urging by the AFL-CIO, officers of the North Carolina state council prevailed on the George Vanderbilt Hotel in Asheville, headquarters for the convention, to accept black delegates as guests.[23] As was true in the case of the Golden Triangle, the integration of the George Vanderbilt

Hotel by the state council broke the color line for hotels in the city. The following year, in 1962, a resolution was passed at the North Carolina state council convention requiring that future conventions be held in desegregated facilities.

The Georgia AFL-CIO, however, was more recalcitrant. Its 1961 convention was scheduled to be held in Macon. Previous conventions had lasted but one day, obviating the need to arrange housing. But the convention in Macon was scheduled for two days at the Dempsey Hotel, which accepted white guests only. The situation was particularly sticky because the AFL-CIO had just boycotted a meeting of the Interstate Conference on Employment Security in Atlanta because housing for conference delegates at the Dinkler-Plaza Hotel was for whites only. For the Georgia state council now to host a segregated conference would be embarrassing and make the AFL-CIO appear hypocritical. When the secretary-treasurer of the Georgia state council, W. C. Crim, arrived in Washington, he was greeted by Boris Shiskin and Donald Slaiman from the AFL-CIO Civil Rights Department, George Guernsey and Larry Rogin from the Department of Education, and representatives from the Social Security Department. They asked Crim to cancel the state council's plan to hold a segregated convention because the AFL-CIO had recently boycotted another convention for the same reason. They proposed that the convention in Macon be limited to one day to eliminate the need to house delegates. Crim declined. They then requested that the Georgia state council move its convention to Atlanta, where at least integrated eating facilities could be found for the delegates. Again Crim refused. Macon was more centrally located than Atlanta, he explained, thus assuring greater attendance of delegates from all parts of the state. Crim then argued with the dexterity of a lawyer that, technically, the Georgia state council was not hosting a segregated convention. The council was not responsible for providing housing to delegates; they were supposed to make their own arrangements. Shiskin and the others were not impressed with such legalisms, but they did no more than slap Crim's wrists. They told him that no staff from AFL-CIO headquarters would appear at the conference in Macon although the AFL-CIO would still supply the state council with literature, films, and reference material it had requested.[24]

The experiences in Virginia and Georgia led the AFL-CIO to draft explicit rules for central labor council conventions. In February 1962, Meany issued a directive requiring all central labor bodies to hold their conventions in integrated facilities, as Randolph had recommended eight months earlier.[25] In the event that only segregated hotels were available, central labor councils were to conduct official convention business outside hotels in integrated auditoriums. This required all delegates, black and white, to make their own eating and housing arrangements, but it also permitted the councils to avoid the taint of sponsoring segregated activities. This awkward procedure was intended to accommodate central labor councils in the Deep South, where desegregated hotels were unavailable. The Mississippi and Alabama state councils did not provide accommodations for their delegates until 1966 because no suitable hotel that would accept black and white delegates was available until then.

Some state councils saw Meany's directive as an opportunity to attract more AFL-CIO-sponsored events to their states. Texas AFL-CIO president Hank Brown recommended to Meany that "any meetings or conferences being held in this part of the country be held in Texas" because desegregated convention facilities were available in Fort Worth, Dallas, and San Antonio.[26] Nor were chambers of commerce above taking advantage of the new AFL-CIO policy to attract convention business. A representative from the Nashville Chamber of Commerce contacted Meany in an effort to draw the Tennessee AFL-CIO convention to his city. He argued that Nashville rather than Gatlinburg, where the convention was scheduled, better met the racial requirements of Meany's directive. Meany replied that a large number of hotels in Gatlinburg already met AFL-CIO conditions and had done so at a time "when adequate accommodations meeting our standards were not available in Nashville or any other city in Tennessee."[27]

If Texas and Tennessee had no trouble complying with Meany's directive, it was an albatross for other southern state councils. The 1962 Florida AFL-CIO convention was scheduled to take place in Jacksonville. A motion passed at the 1961 convention, however, gave state council officers the right to change the location of the convention if desegregated facilities in Jacksonville were unavailable. When such facilities could not be found, the state council chose to use Meany's directive rather than its resolution from the previous convention as the reason for changing the convention site. It informed its affiliates that the matter was "out of its hands" and that it had to comply with Meany's order. The obvious choice was Miami, but the state council ran into trouble immediately when it proposed this site. Central labor councils from the spurned northern parts of the state wrote to Bill Allen, secretary-treasurer of the Florida AFL-CIO, that they would not send delegates and would disaffiliate if the convention was held there. Moreover, Allen was worried that Miami's distance from the rest of the state would hurt attendance. He wrote AFL-CIO coordinator of state and central labor bodies Stanton Smith that, "geographically all of Florida is a long way from Miami except Miami." In addition, the Hotel and Restaurant Workers locals in Miami were not affiliated with the state council. Allen did not want to reward free riders by moving the convention to their city. Finally, the Dade County Central Labor Council refused to host the proposed convention.

These were reasons enough to disqualify Miami as a convention site, and the state council proceeded to search for a more centrally located city with desegregated accommodations. Finally it found a hotel in Sarasota that would accept guests regardless of color. The Saratoga Terrace Hotel was a small facility with only seventy rooms. It had been purchased recently by the Chicago White Sox baseball team so that its black ball players could be housed with the rest of the club during spring training. Unfortunately, the Saratoga Terrace was the only desegregated hotel in the city and could not house all the delegates. The state council thus proposed to make the hotel its convention headquarters and advise delegates to come there first for information on other accommodations. The convention itself was to be held in an integrated auditorium where catered meals would be served.[28]

State conventions in Arkansas and Texas were held on an integrated basis in 1962, but Georgia continued to be the nut that would not crack. Its state council officers never embraced the civil rights movement and were politically the most conservative in the South. When the Georgia state council held its 1962 legislative and education conference in Rome, it directed black and white delegates to different hotels.[29] At an AFL-CIO Committee on Civil Rights meeting, Emil Mazey from the UAW proposed making an example of the Georgia AFL-CIO by removing its officers for flouting policy. But once more the penalties were minimal as staff from AFL-CIO headquarters were again ordered not to appear at the convention.[30] The state council remained unrepentant, however, and the following year it again directed black and white delegates to separate hotels.[31] Not until 1964 were black and white delegates to the Georgia AFL-CIO convention housed at the same hotel. This delay was particularly unpardonable and unnecessary because hotels in Atlanta that would accept black guests were available two years earlier.[32]

The AFL-CIO had more luck when it came to blows with the Alabama state council. Leroy Lindsey, secretary-treasurer of the Alabama AFL-CIO, had invited all affiliated unions to send representatives to the Annual Workers Education Institute that the state council sponsored jointly with the Alabama State Department of Education. Enclosed with the invitation from Lindsey was a letter from the assistant state supervisor of trade and industrial education of Alabama indicating that the week-long institute was for white members only. Meany wrote Lindsey to upbraid him for committing the state council to cosponsorship of a segregated conference in clear disregard of AFL-CIO policy.[33] The Alabama state council withdrew its cosponsorship following Meany's intervention.

AFL-CIO departments also faced difficulties in hosting integrated conventions in the South. The 1960 COPE area conference was shifted to Louisville because the hotel in Lexington that was the original site would not accept black guests.[34] But the following year, the COPE area conference in Texas racially segregated its participants. When instructions to delegates were sent out, Edward Shanklin, Sr., staff representative for the Packinghouse Workers, asked Ray Andrus, the conference organizer, whether the hotel hosting the conference accepted black guests. He informed Andrus that some Packinghouse Workers locals intended to send black delegates. The invitation listed only one hotel to which delegates were to send their reservations, and Shanklin wanted to spare his black delegates the humiliation of being denied rooms. Shanklin recommended that the conference be moved to Corpus Christi, where the Packinghouse Workers intended to hold its district convention in an integrated hotel. But Andrus disregarded Shanklin's suggestion and proceeded to hold the convention in Galveston, where black and white participants were directed to separate hotels.[35] In 1962, COPE was more careful in its selection of conference sites and was able to provide integrated facilities for participants at all four conferences it held in the South. The following year, when the Sheraton Hotel in New Orleans would not give a written commitment to accept all delegates, the COPE area conference was moved to the Hilton Hotel, which would.[36] In 1964, a black newspaper, the *Birmingham World*, noted with approval that COPE conferences in the South were held in desegregated facilities and commented, "COPE seems to be proud of its pioneering in full and open hotel accommodations."[37]

The caution southern state councils displayed in desegregating their events demonstrates the dilemmas the emergent civil rights movement posed to them. State council officers were reluctant to require white delegates to abide by a racial etiquette that violated racial norms they subscribed to in fear of losing their political support. In addition, they feared local unions might disaffiliate in protest over convention arrangements, jeopardizing the income on which the councils depended. Council officers, of course, offered reasons other than political expedience to explain their hesitance to desegregate labor conventions. They claimed that a lack of suitable hotels that would accept all delegates forced them to hold segregated conventions. But, at least in the border South, this wall of segregation crumbled at first touch. Moreover, the liabilities were perceived to be so great that state councils preferred to portray themselves as desegregating their events only under duress from AFL-CIO headquarters. In fact, sanctions were embarrassingly light for those who flouted policy, and the AFL-CIO hardly used more than persuasion to obtain compliance. Members of the Southern state councils were reluctant racial pioneers who approached the desegregation of their events with a mixture of caution and determination that well reflected the risks and rewards the civil rights movement posed to them.

LABOR EDUCATION AND RACE RELATIONS

The desegregation of union conventions, as late and halting as it was, proceeded faster than did getting white members to like it. Union members, like other white southerners, resisted racial change, which segregationists used to drive a wedge between the union leadership and the rank and file. An educational effort that could explain labor's position on race and prevent its members from succumbing to the blandishments of racist demagogues was required to heal this rift. But the AFL-CIO had little experience in conducting educational programs on race relations, no tested method or technique that could convey its views on this sensitive matter, and no staff trained to present it. When the *Brown* decision was issued, the AFL-CIO was utterly unprepared to cope with the hostile response it evoked from members. At the time, the AFL-CIO gave so little attention to labor education on race relations that it depended on outside groups such as the Jewish Labor Committee to provide it. This was not without benefits. In addition to being more experienced, outside groups provided a front behind which the AFL-CIO could address its members on the delicate and volatile issue of race without being implicated directly.[38]

In March 1957, following a year in which southern unions were convulsed by the school desegregation question, Emory Via and Benjamin Segal from the Fund for the Republic invited twenty union education directors to discuss the need for a civil rights program in the South. The Southern Regional Council in Atlanta offered to host the "off-the-record" conference. The meeting in Atlanta began with presentations that reviewed the threat white supremacy groups posed to unions and their success in infiltrating them. This was followed by a discussion among education directors, who agreed that their unions had not responded well to these challenges. They traded stories of local union officials who denied there was a race problem affecting their members, of moderates who feared to speak out, and of flagrant disregard of union antidiscrimination policies. Further discussion revealed that responsibility for responding to racial disturbances should lie with the union staff representative. But if staff representatives were going to defend unions from segregationists, they needed to be trained and educated in the field of race relations. The education directors agreed to provide such training in a workshop to be held in conjunction with the July 1957 Institute on Race Relations conference at Fisk University.[39]

Before the Fisk University gathering, Via participated in a labor education program at Lake Junaluska, North Carolina, sponsored by the Chemical Workers Union. Here, he came into harsh contact with the enormity of the problem to be scaled. He and AFL-CIO assistant director of education George Guernsey were determined to include race relations in the curriculum but could not find a time when it seemed appropriate. Experience warned them that students felt abused if they tried to "slip it in," that it was too important to leave for the last minute, and that students felt hectored if it was a major part of the curriculum. By default they agreed to include it in the National Issues course that Guernsey taught.

Guernsey's course started well enough. Via presented some background to the Supreme Court's *Brown* decision as a prologue to a discussion of a Federal Aid to Education bill then pending in Congress. He reviewed what the Court had said in *Brown*, how the "deliberate speed" formula presumed good faith on the part of the South, and how the Court had provided communities and states with "a good deal of time [to] work out their answers to the problems involved." Guernsey then spoke of the progress school desegregation was making in the South despite the efforts of resisters to prevent it. Guernsey warned that such groups as the Citizens' Councils deviously used the race issue to disguise their conservative, anti-labor agendas. At this, a local union president in attendance from Birmingham stood up and declared that he was a member of the Citizens' Councils which Guernsey had just disparaged, he did not find the Citizens' Councils to be anti-union, and he knew of many other good union members who shared his enthusiasm for the Citizens' Councils. Others in the class took this as a signal to voice their disagreement with *Brown* to Via and Guernsey. The class then took a break to let tempers cool. When Via and Guernsey returned to the classroom, they discovered that someone had written "KKK" on the blackboard.[40]

Results were a shade better when Via gave his talk to a second labor group at Lake Junaluska, though this time Guernsey made no mention of the Citizens' Councils as anti-union. Still, rumblings of discontent could be heard. One participant from Georgia was visibly agitated by the discussion. Another class member confessed privately to Via that he hoped the South would continue to send representatives to Congress who voted against bills that contained school desegregation riders. But Via and Guernsey were more encouraged by this second group because a few class members spoke up who believed that some school integration was unavoidable.

Based on his experience, Via concluded that leaders of civil rights discussions must be present over the course of the entire labor education program or lead sessions that dealt with practical matters if participants were to view them not as moralists but as serious trade unionists. Moreover, Via believed, "There is no way to dodge the race issue." But some methods were superior to others as a way of raising it. Via felt that it should be presented either through an analogy to a situation that participants found less threatening than race or within a larger framework that instructors provided to the students. These approaches had clear advantages over

> raising the specific issues which are symbolic in their significance and call forth a ready-made antagonistic response. Frankly, in many ways, the Supreme Court's decision, national AFL-CIO policy on civil rights, and national civil rights legislation, all fall into this category. Membership, and even leadership, loyalty to the AFL-CIO is not sufficient to get more than a negative response when they are told what national policy on civil rights is. Likewise, their minds are made up on such issues as school desegregation without ever having to think how this issue relates to the rest of their life. In some cases, you can rely on a basic understanding and loyalty as to what unionism itself means; but even here with groups who have not really given any thoughtful consideration as to what their union means in broad terms one may go astray.[41]

Other labor educators agreed with Via that only indirect approaches could avoid the antagonistic responses a more direct appeal would surely encounter. Such approaches were used at a 1956 weekend conference for locals along the Missouri-Arkansas border where opposition to *Brown* was intense. Here, whenever the merits of *Brown* were debated, session leaders used the opportunity to remind delegates that the Citizens' Councils were anti-labor. Labor educators also tried to restore the majesty of the federal government not by defending *Brown* but by reminding students of the freedom they enjoyed to criticize it.[42]

Another technique labor educators used at the weekend conference was to present students with a hypothetical situation that all could decode. In one example, labor educators asked students what they would do if a governor barred legal picketing or if pickets were threatened by a mob. The answer was to get a federal court order to continue picketing and, if necessary, call in the army to protect pickets from the mob. The resemblance of this hypothetical situation to the Little Rock school crisis escaped no one.[43] The key to "successful education programs dealing with civil rights," argued one labor educator, is that "there must be no indoctrination, no 'this must be done because this is AFL-CIO policy.' " Other suggestions for ways unions could promote better race relations included sponsoring integrated recreational and cultural events, inviting black experts to speak to the local on topics other than discrimination, ensuring that black and white delegates represented the local at conventions and workshops, and making resources on race relations available to members.[44]

Labor educators had a chance to test these pedagogical techniques at the Fisk University workshop for staff representatives that the education directors who met in Atlanta five months earlier agreed to host. The plan called for twenty-five union participants to attend the morning sessions of the Institute on Race Relations, followed by separate classes in the afternoon for union conferees only. Classes in the afternoon would cover such topics as southern labor history, background to the resistance and hate groups, use of the race issue against unions, and resources available to assist unions in their civil rights work in the South.[45]

When Segal and Via began planning for the Fisk workshop, they asked union education directors to recommend suitable staff to invite. The level of intimidation was so high that there was some risk to accepting Segal and Via's invitation. Carl Griffin, president of the Alabama AFL-CIO, wanted to know before he responded who else had been invited and whether photographers and reporters would be present. He had recently been attacked for attending a meeting of the Alabama Council on Human Relations and feared that "another incident would finish him with the unions."[46]

The union section at Fisk deserved plaudits because it was the first time labor had been involved in the work of the Race Relations Institute. It achieved enough success to be the target of an editorial attack in the *Chattanooga Free Press*.[47] COPE area director Daniel Powell thought the discussions were thoughtful, but no quick or easy answer emerged to the question of how far "unions could or should go in the field of race relations." But the weakness of the union section was also apparent. Only twelve affiliated unions sent staff to participate. The largest delegation came from the Textile Workers, followed by the United Auto Workers and

United Steel Workers. Union representatives who could have benefited most from the sessions were not present. No building trades business agents attended, only two state councils sent representatives, and no local central bodies officers showed up. "Most of those present," said Powell, "were labor leaders who for years have been facing up to the racial problem and earnestly trying to carry out policy against racial discrimination—so in a sense we were talking to ourselves."[48]

The most significant program on race relations that was delivered in 1958 took place at the advanced institute for southern staff representatives. Discussions there revealed that staff representatives faced different situations from state to state. But regardless of their different experiences, participants admitted that labor had failed to play a positive role in the controversy thus far. Participants then considered steps unions could take to respond constructively to the racial crisis that gripped the South. One proposal called for union leaders to acquaint themselves with the social science literature on race and prejudice. This would give them more perspective on the problems they encountered and help them better understand the reactions of minority groups. Another suggestion was for union leaders to build bridges to such organizations as the SRC and to black organizations in their communities. It was recommended that the latter could be done subtly by getting involved in programs that were for the general community, though the specific service might flow primarily to blacks. Finally, it was suggested that unions defend integration in such a way as to deflect and soften criticism. For instance, the motto "Save Our Schools" that unions used to oppose massive resistance avoided the school desegregation issue in favor of defending public schools, an issue that was more neutral. Or a union could protest acts of violence and intimidation against blacks by appealing to community values in due process, individual rights, peace, and security.[49]

The curriculum and how to present it were not the only issues that perplexed labor educators. Even finding sites in the South that would provide common living and eating arrangements for both black and white participants was difficult. The Gulf Coast Institute for local union officers and stewards from Alabama and Mississippi did not convene in either of those states until 1964 because no integrated sites were available. This was not the only obstacle. In 1957, the Southern Labor School, the premier labor education event in the South, convened at Spring Hill College in Mobile. But the school had to find new quarters the following year because the Jesuits who ran it were uncomfortable with its labor sponsorship, not its integrated format.[50]

By 1958 Via began to notice a thaw in racial attitudes at labor education gatherings. Racial problems were not hushed up as they had been two years before, he told Segal, and he found students looking for new approaches to take to their members.[51] In addition, labor educators were now more confident in delivering labor's antisegregation message to their students. Experience indicated that an indirect approach using analogies succeeded best.

By 1961 all but the most recalcitrant union officers recognized that a change in southern race relations was unavoidable. Daniel Powell attended the 1963 Southern Labor School and was encouraged by the progress he saw. He noticed greater participation from the building trades and was able to distribute a questionnaire on human rights and civil liberties to the participants without protest. He commented to COPE director Al Barkan, "The very fact that I could use the questionnaire without any objections being voiced . . . is in itself a sign of progress." Results from his survey indicated that a majority of the whites (fourteen out of twenty-four) felt public schools should not be segregated, nineteen out of twenty-three believed unions should be open to all, and eighteen out of twenty-three whites felt that union officers should enforce contracts guaranteeing equal job opportunities for blacks.[52]

Another group outside of labor, aside from the JLC, that was intimately involved with labor education on race relations was the National Institute of Labor Education (NILE), established in 1957 to promote labor education within universities. Its board of directors was made up of education directors from affiliated unions, officers of the AFL-CIO Education Department, and representatives from industrial relations programs at universities.[53] Though independent, NILE acted as an arm of the AFL-CIO Education Department in the field of race relations. It was a convenient front behind which the Education Department organized the most sustained, concentrated labor education program on race relations ever undertaken by the labor movement.

In 1959, NILE submitted a grant application to the Taconic Foundation that would form the basis of its labor education program for the future. The grant request, developed by Emory Via, who was now affiliated with the University of Wisconsin School for Workers, acknowledged that "the labor movement could play a most crucial role in overcoming racial prejudice and discriminatory practices. This role is recognized by the top union leadership and it has found clear expression in various statements and resolutions. On the secondary level of union leadership, however, and among rank and file members, discriminatory attitudes still prevail and offer a serious challenge to union leaders and labor education."[54]

To close this gap, NILE suggested a residential training program in the South for full-time union staff representatives and selected local union officers. NILE proposed to recruit twenty to twenty-five union staff representatives to attend classes for four weeks of leadership training on race relations. This would take place in cooperation with a southern university, thereby fulfilling one of NILE's aims of involving universities in the delivery of labor education.[55]

The grant request to the Taconic Foundation, as well as proposals to four other foundations, was not funded. The foundations were sympathetic but skeptical that NILE would be able to entice either universities or unions to participate in its ambitious program. A more modest proposal was submitted to the New World Foundation in the summer of 1961.[56] Joseph Mire, executive director of NILE, solicited letters from union leaders to support the grant application and attest to the need for the program. Amalgamated Clothing Workers education director Marc Karson wrote that NILE's proposed program was needed because unions were not in a position to provide the service themselves. He admitted, "Because trade union officials feel that they cannot go further than the social views of their membership it would be unrealistic to expect the unions themselves today to hold education conferences in the South for the purpose of lessening prejudice and discrimination." For this reason, Karson argued, NILE's sponsorship was necessary and would not duplicate or replace union efforts.[57] Other union officers complied and sent letters to the New World Foundation in support of NILE's proposal. In February 1962, NILE was informed that the New World Foundation had approved its application and would contribute $10,000 to cover half of the estimated expense for a four-week residential institute. Unions that sent participants were expected to pay the remainder of the costs.

The first Southern Union Staff Training Institute was held at the University of North Carolina at Chapel Hill from March 7 to April 3, 1963. Ronald Donovan, a professor at the New York State School of Industrial and Labor Relations at Cornell University, was appointed director of the institute and George Guernsey was selected as co-director.

One of the first problems the NILE institute faced was recruiting students. Unions were not anxious to sacrifice their full-time staff for a month or to subsidize them for training they did not perceive as essential. The deadline for applications was extended twice because not enough participants were enrolled. Guernsey and Donald Slaiman from the AFL-CIO Civil Rights Department appealed personally to international union presidents to recommend students. Two lunches for union education directors in the Washington, D.C., area were organized to aid recruiting. Even with these efforts, only eighteen students enrolled for the four-week institute.

More than half of those who attended the institute were from former CIO unions. The Electrical Workers was the only building trades union to send a representative. Fourteen of the participants were full-time union employees; the rest were local union presidents. Among those in attendance was the president of Textile Workers Local 371 in Front Royal, Virginia. Three years earlier this local had been placed under trusteeship by its international for donating money toward construction of a segregated private school when public schools in its area were desegregated. Four of the participants were black, and only one held a position that permitted even limited contact with white members.

The curriculum reflected Donovan and Guernsey's belief that the purpose of the institute "could best be served by a less direct approach to the subject of race relations."[58] They reasoned that most of the students who attended the institute were interested in building and maintaining their unions. The best way to convince these students of the relevance of race relations would be to demonstrate that union discriminatory practices thwarted these goals. A preoccupation with race relations in the curriculum would also make it difficult to sell the institute idea to union presidents who favored more practical training for their staff, and it might also frighten away students with segregationist attitudes. Only the course entitled Labor and Civil Rights would deal with the issue directly. Donovan and Guernsey were confident, however, that discussions of race relations would permeate the other classroom presentations and that the integrated living arrangements would ensure that students were conscious of race at all times.

The Labor and Civil Rights course was taught by Donald Slaiman. One optimistic student wrote his union education director that he was "greatly encouraged following the course on Labor and Civil Rights. We had eight hours of this and nobody walked out."[59] Although the students may have been too polite to leave their seats, they clearly had reservations regarding the course. Labor and Civil Rights received the lowest evaluations from the students of any major course (six hours or more) offered. Students were uneasy with the description of union discriminatory practices that Slaiman presented and were reluctant to discuss questions that he posed. Whites and blacks separated at coffee breaks though they did not do so in other classes. Comments by whites revealed defensiveness such as when the most outspoken segregationist in the group asked one of the blacks,

"How many whites do you have in your union?" But even the moderate students expressed dismay at black responses to discrimination. One remarked that he could not understand why blacks at Atlantic Steel petitioned for decertification in protest over racial job classifications when "they have some of the best paying jobs for Negroes in the city." The class deteriorated to the point that on its last day Slaiman shifted the topic away from race because it was apparent that further discussion would be "counterproductive." In his analysis of this class Donovan questioned whether the indirect approach to race relations was sufficient and whether labor education was up to the challenge in this field. He wrote: "Most of the matters discussed in these sessions must be confronted directly if any headway is to be made in changing attitudes. What is greatly needed is more experience and experimentation in method before we can claim genuine proficiency as educators on these problems. . . . The need for improving teaching skills in this area is . . . pronounced."[60]

Relations between whites and blacks at the institute were cordial and polite, if not close. This was the first time many of the white students had lived, shared meals, or sat in the same classroom with a black. Although no embarrassing incidents occurred as a result of the interracial living arrangements, the students were sensitive about them. When a photographer arrived to take pictures of a pair of white and black roommates at various activities—in class, in the dining hall, and studying in their room—the white asked the photographer privately not to take a picture of them sharing a room. He explained that such a picture "would cause him trouble back home if his members were to see it."[61]

The New World Foundation was impressed enough with the first institute to contribute $15,000 for two more. The second Southern Union Staff Training Institute was scheduled to begin September 9, 1964, at the University of Texas at Austin. Emory Via was chosen as director of the institute, and Guernsey was again selected as co-director. But recruitment of students became impossible once the Republican party nominated Senator Barry Goldwater as its presidential candidate. Unions felt they could not release staff for a month to the institute because the election was so important to them. Consequently, NILE was forced to reschedule the institute for January 1965.[62]

Eighteen students attended the Texas institute, including three blacks, two Hispanics, and one Native American. Participants came from a more diverse group of affiliated unions than those who attended the North Carolina institute. With one exception, every union that sent a student to the institute at North Carolina was represented at Texas. But now more building trades unions sent students, and even unions from the printing trades and railroads were represented.

The curriculum at the Texas institute again reflected a mixture of practical and liberal education courses. One session was designed so that students could experience the obstacles blacks faced by having them take the Alabama voter registration test. Only three students passed. But accommodations were less satisfactory than those at Chapel Hill. Students were forced to live off campus in a hotel because housing at the University of Texas was still segregated.[63]

The third institute, held at the University of Georgia Center for Continuing Education in 1966, followed the pattern set in previous meetings. Students were again drawn from a variety of affiliated unions, the curriculum again included practical courses as well as those with a broader, more sociological perspective, and the interracial living arrangements again demonstrated the integrity of the institute's program. The Georgia institute also included more blacks as instructors. From the start, the NILE institutes made a conscious effort to use black instructors. Philip Weightman, head of the minorities division at COPE, led a session at the first institute in North Carolina and was joined by Vivian Henderson, an economics professor from Fisk University, at the institute in Texas. At Georgia, Henderson led one session while black civil rights leaders led another. Students met with Vernon Jordan, director of the Voter Education Project, and Aaron Henry, president of the Mississippi NAACP. The institute hosted a talk to the college community by Roy Wilkins, executive director of the NAACP. Wilkins's appearance was the first time that a major national civil rights figure spoke on the University of Georgia campus.

But the civil rights portion of the curriculum continued to get low marks from the students. They felt uncomfortable discussing some of the issues raised and complained of overexposure to the material. Only when the subject was immediately relevant to their jobs, such as a description of the work of the Equal Employment Opportunity Commission, did they respond. Otherwise, reactions were less favorable to this portion of the institute—ostensibly its raison d'être—than to any other.[64]

CONCLUSION

In 1958, one critic of labor education efforts charged that racial issues "got a real soft pedal, becoming inaudible the further South you go."[65] This criticism may have been accurate in 1958, when southern unions were paralyzed by the inroads segregationists made among their members, but after that, racial issues received a full hearing at labor education meetings in the South. In addition to the NILE institutes, southern state councils introduced racial issues into leadership and weekend institutes they hosted. The need for unions to oppose segregation was also raised at sessions of the Southern Labor School, the Gulf Coast Institute, and the Tri-State Labor School sponsored by the Virginia, North Carolina, and South Carolina state councils.[66] In fact, the "inaudibility" this critic refers to runs in the other direction. Less attention was paid to racial issues in labor education gatherings in the North, where the issue did not have the same significance to unions as it did in the South.[67]

The four-week residential NILE institutes were ambitious, expensive, and, in their integrated living arrangements, positively bold. But the NILE institutes also had their shortcomings.

First, F. Ray Marshall is accurate when he says that unions that already agreed with AFL-CIO policy were most likely to send students.[68] Of course, students from these unions did not necessarily share their unions' views and could thus profit from the NILE institutes. But as Marshall suggests, labor education programs on race relations did not generally reach members in unions that needed them most, such as the building trades, where segregationist sentiment was strongest.

Second, it is difficult to judge the effectiveness of the NILE institutes because little effort was made to follow the progress of participants once they left. In his evaluation of the first institute, Ronald Donovan acknowledged that "four weeks cannot reverse the . . . prejudices acquired over a lifetime."[69] But none of the institute planners expected a conversion experience on the part of students, and it would be unfair to judge them on that basis. They hoped the institutes would broaden the perspectives of the participants, leading them to raise new questions and confront old shibboleths. Via describes the modest task that labor educators in the South tried to accomplish:

> Our effort has been to get union members to think. . . . It is hoped that they can begin to shake away from a negative and antagonistic view of civil rights progress and find an understanding that can hold some promise of a South of decency, equality and mutual progress. . . . Another important goal is a reasoned and reasonable "other view" of events in the South and the Nation. They may discover that the Supreme Court is not always villainous, that the Constitution and democracy have a certain compatibility and that Negro gains do not mean white losses. Simple lessons, but it is often the first exposure to such an approach for many in a society where few efforts are made to reach working whites.[70]

Whether the institutes met even this standard is difficult to determine because of the lack of follow-up of those who participated.[71]

Finally, the NILE institutes were undermined by the labor movement's economism, its strategy of "pure and simple unionism." Students did not perceive the relevance of the race relations lessons to the skills they would need in defending the workplace interests of their members. Regardless of the arguments labor educators made to demonstrate the value of the race relations sections—that sit-ins by blacks in the 1960s resembled the sit-downs of the great CIO organizing drives in the 1930s, that blacks would undercut union wages unless they were organized, that blacks were a potential political ally, that unions and blacks shared the same opponents in the South—NILE participants continued to perceive the race relations part of the curriculum as tangential to the skills they needed.[72] The labor movement's strategy of pure and simple unionism posed as much of an obstacle to the simple lessons labor educators sought to impart as the prejudices they tried to overcome. If the South's racial culture led some students to reject labor's views on race relations as heresy, labor's economism led others to ignore them as irrelevant.

Perhaps the critic who complained of the "inaudibility" of labor education on race relations was less disappointed with the absence of racial issues from labor education programs than with the slight effects of their presence.

4

In Search of Realignment

Up until now the Democratic party has been affiliated with
the . . . Liberals and Conservatives, all in one party, and you
couldn't tell one from the other. If we can have some place else
for some of these to go, then we have a choice we can make and I
think . . . in the long run it will help the Labor Movement.

—Stanton Smith, AFL-CIO coordinator of
state and local central bodies

A S THE CIVIL RIGHTS MOVEMENT gained momentum, labor no longer
viewed it as a nuisance and a liability that created unwanted
conflicts. On the contrary, labor came to regard the civil rights
movement as an opportunity to defeat southern Democracy on its own
turf. If the movement succeeded, the South would no longer block progressive legislation in Congress, vote for restrictive labor legislation under the
Democratic party label, or disorder party identities with its conservatism.
The civil rights movement would supply the shock troops, newly enfranchised black voters who would realign the South and end this confusion.
This shift in perspective can be traced to the 1960 sit-ins to protest
segregation. The sit-ins were so reminiscent of the sit-downs used in the
CIO organizing drives of the 1930s that, for a moment at least, unions
could see themselves in the civil rights movement. AFL-CIO Civil Rights
Department director Boris Shiskin was so taken with the sit-ins that he
wanted to bring some participants to summer labor schools in the North to
tell of their experience. But the sit-ins had a psychological meaning that
went deeper than their ability to evoke fond memories of the past. One
report of their impact on union leaders revealed that the sit-ins "demolished
any remnants of the fantasy" that blacks were content with segregation and
demonstrated "the implacable determination of southern Negroes to
achieve integration." "One thing is clear from all this," the report continued, "the situation has changed so much in the last year that only for the

first time do real possibilities now exist for southern liberal labor opinion to speak and make itself heard."[1]

The AFL-CIO Industrial Union Department (IUD) displayed this new conviction in 1961 when it publicly contributed $5,000 to CORE, the sponsor of the Freedom Rides. News of the contribution brought the usual outbursts of rage and protest from southern members. Local unions in Alexandria, Louisiana, issued a statement to assure the public that they were opposed to the Freedom Rides and that "as far as we can determine no union money from the state of Louisiana was contributed to these law-breakers."[2] CWA Local 3902 in Alabama wrote to Meany and their international president to request a refund of the portion of their dues that went to the IUD.[3] Plumbers Local 548 in Elmore, Alabama, asked Alabama AFL-CIO president Barney Weeks whether any of the dues it contributed to the state council went toward the contribution to CORE. The local was satisfied only after Weeks assured them that "not one penny" of the money donated to CORE came from the state council. Mississippi AFL-CIO president Claude Ramsay wrote Meany to describe how disturbed his members were over the IUD contribution. Ramsay told Meany he understood that "the AFL-CIO can take only one position, and that is against racial discrimination. . . . Unfortunately, a wide segment of our membership doesn't know these things or don't give a damn, for today alot [sic] of turmoil exists because of this contribution. . . . The thing boils down to this, we can overcome everything but the contribution of union funds. No explanation will satisfy these people in this respect."[4]

Most southern unionists were unaware that the AFL-CIO had quietly financed civil rights activity before the Freedom Rides. In 1957 AFL-CIO COPE funded a registration drive among blacks in Birmingham conducted by the Alabama State Coordinating Association for Registration and Voting (ASCARV). COPE then made ASCARV a generous offer to underwrite three-quarters of the salary and expenses of a full-time worker on black voter registration.[5] COPE also invested in voter registration activity conducted by the Montgomery Improvement Association (MIA). Under the dynamic, effective leadership of a young minister, Martin Luther King, Jr., MIA boycotted segregated buses in Montgomery, organized an alternative transportation service, and maintained the spirit and solidarity of the black community in the face of threats and intimidation. When the boycott came to a successful conclusion, MIA turned its attention to electoral politics. In 1958, COPE minorities director Philip Weightman and his assistant Earl Davis enlisted MIA's support for Alabama COPE-endorsed Wilbur B. Nolen in the Democratic primary against

Representative George M. Grant. Davis reported that MIA was most cooperative in the campaign. "But most significant," Davis wrote, "was the cooperation of MIA President Reverend Martin Luther King. He came through on every request that we made of him. His expressions of appreciation at the mass meetings, of AFL-CIO's efforts in Montgomery, and the desire for complete cooperation between Labor and the Negro was most impressive."[6]

But these sporadic contributions were inadequate as the civil rights movement gained momentum. The number of requests that labor received for contributions from black voter registration groups overwhelmed the ability of Weightman's minorities office at COPE to evaluate their merit. A more effective, regular, yet discreet channel to funnel money to the civil rights movement was required. The formation of the Voter Education Project (VEP) under the auspices of the Southern Regional Council provided the perfect cover. Unions were attracted to the SRC because it was a multiracial, multipurpose organization that represented liberal white opinion in the South. This did not make the SRC lovable in the eyes of southern white union members, but it was more defensible and certainly preferable to the other alternative of contributing money directly to black civil rights organizations. The labor movement had already experienced the outcry it could expect if it contributed money directly to such organizations. The AFL-CIO wanted to avoid a repeat of the backlash and resentment that occurred following the IUD contribution to CORE in 1961.

During the summer of 1962 VEP director Wiley Branton met with COPE assistant director Al Barkan, Philip Weightman, COPE director James McDevitt, and Victor Reuther from the UAW. They agreed that labor and VEP should exchange information regarding groups and personalities they worked with in the South. COPE officials told Branton that they could not spend much money in the South but would consider VEP's requests seriously.

The first request VEP submitted to COPE concerned the Coordinating Council of Greater New Orleans (CCGNO), a group of 125 black social, fraternal, and religious groups that planned to conduct a black voter registration campaign in the Crescent City. COPE told VEP that it would contribute $5,000 to CCGNO, and the first check for $1,500 was sent. But the registration effort in New Orleans stalled when the director of the project took another job outside the city. CCGNO reorganized and submitted a new project description to VEP for approval. The new plan was budgeted at $25,000 with VEP responsible for raising $15,000 of that total. Earl Davis assured Branton that the remaining $3,500 which COPE still owed CCGNO on its original commitment could be part of the money VEP pledged to raise. COPE then promptly sent CCGNO $1,750, half of its remaining commitment. On February 5, 1963, Branton flew to Washington to discuss the New Orleans project with COPE officials. Branton argued that VEP had relieved COPE of some of its burdens in the South and consequently COPE "should seriously consider any request for financial assistance to a project from VEP." McDevitt assured Branton that COPE intended to pay the remaining $1,750 it owed on its original commitment. McDevitt then asked Branton how much additional money VEP was requesting of COPE. Branton wanted COPE to provide the remaining $12,000 VEP said it would raise for CCGNO. McDevitt demurred. Branton reminded McDevitt that VEP had refused a request from a group in Memphis that opposed a COPE-endorsed candidate. If VEP could not expect support from COPE, Branton told McDevitt, then there was no need "for VEP to keep COPE informed of our activities or even welcome suggestions from them as to where VEP might work." McDevitt reluctantly offered $6,500 more to CCGNO, in addition to COPE's original $5,000 contribution. By 1964, when the civil rights movement was in full stride, COPE was sending CCGNO $1,000 per month.[7]

Disclaimers, even when false, that COPE did not give money to civil rights organizations did not pacify outraged southern members.[8] Contributions to COPE from the South declined as members determined to punish the AFL-CIO for its support of civil rights. Arkansas AFL-CIO COPE director George Ellison explained to McDevitt that "some of the officers of this council are a little hesitant to start the COPE dollar drive because propaganda has been spread by local politicians that COPE is one of the largest contributors to the NAACP."[9] Printing Pressmens Local 211 in Montgomery informed Barney Weeks that it would pay its regular assessment for affiliation but would not contribute to the dedicated fund for COPE. The local explained that a majority of its members "refuse to support COPE because of their [sic] national views." The local understood that failure to contribute to the COPE fund would force the state council to suspend it, but this seemed a small price to pay to maintain its integrity in defense of segregation.[10] One local union was so upset at the alliance between the AFL-CIO and civil rights groups that it wrote into its bylaws the provision that, "no member shall at any time take, or spend any money from or out of the Local Union #183 treasury for anything pertaining to COPE."[11]

As precarious as such AFL-CIO organizations as COPE were in the South, the situation of AFL-CIO state councils was even more desperate.

Yet, with a few exceptions, these councils opposed segregationists, defended the national Democratic party's record, and in some cases worked with black organizations in voter registration campaigns. Southern state council officers provided courageous leadership in the face of a resistant membership and antagonistic political culture. Their leadership on civil rights is surprising because there is little in the union background of state council officials to indicate they would be so inclined. No southern state council president came from the liberal, industrial wing of the labor movement; almost all of them began their careers in segregated union locals. Louisiana AFL-CIO president Victor Bussie came from the Firefighters, Barney Weeks of Alabama from the Typographers, Claude Ramsay of Mississippi from the Papermakers, Sinway Young of South Carolina was an Electrical Worker as was Hank Brown from Texas, Harold Boyd of Virginia was a Plumber, and Bill Becker of Arkansas came from the Teachers union.

Their sympathetic response to the civil rights movement is attributable to the office they held. State council officers are responsible for defending labor's political interests. Representing only a fraction of the labor force in their states, held in low esteem by the public, maligned as an obstacle to their states' industrial development, and distrusted as Yankee agents who would change the South's racial customs, state council officers could not prevent the passage of right-to-work laws or any other restrictive labor legislation their state legislatures might propose. State council officers found themselves stymied politically by the overwhelming power of southern Democracy. The limited franchise, the one-party system, the issueless campaigns, and the preoccupation with race all conspired to permit conservative elites and their anti-labor policies to prevail. Even more than COPE in Washington, southern state councils recognized that only black enfranchisement could overcome southern Democracy and bring about the realignment labor desired. George Ellison confessed to Philip Weightman: "I feel very strongly about registering Negro voters in the state of Arkansas. I think it is the only way labor can ever achieve its political program in this state."[12] Even in such unlikely and unreconstructed outposts as Mississippi, state council officers viewed the civil rights movement as an opportunity to escape their political impotence. As early as 1959, Mississippi AFL-CIO secretary-treasurer Ray Smithhart told COPE that he was "very interested in lining up the minority people with the labor movement."[13]

Not only were black voters politically dependable, but they were strategically located in agricultural black-belt counties. These counties were the home of anti-labor legislators whom state councils could not threaten because few members lived in these legislative districts. If these legislators were to be removed from office, black voters would have to do it. Mississippi AFL-CIO president Claude Ramsay explained why a black-labor coalition in his state was necessary: "Twenty-six counties in Mississippi have a Negro popular majority. Many of labor's worst enemies in the Mississippi state legislature live in these counties: If these people are to be removed from office it will have to be with the Negro vote. To a large degree our legislative program is dependent on our ability to form alliances with these people and this we are trying to do."[14] Other state council officers in the South could also do arithmetic and recognized that black votes were necessary to defeat conservative, anti-labor legislators.

A second reason why southern state council leaders were willing to antagonize their members in pursuit of a black-labor coalition was that blacks and organized labor faced common problems and shared common enemies. Laws intended to restrict civil rights marches and demonstrations could be and were used to restrict picketing. For instance, a bill intended by the Mississippi state legislature to prevent sit-ins was first used to break a Paperworkers strike in Hattiesburg.[15] Similarly, civil rights groups suffered when laws intended to weaken unions were used against them. Laws were invoked against the Montgomery Improvement Association that were designed originally to hamper strike activities by unions.[16] Moreover, unions and blacks attracted similar enemies. Unions were not far behind blacks in the demonology of the Klan and the Citizens' Councils. A coalition of blacks and labor thus seemed appropriate if for no other reason than to defend themselves from common threats.

Third, southern AFL-CIO leaders believed that a black-labor coalition would assist in organizing new workers. The ability of unions to organize in rural counties was hindered by labor's lack of political influence in such areas. Yet the dispersed geography of southern industrialization meant that industrial jobs were increasing fastest in these rural areas.[17] For instance, between 1951 and 1964, twice as many industrial jobs were created in counties north of Jackson, Mississippi, than south of it in the more developed regions of the state.[18] Labor had no political influence in these rural areas and, consequently, organizers encountered great resistance from local officials and police. State council leaders hoped that black voters would challenge local officials and make organizing in rural areas easier. Southern union leaders were also aware of the good public relations their opposition to segregation could earn them in the black community. Black workers, who were already strong union supporters, would now be even more receptive to organizing appeals because of labor's credible civil rights record.

But the risks were as apparent as the rewards. Louisiana AFL-CIO president Victor Bussie suffered a cross burning on his lawn one night, and in another incident his car was firebombed.[19] Claude Ramsay received so many death threats that he went armed at all times. In addition to the personal danger their policies invited, state council leaders also had to contend with the political and institutional costs. Local unions disaffiliated when state councils opposed segregationists, defended the national Democratic party, and allied with blacks. Disaffiliations threatened to bankrupt state councils. Their political credibility also suffered when local unions repudiated their policies and labor-endorsed candidates were defeated. The story of a legislator from Birmingham, Alabama, illustrates vividly the degree to which members disregarded COPE recommendations and the pleading to which this reduced state council leaders. When state council officers requested the legislator's vote on a pending bill, he reminded them that they had campaigned for his opponent. "Yes," replied one of the union supplicants, "but you got most of our votes."[20]

The following chapters present case studies that reveal how southern state councils attempted to take advantage of the civil rights movement to realign their state's party systems. State councils in Arkansas, Texas, Alabama, and Mississippi tried to form biracial coalitions that would bring their state's Democratic party in line with the liberal policies of the national party. State council leaders in these states were interested in moving beyond southern Democracy because it protected conservative legislators who were hostile to unions. But they were accountable to a rank and file who, much to their dismay, were less interested in the political benefits of realignment than they were in preserving the racial status quo. This chapter details the relative success state council leaders in Arkansas and Texas had in forging "Night and Day" coalitions. The next two chapters will focus on the more demanding trials state council officials encountered in the Deep South states of Alabama and Mississippi. These states not only presented the sternest tests for civil rights activists but also posed the greatest challenge to labor's political strategy.

ARKANSAS

The greatest obstacle the Arkansas state council encountered in forging a black-labor coalition and in nationalizing the Arkansas Democratic party was Governor Orval Faubus. Attracted by his populism, the Arkansas AFL-CIO supported Faubus in 1956 when he won the second of six consecutive gubernatorial races. But labor broke with Faubus two years later when the governor surrendered to racial demagoguery and closed schools in Little Rock to prevent their desegregation. This action left the state council paralyzed by conflict between rank-and-file members who defended the governor's racial record and state council leaders who opposed it. The statewide labor movement was so split over Faubus that the 1962 Democratic gubernatorial primary marked the third consecutive time the Arkansas COPE convention failed to issue an endorsement. But the state council leadership made its views known through the *Arkansas Union Labor Bulletin*, which warned its readers that "the reelection of Governor Orval Faubus would be of great harm to the working people of our state."[21] Many of the *Bulletin*'s subscribers, however, believed otherwise. Faubus won the 1962 primary with 51 percent of the vote, and the *Bulletin* conceded that the governor polled well in working-class districts "out of past loyalties and his record on segregation."[22]

As long as Faubus dominated the Democratic party, and the Democratic party dominated politics in Arkansas, the state council would be politically homeless. State council president George Ellison was in such despair over the situation that he even considered working with the Republican party if that would break the mold of one-party politics in Arkansas. The chair of the Republican party in Arkansas asked Ellison what his party's candidates must do to earn the state council's endorsement. Ellison wrote to James McDevitt for advice:

> The big question for the AFL-CIO in Arkansas is whether or not we should give them any assistance. Most of the candidates . . . are more reactionary than their Democratic opponents. Which, of course, would mean if the Republicans were elected, Labor would take a beating for the next two years. But, if the Republicans gain control of some of the state offices, this would make available some of the state patronage and enable them through patronage to build a fairly strong party. Our question is if the Republicans were strong in Arkansas, would this force the Democratic Party to more closely align themselves with the National platform and eventually put up liberal candidates for the Democratic nominees? If this were to happen, then perhaps over a period of time it would be to labor's advantage to build a Republican party now. I would certainly appreciate your opinion as to the right course Labor should pursue in this matter.[23]

Ellison's proposal may have been only half-serious, but there was nothing frivolous about the lack of alternatives offered by the party system in

Arkansas. The dilemma created by one-party politics was real, as others besides Ellison acknowledged. AFL-CIO coordinator of state and local central bodies Stanton Smith told delegates to the 1962 Arkansas AFL-CIO convention that he welcomed Republican gains in the South. Labor needed "some means of separating the sheep from the goats here in the Southern states. Up until now the Democratic party has been affiliated with the . . . Liberals and Conservatives, all in one party, and you couldn't tell one from the other. If we can have some place else for some of these to go, then we have a choice we can make and I think . . . in the long run it will help the Labor Movement."[24] The *Arkansas Union Labor Bulletin* was pleased when Winthrop Rockefeller agreed to run for governor on the Republican ticket in 1964 because of the boost this would provide the Arkansas GOP. The *Bulletin* found virtue in Rockefeller's candidacy, not because it found merit in his platform, but because it would revive the Republicans and contribute to a two-party system in Arkansas.[25]

The Arkansas AFL-CIO flirted with a Republican resurgence but in the end did nothing to assist it, and instead tried to bore from within the statewide Democratic party. When the party refused to include liberal planks suggested by labor in its platform, the state council formed a group called Democrats for Arkansas to fight for these reforms within the party. Democrats for Arkansas was organized in 1964 "to change the course of the State Party in the image of Presidents Roosevelt, Truman, Kennedy and Johnson" and to have such measures as a state minimum wage law and permanent voter registration included in the party's platform.[26] A year later, in 1965, the state council allied with the Young Democrats of Arkansas in another attempt to bring the Arkansas Democratic party into conformity with the national party.

The Arkansas Young Democrats' convention in May 1965 was a raucous affair. Liberals led by Samuel Boyce, district attorney for the Third Judicial District of Arkansas, engineered a quick vote that elected delegates to the Young Democrats' national convention who were loyal to the national party. Boyce was well supported at the convention by members of organized labor, including Herb Bingaman, Arkansas director of the UAW, Bob Parker, a state council executive board member, and Lee Pritchard, secretary of the Central Arkansas Labor Council.[27] Outmaneuvered and defeated, conservatives walked out, held a rump convention, and selected their own delegates.[28] The Democratic national committeeman for Arkansas and the chair of the state Democratic party immediately certified the rump group and denied Boyce a hearing. Boyce appealed to Arkansas AFL-CIO president Bill Becker, who then alerted AFL-CIO COPE director Al Barkan about the ferment in the Young Democrats. Becker flew to Washington, where he and Barkan visited the Democratic National Committee and the president of the Young Democratic Clubs of America to discuss the situation in Arkansas.[29] The Arkansas AFL-CIO subsidized the Boyce faction, contributing $600 per month until the credentials challenge could be settled at the Young Democrats' national convention in New York.[30] In October, Becker traveled with Boyce to the Young Democrats' convention. The convention listened to both groups' arguments for credentials and, for the first time in its history, refused to seat a delegation certified by state party officers and instead awarded credentials to Boyce's delegation.[31] The *Arkansas Gazette* editorialized that the formation of Democrats for Arkansas and the success of the Boyce faction of the Young Democrats provided "new evidence for a belief that Arkansas politics and government are on the threshold of a reformation."[32]

To cross that threshold, however, the formation of a black-labor coalition was necessary. Blacks and state council leaders were familiar with each other from their alliance to keep Little Rock schools open in the late 1950s. The first steps toward a black-labor political coalition occurred in 1961, when George Ellison was approached by a delegation of black women from the Women's Emergency Committee (WEC). WEC was formed during the Little Rock school crisis. When that crisis passed, WEC followed the direction of MIA in Alabama and turned its attention to black enfranchisement. WEC indicated to Ellison that it was interested in conducting a voter registration campaign among blacks. The group said it could raise the money for a registration drive, but needed help planning and executing the campaign.

Ellison was discouraged when WEC raised only $500, but he was not prepared to let this opportunity slip away. He asked COPE minorities director Philip Weightman to visit Arkansas "on what appears as a wild goose chase. But I feel very strongly about registering the Negro in the state of Arkansas. I think it is the only way Labor can ever achieve its political program in the state."[33] Ellison also wrote McDevitt, excited that WEC's new direction "will benefit the county COPE program [in Little Rock] as a large majority of the members of the committee support the same political program, particularly economic issues, as organized labor."[34]

Other civil rights groups in Arkansas made efforts to familiarize themselves with state council leaders, who responded warmly to their overtures. For example, the Arkansas coordinator of SNCC inquired if the state council would assist his organization with a registration drive it planned to conduct.[35] In 1962 the Central Arkansas Labor Council endorsed the first black candidate in its history when it supported Dr. W. H. Townsend, president of the Council on Community Affairs (COCA), a federation of black religious, civic, and fraternal groups in Little Rock, for a seat on the Little Rock City Managers Board. Ellison proudly informed Barkan that "the most promising news regarding labor's political future is the eagerness of the other minority groups in the state to work with us. . . . They are not only willing but anxious to work with labor in accomplishing our common goals."[36]

The black-labor coalition congealed in the 1964 elections. COPE forgave Faubus for his past transgressions and endorsed him for the first time since 1956. Faubus rode on President Lyndon Johnson's coattails to win 86 percent of the black vote.[37] Blacks and labor also allied in a referendum campaign to abolish the poll tax, a goal the state council had pursued in vain for some years.[38] The state council underwrote the Committee for Voter Registration that was formed to lead the poll tax campaign. The Arkansas AFL-CIO made an initial investment of $10,000 to the committee, $3,500 of which was supplied by national COPE, with more money promised as needed.[39] Daniel Powell estimated that labor furnished 95 percent of the money and 80 percent of the personnel in the campaign to abolish the poll tax. In addition, the state council financed registration drives by black organizations and contributed to the new spirit of unity among them. Ellison told Barkan that the state council's participation in the Committee for Voter Registration was "public relations that will definitely change the public image of Labor in the State of Arkansas that no amount of paid advertising and publicity could ever buy." When the referendum initiative passed by fifty-eight thousand votes, Becker confided to Barkan that labor was in the "best political shape we have been in for a long time." He cited the development of a two-party system in Arkansas, a good registration law, and his "high hopes that we'll be able to form good working relationships with Negro and other organizations" as the reasons for his optimism.[40]

Another notable contest in which blacks and unions cooperated was the 1964 state senate race in Pulaski County. The Central Arkansas Labor Council and black organizations in Little Rock allied to elect Jim Brandon in the Democratic primary.[41] Brandon was opposed by Everett Tucker, one of the Little Rock school board members who in 1959 had voted to dismiss teachers for encouraging desegregation. While Brandon came out publicly in support of the 1964 Civil Rights Act passed by Congress, Tucker told voters, "When I was elected to the Little Rock School Board in 1958 my position as a segregationist was known and my position has not changed."[42]

Tucker circulated hate literature during the campaign that showed Arkansas AFL-CIO president Bill Becker flanked by two SNCC activists and charged Brandon with being the tool of labor bosses and black extremists. Becker reported to Barkan that "a coalition of labor and the Negro is evident in this race and both groups are working well together." When Brandon defeated Tucker, the *Pine Bluff Commercial* called it "a turning point in Arkansas politics."[43]

The black-labor coalition that emerged in the 1964 elections continued to blossom. Powell reported to COPE officials in Washington that Becker was "working with Liberal and Negro leaders in the formation of a Liberal-Negro coalition for the 1966 elections." The *Arkansas Gazette* reported that at the 1965 Arkansas AFL-CIO convention "speaker after speaker spoke out against discrimination." A resolution that called on unions to "set their own house in order" and provide leadership to the community in bringing about compliance with the new federal civil rights law was passed without dissent. AFL-CIO Civil Rights Department director Donald Slaiman told the delegates how civil rights leaders had lobbied Congress to repeal 14(b) of the Taft-Hartley Act, and Texas AFL-CIO president Hank Brown urged delegates to ally with minorities but to come with clean credentials, no taint of discrimination.[44] Later in the year, members of the Central Arkansas Labor Council and COCA cooperated successfully to pass a millage increase in school taxes and to elect candidates to the Little Rock school board.[45] Becker hosted a luncheon for local union leaders in Little Rock at which Townsend spoke of the benefits a black-labor coalition could bring. In November, Becker was invited by the Little Rock Urban League to chair Equal Opportunity Day, which recognized employers who did not discriminate. Becker also held regular meetings with COCA and the state chapter of the NAACP to discuss cooperative strategies blacks and labor might pursue in the next spring's primaries.[46]

The black-labor coalition was sealed in the 1966 Democratic gubernatorial primary runoff when Arkansas COPE endorsed Frank Holt over his opponent, Jim Johnson. Arkansas COPE acknowledged that Johnson had a superior record on strictly labor issues but that he forfeited labor's support because he was an avowed segregationist. Becker accused Johnson of spreading racial hatred and explained that the state council could not endorse him despite his superior labor record because the issues in the runoff were "larger than minimum wage, larger than social security. These issues go to the heart of our democratic institutions. . . . We've said we're citizens first and labor members second and it's time to demonstrate our belief in that statement."[47]

A letter Daniel Powell sent to COPE headquarters in 1968 indicates how far unions in Arkansas had progressed since the Little Rock school crisis. Ten years before, Powell told COPE that he found more racist views expressed in locals from Arkansas than even those from Birmingham, Alabama. Powell now wrote to COPE director Barkan that there was "less racial antagonism within the ranks of the local union leadership in Arkansas than in any other state." The Arkansas state council not only participated in a political coalition with minorities but was the only state council in Powell's territory to endorse a strong civil rights bill before the state legislature. Credit for this remarkable achievement, Powell believed, belonged to the officers of the Arkansas AFL-CIO, Bill Becker and George Ellison. Their leadership had steered unions in Arkansas from the paralysis that afflicted them during the Little Rock school crisis to the benefits of the coalition with blacks they now enjoyed.[48]

TEXAS

Both Arkansas and Texas were one-party states, dominated by conservative Democrats, in which unions were isolated politically. Consequently, the labor movement in both states perceived the civil rights movement as an opportunity to realign the party system and break finally the mold of one-party domination that was the source of their political impotence. But Texas officials encountered far more protest from below to their political strategy than did officers in Arkansas.

The Texas labor movement did not escape the turmoil that swept through the South in the wake of *Brown*. Civil rights issues dominated the 1957 merger convention of the AFL and CIO state councils. Conflict over civil rights policy had not abated when delegates convened again a year later. At the 1958 Civil Rights Committee meeting, supporters and opponents of segregation each promised to take the issue to the convention floor with a minority report if they found the committee's recommendations objectionable. When a black delegate on the committee commented that "we could not be proud of Little Rock or Governor Faubus," a white delegate interrupted: "Maybe we are not proud of the NAACP but we are not popping off about it."[49] At the convention, state council leaders were forced to concede and modify a resolution that condemned the Citizens' Councils and Ku Klux Klan as subversive organizations. So many union members had joined these organizations and took umbrage at their characterization as "subversive" that the resolution was amended so that no organization was identified by name.[50] Texas AFL-CIO president Jerry

Holleman acknowledged that the state council experienced "a riffle of excitement" when it hired a black secretary and encountered some "resentment" when it hosted a mixed banquet and dance at its convention. But he assured Stanton Smith, "The progress is slow and steady and our pressure shall remain constant."[51]

The Texas AFL-CIO could also report progress on the political front. The labor movement in Texas and its liberal allies had been sorely disappointed with the record of the Texas Democratic party. The party was dominated by conservatives from the banking, ranching, and oil industries who refused to cooperate with the national Democratic party and supported policies indistinguishable from those offered by the Republicans.[52] Open conflict exploded finally at the 1956 Texas Democratic party convention when liberals charged conservatives with violating party rules to steal the convention from them. Three months later, the Texas AFL-CIO and liberals formed the Democrats of Texas (DOT) to democratize party procedures and ensure loyalty to the national party. One speaker at DOT's founding convention articulated the view of labor officials and liberals in Texas when he complained, "Wouldn't it be nice to have all those who really believe in Republicanism opposing us honorably . . . rather than having to continue this practice of having to watch more closely the traitors in our own party than we do the honest Republican opposition?"[53] The Texas labor movement was DOT's most generous benefactor, and Holleman and Texas AFL-CIO secretary-treasurer Fred Schmidt served on DOT's executive committee.

But alliance with the state's liberal Democrats did not offset the newly merged Texas AFL-CIO's lack of rapport with the black community. COPE area director Donald Ellinger confessed, "Our relationship with the Negro organizations in Texas is at an all-time low." In August 1957, state council officers met with black leaders but came away without an agreement on a coordinated statewide poll tax drive. The best Ellinger could recommend was cooperation between labor and blacks at the county level. Later in the year, Ellinger attended the NAACP state convention but again found the NAACP's plans for a poll tax drive "completely inadequate." He reported to McDevitt that the NAACP "is not going to produce the kind of response we need from the leaders of Texas in 1958." When the NAACP registration drive finally got under way, Ellinger was skeptical that it would produce any results.[54]

But blacks were as disappointed with labor's civil rights record as labor was with the black community's political disorganization. Segregationist outbursts from local unions in East Texas and along the Gulf Coast did not enhance the reputation of unions among blacks, and when a black ran for a seat on the Houston school board in 1958 she was all but ignored by the state council and unions in the city.[55]

Ellinger was discouraged and asked Philip Weightman to visit Texas to see if bridges to the black community could be built. Weightman arrived in Texas on August 13, 1959, and after touring the state reported that blacks were "very anxious to work with us on a poll tax campaign." Weightman suggested that the state council hire a black trade unionist to work with the NAACP on voter registration. Erma LeRoy, who was active in the NAACP and whose husband was president of a Railway Clerks local union in Houston, was chosen for the job. National COPE agreed to subsidize half of LeRoy's salary with the Texas AFL-CIO responsible for the rest.[56]

LeRoy's reports to the state council were an invaluable source of information on the political status and mobilization potential of the black community in Texas. She provided the state council with the names of political organizations in different black communities, their leaders' names, whether the tax assessor in a particular county would deputize blacks to collect poll taxes, and whether local black and trade union leaders were familiar with each other. Although she acknowledged that "the great majority of the Negro voters . . . are outside of the labor movement and don't know and haven't heard of our Labor Leaders in the immediate area," the reception she received as a labor ambassador left her encouraged. According to LeRoy, black leaders appreciated the interest labor showed in their welfare and expressed a desire to work with the labor movement on voter registration.[57]

LeRoy's work paid off in the 1960 elections. The statewide Council of Negro Organizations worked closely with the Texas AFL-CIO, and there was notable black-labor cooperation at the local level in Houston and San Antonio. Ellinger told McDevitt, "I think the movement in Texas throughout the state, top to bottom, did an excellent job . . . coordinating with the necessary minority groups here."[58] But the fight within the Texas Democratic party that preceded the election fractured labor's relationship with DOT. Labor was content to secure a loyal delegation from Texas to the national Democratic party convention and announced that it would support any candidate the convention nominated for president, even Texas senator Lyndon Johnson. DOT liberals, however, were far more determined to spoil Johnson's bid for the nomination and wanted to challenge the Texas delegation that was instructed for Johnson on the floor of the convention. Labor withdrew from DOT when liberals continued to challenge the Texas delegation despite its pledge to support the Democratic ticket.[59]

Labor's departure dealt DOT a crippling blow. The demise of DOT left the coalition of labor, blacks, Hispanics, and independent liberals without an organizational vehicle. This became painfully apparent in the 1961 special election to fill Lyndon Johnson's Senate seat. So many candidates bid to inherit the Kennedy-Johnson coalition that carried Texas in 1960 that the liberal vote split among them. Two conservatives, "Dollar" Bill Blakley, a Democrat, and John Tower, a Republican, survived into the runoff. There was some sentiment in the state council to support Tower in the hope that a Republican victory would attract enough conservative Democrats to vote in the 1962 Republican primaries that a liberal would prevail among the Democrats.[60] But the state council reluctantly and unenthusiastically opted for Blakley so it could plead for "party loyalty in subsequent campaigns."[61]

State council leaders were discouraged and appalled at the division of the liberal vote in the 1961 special election. Beginning in July, executives representing black political groups, Hispanic organizations, the Farmers Union, the Texas AFL-CIO, and the remains of DOT met in Austin to discuss how liberals could avoid dissipating their strength in future contests. These meetings bore fruit two years later when the Democratic Coalition (DC) was formed. The coalition was composed of black, brown, labor, and liberal organizations, which allied "for the objective of securing candidates and assuring their election to congressional and state governmental offices and to prepare for a poll tax drive."[62] The DC would evaluate candidates and recommend one as most favorable to its affiliated organizations. Although affiliates were not bound to follow the coalition's recommendations, they would obviously carry some weight.[63]

In 1963 the coalition was absorbed in the referendum campaign to repeal the poll tax. A block-worker program funded by the Texas AFL-CIO was set up in sixteen cities, each with a full-time director, to increase turnout from minority precincts. Over eight thousand block workers were recruited, trained, armed with walk lists, and given repeal literature to distribute to prospective voters. The block-worker program was truly impressive. Black turnout in the 1963 poll tax referendum increased 90 percent over its turnout in the 1962 Democratic primary and was triple the normal black turnout in Texas off-year elections. Hispanic turnout equaled that in the 1962 primaries instead of dropping, as would be expected in an off-year, while white turnout declined from 56 to 20 percent. But poll tax repeal was defeated. Whites were so opposed to repeal and constituted so large a majority in the state that they defeated the measure despite their poor turnout.[64]

"The Coalition concept is strong among our leadership but still has not been accepted by local union leaders," Texas AFL-CIO president Hank

Brown confessed in a letter to Al Barkan. Brown acknowledged that there was considerable backlash against civil rights among white union members, as indicated by a letter he received from a member of OCAW Local 4-228 in Port Neches:

> [Given] the deep-seated feelings that exist and which show little signs of subsiding in the immediate future, it is obvious that we jeopardize our own security and growth by a too aggressive pursuance of our Civil Rights policy. . . . Today there is widespread discontent in this local and others. The list of non-members is growing. A very serious condition exists and over-emphasis on Negro rights will surely result in decreased C.O.P.E. contributions, less political effectiveness, adversely affect collective bargaining and make organizing in the South practically impossible.

At times Brown was bewildered by the racism he encountered within the affiliated locals. He wrote C. J. Haggerty, president of the AFL-CIO building and construction trades department, that he could not understand how some union leaders could "have such a strong dislike and contempt for their Negro and Latino brothers," when they needed to cooperate with such groups to overcome powerful anti-labor forces in the state.[65]

Racism was not the only obstacle state council leaders had to overcome when they participated in the coalition. Some union leaders disagreed with the coalition's strategy of challenging the Texas Democratic party. These officials believed that the state council should cooperate with the existing power structure led by Governor John Connally and not ally with minorities, who lacked the power to deliver politically. This conciliatory strategy was articulated especially by representatives from the Carpenters, Machinists, Auto Workers, and Steel Workers.[66] They were powerful enough to prevent Texas COPE from endorsing the coalition slate for statewide races in 1964. This had calamitous results for liberal candidates. Local union leaders hoping to earn credit with Governor Connally supported him while the other members of the coalition canvassed for Connally's opponent, Donald Yarborough. Coalition partners retaliated and refused to support labor-endorsed candidates in other contests. Relations deteriorated further when coalition members held labor's desertion responsible for the defeat of their candidates. Blacks now voiced publicly what they had felt in private: labor dominated the coalition by virtue of its financial support and labor-endorsed candidates received far more support from blacks than black candidates received from labor.[67] In the aftermath of the election, Brown acknowledged the damage that had been done when he told Barkan, "We must now begin the hard task of again consolidating our forces to maintain a working coalition in Texas."[68]

But before the Texas AFL-CIO could repair its relations with the coalition, it would have to defend its political strategy from critics inside the state council. Building trades unions and Steel Workers locals disaffiliated in protest over the state council's attempt to rebuild its damaged coalition with minorities. The Auto Workers' district director threatened to take his locals out of the state council if it did not change its political strategy. COPE area director Walter Gray informed Barkan that the Texas AFL-CIO had suffered so many disaffiliations that it could no longer financially support all its programs. This left "the Democratic coalition on pretty shaky ground mostly because we are no longer putting in all the finances." Brown invited Haggerty to intervene and convince the building trades to reaffiliate. He informed Haggerty that "the Texas Labor Movement is today standing at a crossroads" and argued for the path that led toward coalition. Brown acknowledged that the "Texas COPE program is definitely a departure. . . . We do not seek primarily patronage but rather political change," which, he told Haggerty, was within grasp only if labor was united. A similar appeal was sent to UAW president Walter Reuther in which Brown lamented, "Where the UAW is strongest in Texas, the coalition concept is weakest." Brown informed Reuther that deals between Governor Connally and the Auto Workers leadership in Texas had tarnished labor's reputation among minorities and imperiled the coalition strategy. He urged Reuther to ensure that his locals remained affiliated and encouraged him to visit Texas and "provide the Texas Labor Movement with the stimulus and wisdom it needs in this crucial period." Brown made one last plea, flying to Washington to discuss with AFL-CIO officials the state council's affiliation problem and to request a $30,000 loan that would permit the Texas AFL-CIO to continue to underwrite the Democratic Coalition.[69]

Although the state council's relations with its coalition partners would heal, it continued to be beset by internal cleavages and disaffected members. Local unions that disagreed with the state council's realignment strategy were slow to reaffiliate, and union members continued to disregard COPE endorsements. In the 1968 presidential election, a majority of union members in Texas either voted Republican or for third-party candidate George C. Wallace.[70]

CONCLUSION

State council officers in Arkansas and Texas were stymied by the one-party system in their states. Labor officials felt unwelcome within their state's Democratic party because it was controlled by conservatives in Texas and the Faubus machine in Arkansas. Labor officials felt like orphans who had been placed in a foster home where they were more likely to be punished than appreciated. In each case, they turned to the potential of black enfranchisement as a solution. They tried to build bridges to blacks but to their dismay discovered that their members were unwilling to cross them. Members were less interested in the organizational and political benefits a black-labor coalition could deliver than they were in preserving Jim Crow. This was especially the case in Texas, where the Klan and the Citizens' Councils captured several local unions. The coalition strategy was less successful in Texas than in Arkansas because industrial unions in the Lone Star State defected from it.

Jack Bass and Walter DeVries acknowledged in their review of southern politics that "AFL-CIO presidents in every southern state . . . stood with blacks on civil rights issues."[71] This statement is overly generous. The response of southern state councils to the civil rights movement differed according to the potential influence of the black vote within the state, the strength of the building trades within the state council, and the courage and liberalism of the state council leadership. For instance, leaders of the Georgia AFL-CIO were racial conservatives who were allied politically with the Talmadge wing of their state's Democratic party, and the Florida AFL-CIO was apathetic. The Tennessee AFL-CIO was also unresponsive to the opportunities the civil rights movement presented. Under President Stanton Smith the Tennessee AFL-CIO had supported black voter registration. But when Smith was defeated in 1960 over this issue, his successor, Matt Lynch, severed relations with black voter registration groups. He even forbade anyone from Philip Weightman's minorities division at COPE to do registration work in his state.[72]

Other state councils performed erratically. At times, North Carolina AFL-CIO president William Barbee was genuinely interested in forging a political coalition with blacks. The 1960 North Carolina AFL-CIO convention passed a resolution applauding the student sit-ins at lunch counters.[73] A year later, the state council executive board met with black leaders in Raleigh to discuss forming a political coalition. At the 1965 state council convention Barbee denounced the Klan, which had infiltrated some locals to the extent that Klan literature circulated openly in the convention hall. A few delegates walked out when Barbee spoke, and Daniel Powell was impressed that Barbee risked loss of political support by his brave attack.[74]

But at other times Barbee showed disinterest in civil rights matters and exceedingly bad judgment. Nothing beyond an exchange of good faith came out of the meeting with black leaders in Raleigh. By 1966 Barbee was being criticized for being unfamiliar with the black leadership in North Carolina.[75] In 1963 Barbee was forced to withdraw a job offer to CWA Local 3060 president Roger Baugess to be North Carolina COPE director because Baugess had signed a petition to resegregate the bathrooms at the Western Electric plant that his local represented in Winston-Salem. Barbee reluctantly withdrew the offer only after Powell explained that Baugess's appointment would embarrass the AFL-CIO and the state council.[76]

Other state councils, however, produced better results and confirm Bass and DeVries's judgment about their support of black political equality. In South Carolina, state council president Sinway Young was supportive of civil rights. In Louisiana, AFL-CIO president Victor Bussie opposed massive resistance and defended the national Democratic party from a slate of unpledged electors in 1960. Following passage of the 1965 Voting Rights Act, Bussie joined with civil rights groups in Louisiana to request that U.S. Attorney General Nicholas Katzenbach assign more federal registrars to the state. A year later Bussie wrote Emory Via at SRC that "we have sponsored efforts jointly with the Negro community throughout Louisiana to step-up the registration program."[77]

These actions provoked the customary response from local union leaders and members in Louisiana. The state council lost fifteen thousand members because of its support of public schools and the Democratic party, and another six thousand left when Bussie intervened on behalf of blacks in the 1965 race wars in Bogalusa.[78] The defeat of Representative James Morrison in 1966 also confirmed that Bussie's constituents would be unwilling accomplices in the coalition he was trying to form. Morrison had a distinguished labor record of opposing Taft-Hartley in 1947, Landrum-Griffin in 1959, and of voting for repeal of section 14(b) of Taft-Hartley in 1965. But Morrison's fealty to President Johnson's program, including a vote for the 1965 Voting Rights Act, earned him the enmity of voters back home. The state council highlighted Morrison's labor record, but members were more concerned with his votes on civil rights. Mailings from the state council supporting Morrison were returned defaced, and Morrison was turned away from union halls where he had once been welcome.[79] Despite these defeats, threats, and disaffiliations, the Louisiana AFL-CIO continued to support black enfranchisement and civil rights.

The Virginia AFL-CIO also earned a good record on civil rights. Labor gave generously to increase black voter registration in Richmond, Portsmouth, and Norfolk in 1959. Earl Davis and Fannie Neal of COPE worked with the Crusade for Voters in Richmond, the Citizens Committee in

Norfolk, and the Central Civic Forum in Portsmouth to bring out the black vote.[80] Two years later, in the 1961 Democratic primary, the COPE-endorsed slate led by A. E. Stephens for governor received more support from blacks than from union members.[81] COPE officials and the Virginia state council drew the obvious lesson from these results: the only way to defeat the anti-labor Byrd machine and redeem the Democratic party in Virginia was to enfranchise blacks. Davis urged delegates to the 1963 Virginia AFL-CIO convention to ally with their natural partner, and Barkan made a similar plea two years later.[82] The black-labor coalition experienced its finest hour in 1969, when it finally defeated the Byrd machine and elected Virginia's first Republican governor since 1885.

Although the record of southern state councils was not as unambiguous as Bass and DeVries suggest, many did attempt to build "Night and Day" coalitions. This political strategy was pursued in both Arkansas and Texas, and the former even derived some benefit from it. The Alabama AFL-CIO was not so lucky. Alabama was the cradle of the Confederacy and defended its memory with a tenacity that frightened even the bravest of civil rights activists. It was the site of some of the most fierce civil rights struggles: the test of strength and endurance in Montgomery, the uncontrolled savagery the Freedom Riders encountered in Anniston, the fire hoses and dogs that were unleashed on protesters in Birmingham, and the police violence in Selma. Racial antagonism ran so deep throughout the state that the Alabama AFL-CIO waged a purely defensive struggle to maintain an organizational presence and to prevent its members from falling victim to the segregationist appeal of Governor George Wallace.

5

Fighting the Good Fight in Alabama

I am afraid that a majority of our union membership in the South
today is more aware of and in sympathy with the program and
policies of the John Birch Society than they are with the program
and policies of the AFL-CIO.

—Daniel Powell, COPE area director

I N MARCH 1958, the newly merged Alabama AFL-CIO prepared for its
first Democratic primary. The state council gave a favorable evaluation to five of the thirteen candidates, and when only one of them
made it to the runoff, the state council endorsed him. This candidate was a
former circuit court judge who compiled an impressive record while
serving in the state legislature. He opposed Alabama's right-to-work law,
voted against regressive sales taxes, favored more liberal unemployment
compensation laws, and remained loyal to the national Democratic party
in 1948 when other southerners bolted.[1] His legislative record was so
progressive that the Alabama Chamber of Commerce once labeled him a
"radical."[2] His name was George C. Wallace.

Wallace lost the Democratic primary runoff in 1958 but returned four
years later in another bid for governor. On March 9, 1962, the Alabama
COPE executive board met to evaluate Wallace and the other candidates
in the Democratic gubernatorial primary. A screening committee reviewed their records and gave a favorable rating to three of the nine
candidates: former governor James E. Folsom, state legislator Ryan de-
Graffenried, and Judge George C. Wallace. A brief attempt was made in
the executive board meeting to give a favorable rating to a fourth candidate, Birmingham police commissioner Eugene "Bull" Connor, but his
states'-rights past was too great an obstacle and this effort died quickly.[3]
The executive board finally settled upon its three preferences but was

unsure whether it should single out one candidate or report all three favorably. It left this decision to the full COPE committee, which held its own version of a southern primary to determine whether any of the candidates had enough support to warrant a single endorsement. Wallace won the first primary against both Folsom and deGraffenried in the COPE committee and then defeated Folsom 34 to 23 in the runoff.[4] But Wallace was still three votes shy of the two-thirds majority he needed for an endorsement, according to AFL-CIO central body rules. Despite its clear preference for Wallace, the COPE committee forwarded a favorable rating for all three candidates to the COPE convention, which ratified it by a vote of 314 to 211.[5]

The results of the May primary did not clarify the picture for the state council because both Wallace and deGraffenried survived into the runoff. Wallace lobbied the Alabama AFL-CIO executive board before the runoff and reportedly promised to recommend a Speaker of the House and chair of the House Business and Labor Committee who would be acceptable to the state council in return for its support.[6] When asked for his views on racial matters, Wallace did not mince words and told the executive board, "I am for segregated schools." But this did not distinguish his response from deGraffenried, who assured the state council that he "would do everything in his power to preserve segregation" if elected governor.[7]

Wallace crushed deGraffenried in the runoff, which assured his election as governor. When the Alabama AFL-CIO convention met in October, an appreciative and victorious George Wallace appeared to address the delegates. He expressed his gratitude to the state council for its faith and support over the course of his political career, in both victory and defeat. He assured delegates of his sympathy for their concerns and promised that his pro-labor record as a legislator was just a precursor of what they could expect from his administration.

But the state council never profited from the investment it had made in Wallace's career. Instead of the access and influence it hoped to receive in return for its loyal support, the state council's political profile deteriorated precipitously during Wallace's first administration. When Wallace emerged as the South's most popular and defiant defender of segregation, the state council opposed him openly and paid dearly for doing so. Local unions disaffiliated, membership declined, and the state council was discredited politically when candidates it endorsed were defeated. Despite Wallace's promise that the "door of the Governor's office would be open" to them, state council officers were not consulted on bills pertinent to their members, they were not appointed to state commissions on which they traditionally had served, and Wallace campaigned against the candidates they endorsed. The political career they had nourished now threatened to ruin them.

This chapter recounts the challenge that Governor George Wallace and his defense of white supremacy posed to the Alabama AFL-CIO in the 1960s. The state council was accountable to and financially dependent on local unions whose members believed in white supremacy and supported George Wallace. Yet the Alabama AFL-CIO braved these threats and was a persistent critic of Wallace's racial demagoguery. It endorsed loyal Democrats over candidates favored by Wallace and fought with Wallace supporters to ensure that the Alabama Democratic party remained faithful to the national party.

The Alabama AFL-CIO opposed Wallace because its leaders sympathized with black demands for civil rights. In addition, Wallace's defense of white supremacy threatened the state council's political strategy which depended on black enfranchisement. Black political participation, state council leaders believed, would increase the influence of liberals inside the Alabama Democratic party and the state legislature. It would also realign the state's party system, giving voters a choice at last between conservative Republicans and liberal Democrats.

But the courage required to pursue these goals and resist the Wallace juggernaut took a toll. The more the state council found itself at odds with the governor over civil rights, the more institutional and political costs accumulated. A decade would pass before the state council was rewarded for the political courage it displayed in the 1960s. The civil rights record it assembled in the 1960s laid the basis for the black-labor coalition that sustains the Alabama Democratic party today.

THE ALABAMA AFL-CIO AND GOVERNOR GEORGE WALLACE

The Alabama AFL-CIO was as sympathetic and sensitive to black demands as its location in the Deep South would permit. The 1956 unity convention of the Alabama AFL and CIO state councils took place in Mobile because it was the most racially tolerant and least segregated city in the state. Mobile prevailed over the objections of some AFL executive board members who complained that it was too isolated from the rest of the state, which might discourage attendance. They preferred that the convention be held either in Montgomery, where it was scheduled originally, or in Birmingham, closer to most locals. But both cities had been the sites of recent racial turmoil, which disqualified them as hosts for the convention.[8] The newly unified state council also took pains to ensure black representation on its executive board. The new Alabama AFL-CIO constitution provided for six vice-president positions that were to be elected at large. According to a gentleman's agreement reached during the merger negotiations, four of these posts were reserved for blacks and two for women.[9] But the Alabama AFL-CIO was circumspect enough not to comment directly on the racial matters that so exercised its members. It did not demand repeal of the poll tax because of its racial implications, nor did it denounce Jim Crow. The state council was occupied enough with reconciling local unions and local central bodies to the merger without antagonizing them further over civil rights.[10]

The state council was encouraged when Wallace took office in 1962 and looked forward to a warm relationship with the new governor. But the more Wallace became the tribune of those who defended segregation, the more the state council recoiled from him. The divergent paths of these former allies became clear when the state council failed to endorse Wallace in the 1964 presidential primaries and opposed his slate of unpledged electors in the Alabama Democratic primary.

Governor Wallace announced his candidacy for the 1964 Democratic presidential nomination on March 7 and declared that his first test would be the Wisconsin primary. The Wisconsin AFL-CIO responded quickly in a letter to its affiliated locals accusing Wallace of being a "carpetbagger, a bigot, a racist and one of the strongest anti-labor spokesman in America." Wallace supporters moved quickly to parry this charge and to portray the governor as a friend of workers. H. L. Welch, a business agent for the Carpenters and president of the Montgomery Building Trades Council, told the UPI wire service that the Wisconsin AFL-CIO's statement was "false and malicious" and that "the rank and file membership of the AFL-CIO in Alabama . . . is 100% behind Governor Wallace."[11] Alabama AFL-CIO president Barney Weeks alerted the news media immediately that the Alabama state council had not endorsed Wallace, as the wire service story implied, and that Welch spoke only for himself. Wallace campaign aides then pressed Weeks for a statement they could use to offset the attack by the Wisconsin state council. Weeks refused. The aides then approached local union officers in Alabama to attest to Wallace's pro-labor record. Communications Workers Local 3902 complied and informed the Milwaukee Labor Council of Wallace's outstanding labor record, urging it to support him. William T. Thrash, business manager of Operating Engineers Local 312 in Birmingham, sent a telegram to the Wisconsin AFL-CIO informing it that the governor had a "perfect labor record in

Alabama" and demanded that the state council retract its statement. When Wallace spoke on Milwaukee's Polish south side, two local union officials from Alabama joined him on the stage of Serbian Memorial Hall. John Stone of the Bessemer Labor Council and Jack Pratt of the United Steel Workers received resounding applause when they unrolled a sixty-two-foot list of 1,734 names of union members in Alabama, each of whom had contributed one dollar to Wallace's campaign. Stone then told the packed auditorium that "irregardless [sic] of what you have heard, George Wallace is a friend of labor and we are behind him 100%."[12]

Wallace returned to Alabama from his surprisingly strong showing in Wisconsin to prepare for the Indiana primary. In Tuscaloosa, Wallace was greeted by an independent committee from the Rubber Workers. They contributed $600 toward his presidential campaign and presented him with a petition signed by four hundred members urging him to continue his fight against the 1964 Civil Rights Act. Papermakers Local 297 furnished Wallace with a letter of endorsement that praised his labor record and his defense of states' rights. The Papermakers local and Pulp and Papermill Workers Local 157 then presented Wallace with a donation to his presidential campaign.[13] Weeks sent a letter to Dallas Sells, president of the Indiana AFL-CIO, warning him that local union leaders from Alabama would appear in Indiana claiming Wallace had labor's support. "Needless to say," Weeks informed his colleague, "no such statement is true nor are they authorized to make such statements."[14]

Friction between the governor and the state council also occurred in the 1964 Alabama COPE convention over the selection of presidential electors for Alabama. Alabama COPE recommended that the delegates endorse a pledged slate of electors who would be loyal to the Democratic party candidate. Wallace proposed that Alabama elect a slate of unpledged electors so the state could bargain with presidential candidates for civil rights relief in return for its electoral votes. Independent electors, Wallace advised, "would put them on notice in Washington, especially about the so-called Civil Rights Bill" which threatened "to destroy the seniority rights" of every union member.[15]

The Alabama AFL-CIO and the governor crossed swords at the 1964 COPE convention even before the question of presidential electors was called. Former governor James E. Folsom opposed Birmingham police commissioner Eugene "Bull" Connor in two races, for national Democratic committeeman and for president of the Alabama Public Service Commission. Alabama COPE had endorsed Folsom when he ran for governor in 1954 and had given him a favorable review when he ran again in 1962. But

Connor also had a background of friendly service and labor support to which he could point. He had voted for a civil service bill, to create an Alabama Department of Labor, and for a more generous workers' compensation law when he served in the state legislature.[16] In 1957 Connor was endorsed by the Joint Labor Committee of Jefferson County when he ran for Birmingham police commissioner because his opponent had used police to break strikes. At the time, COPE area director Daniel Powell described Connor to his superiors in Washington as a "segregationist de luxe who was very friendly to labor while in office."[17] When state council officers argued against endorsing Connor, they did not condemn his brutal treatment of blacks as much as his past disloyalty to the Democratic party.

The Connor-Folsom contests were just a prelude to the main event, choosing a slate of presidential electors to endorse. State council vice-president Earl Pippin spoke for the Alabama COPE committee and argued that the unpledged slate was composed of right-to-work advocates, Dixie-crats, strikebreakers, and reactionaries. A delegate rose immediately to oppose the recommendation and argued that to vote for the pledged electors was to commit Alabama to President Johnson, who had betrayed the South by supporting civil rights. A vote for the unpledged electors, on the other hand, was a vote for George Wallace, "a true friend of labor," in whom the state council leadership had enough confidence to recommend him for governor in 1958 and 1962. Wallace, argued the delegate, had done nothing since then to forfeit labor's support. "How can we go against the best friend we have had in many a day?" he concluded and was greeted with applause. Another delegate spoke for Alabama COPE and reminded his colleagues that civil rights was but one issue. None of the groups that supported unpledged electors stood for other programs that labor advocated such as social security, better schools, or medical care for the needy. Delegates should not be swayed by one issue, he cautioned, but should consider the entire program when voting on the question.[18]

Pledged electors were approved by a voice vote. Daniel Powell congratulated the delegates for their decision. Now they needed to go back to their local unions and tell their members what was at stake in the May 4 Democratic primary. Support for the unpledged slate of electors would isolate Alabama from the rest of the nation, relieve President Johnson of a sense of obligation to the state, and imperil the flow of federal funds to Alabama.[19]

When the delegates returned home, George Wallace was waiting. His partisans often had enough support within local unions to repudiate the endorsement of pledged electors after lengthy and boisterous meetings.

Local central bodies and building trades councils violated their charters and endorsed candidates, including "Bull" Connor, in opposition to Alabama COPE-endorsed candidates. As early as March, Weeks was sending distress signals. He wrote Al Barkan of Wallace's attempts to sow discord within the state council and said plaintively, "I don't know what you can do about this, but wanted you to know the present situation, which is steadily deteriorating." Powell also tried to sound the alarm at COPE headquarters and wrote Barkan, "No elected state or municipal official, no large local union officer, city central body official or no state council officer in Alabama today can survive if Wallace actively opposes him. I know this statement sounds fantastic and almost unbelievable, but the situation in Alabama today is without parallel in the history of this nation. . . . From recent reports . . . there is every indication that Wallace intends to oppose Weeks and the other officers in October." Meany intervened and sent a letter to international union presidents informing them that some of their locals in Alabama were "actually aiding and abetting the forces of race hatred" that threatened the state council. Meany requested that the union presidents assist Weeks, presumably by disciplining their wayward locals. In April, Weeks sent Powell several items that confirmed the success of Wallace's strategy of bypassing the state council to appeal directly to the local union leadership and rank and file. "The reason for sending you all this is to show you some small evidence of the total concentration on the race issue (because of George Wallace's activities) by so many of our members, which is costing us the loss of thousands of members in affiliations."[20]

Rebel locals attached to George Wallace disaffiliated from the state council to protest its failure to endorse either the governor's slate of unpledged electors or his candidacy in the Democratic primaries. These defections weakened a state council that had been losing members even before the present crisis broke. The Alabama AFL-CIO first began to lose members when it doubled its per capita tax in 1960. Membership declined even more when twenty-five United Steel Workers locals withdrew in a tiff over the removal of one of their members as secretary-treasurer of the state council. Just as this drama was ending, the state council's conflict with Wallace led to even more disaffiliations. From a peak of 107,000 members in 1958, the state council had lost nearly half by 1965, collecting per capita taxes on only 55,568 members. Whereas the state council represented 58 percent of all AFL-CIO members within the state in 1958, it represented just 30 percent seven years later. In 1958 the state council listed 485 affiliated local unions. By 1964 only 349 local unions were affiliated out of a total of 740 AFL-CIO local unions statewide.[21]

Local union disaffiliations had a devastating effect on the state council. Because 80 percent of its revenue came from membership dues, the Alabama AFL-CIO had to cut costs. In 1963 the state council closed the office it maintained in Montgomery and laid off its full time lobbyist. In addition, the loss of so many members damaged the state council's political credibility and reduced its ability to assist endorsed candidates either financially or organizationally.

Worse than the organizational decay the state council suffered was the outright political rejection it experienced, as the fate of Congressman Carl Elliot revealed. Elliot was the most liberal member of Alabama's congressional delegation and had compiled a COPE voting record of 82 percent, nine "right" votes and only two "wrong" in the Eighty-eighth Congress. His district included the hills of northern Alabama, where pro-Union sentiment flourished during the Civil War, and which in more recent times benefited from various federal projects including the Tennessee Valley Authority. But in 1964 candidates for the House had to compete under extraordinary conditions. Alabama lost a House seat as a result of the 1960 census, but the legislature refused to redistrict the state. Rather, it adopted the "8-9" plan under which Democratic candidates had to run three times to be elected. Candidates would run first in their old districts, then the nine winners of the district races would compete at large in a statewide election and the candidate receiving the fewest votes would be dropped from the ticket. The surviving eight candidates would then be assigned to districts to compete against the Republicans in November.

The Wallace camp entered Alabama House floor leader Tom Bevill against Elliot in the first-round district primary. Bevill attracted money from national conservative pressure groups and attacked Elliot for being soft on integration. The AFL-CIO was interested in Elliot's future and COPE director Barkan asked Weeks to keep him apprised of Elliot's prospects. Weeks's reply was discouraging. Local unions of the Bricklayers, Carpenters, and Painters were deserting Elliot over segregation. The Jasper Building Trades Council disregarded Alabama COPE's endorsement of Elliot and endorsed Bevill in violation of its charter. Local unions of the International Ladies' Garment Workers' Union and CWA that had campaigned for Elliot in the past refused to do so now. Union staff representatives were assigned to Elliot's campaign at Weeks's request when it was clear that local unions from the district would not campaign for him. Following Elliot's victory in the May primary, Weeks wrote Barkan: "Many of our members left us, because of their loyalty to Wallace, and their preoccupation with the race issue. Those who stuck with us were apathetic, and did not work in the campaign. . . . [The] full-time paid union representatives assigned to the campaign . . . in my judgment, was the one thing which meant the difference between victory or the defeat of Congressman Elliot."[22]

But a month later Elliot fell victim to the second hurdle when he received the lowest total of any of the nine district survivors in the statewide runoff. Weeks was mortified by Elliot's defeat. He told Barkan, "This is the worst blow we've suffered here in Alabama in a long time, and it will be some time before we recover from this." With Elliot's defeat, the climate in Alabama "had gone from bad to worse," according to Weeks. Weeks informed COPE that he would not be able to use the voting records of Alabama's congressmen and senators which COPE had prepared for distribution because they included civil rights votes. Instead, the state council would produce its own voting records that omitted a candidate's civil rights record.[23]

Fratricide within the Alabama AFL-CIO even attracted the attention of the *New York Times*, which carried a story on the exodus of dissatisfied members from the state council. A follow-up story disclosed that opposition to President Johnson was "greatest in Alabama where Governor George C. Wallace has achieved great influence among the rank and file." Members reportedly were disenchanted with the Democratic party's civil rights record, and radical right-wing groups such as the Ku Klux Klan had taken advantage of this sentiment to infiltrate and in some cases seize control of local unions.[24] Representatives of the Klan in Alabama who held union cards included Imperial Wizard Robert Shelton, who was a member of the United Rubber Workers. The president of a United Steel Workers local in Fairfield was also a former officer in the Klan. Two of the three Klansmen accused of the murder of civil rights marcher Viola Luizzo in 1965 were members of the United Steel Workers.[25] But it was almost irrelevant whether there were direct organizational links to the Klan because so many union members shared its views. Although Powell's report is a bit exaggerated, it does indicate how far and how deep reaction to the civil rights movement went. Powell wrote: "In several large locals in Mississippi and Alabama the presidents are either members of the John Birch Society or are cheating the society out of dues. In state after state I find a frightening number of local union leaders and members, wittingly or unwittingly, expressing opinions and taking positions identical with those espoused by the radical right-wing. I am afraid that a majority of our union membership in the South today is more aware of and in sympathy with the program and policies of the John Birch Society than they are with the program and policies of the AFL-CIO."[26]

Despite the financial and organizational costs it suffered, the Alabama state council remained steadfast in its support of the national Democratic party. Speaker after speaker at the 1964 Alabama AFL-CIO convention in October urged delegates to vote the entire Democratic party ticket. Senator John Sparkman appeared at the convention and reminded delegates that Alabama received three times from Washington what it paid in taxes. In his farewell address Congressman Elliot warned delegates to beware of "deceitful promises and false hopes." He insisted that both President Johnson and his opponent, Republican senator Barry Goldwater, supported civil rights. "The only issue" in November, according to Elliot, "is prosperity and Johnson has a proven record on that." Stanton Smith alerted delegates that the real meaning of states' rights was more regressive taxes and more restrictive labor legislation. Finally, Al Barkan appeared on the last day of the convention and gave a rousing speech. Barkan accused Goldwater of hypocrisy for embracing the 1964 Civil Rights Act when he spoke in the North and condemning it when he appeared in the South. He warned delegates not to be duped by promises that Goldwater would put blacks in their place because Goldwater intended to put union members right beside them. Barkan warned that union members could not take only the anti-civil-rights Goldwater, but also the anti-labor Goldwater who had voted for Taft-Hartley and Landrum-Griffin. Barkan urged delegates to vote a straight Democratic ticket because what was at stake in November was not the end of segregation if Lyndon Johnson won but the end of trade unionism if Goldwater did.[27]

But the final word belonged to the rank and file, most of whom were no longer affiliated with the state council and disagreed with its fealty to the national Democratic party. On November 1, two days before the election, an advertisement appeared in the *Mobile Press-Register* that endorsed Goldwater for president. It was signed and paid for by over three hundred members of AFL-CIO unions.[28]

Alabama was one of the six states that President Johnson lost when he accumulated a national margin of 16 million votes. Not only did Goldwater carry Alabama, but Republicans won five congressional seats from the Democrats. In 1960 Alabama COPE-endorsed candidates were victorious in every statewide and congressional contest but one. In 1964 the results were just the opposite. Congressman Robert Jones, who faced meager competition in the primaries and ran unopposed in the general election, was the only COPE-endorsed candidate to survive the 1964 election.

By 1965 all contact between the Wallace administration and the state council had ceased. The state council did not invite members of the

Wallace administration to speak at labor conferences, and Wallace did not solicit the council's recommendation for pending appointments. The Alabama AFL-CIO was even excluded from negotiations to consider changes in the state unemployment insurance law.[29] Disaffiliations continued to sap the state council's strength. Asked by COPE how the council proposed to take advantage of the 1965 Voting Rights Act, Weeks replied that "due to the loss of so many members because of the civil rights issue, the state council was unable to do anything financially at this time."[30] And Governor Wallace continued to drive a wedge between the state council and its membership. Alabama COPE director William Mintz told the state council executive board that "interest in COPE has declined" because of the influence of Governor Wallace and the Radical Right. A 1965 Oliver Quayle poll of the Alabama electorate confirmed Mintz's suspicions when it found that no demographic, economic, or occupational group was more devoted to Governor Wallace than members of organized labor.[31] When the Alabama AFL-CIO executive board voted to oppose a bill that would have permitted Wallace to succeed himself as governor, one board member confessed ruefully, "My members have got their minds made up and it would do no good to go back and tell them how we voted here."[32] Wallace's influence was so great that the Anniston central labor council presented him with a lifetime membership in its organization. The following year, in 1966, Weeks pressed charges against the Anniston council and tried to have its charter lifted when, contrary to the state council, it endorsed Lurleen Wallace for governor. Weeks warned AFL-CIO coordinator of state and local central bodies Stanton Smith: "We need action on this as quickly as possible. . . . Several groups outside of Labor are watching to see what kind of discipline we have."[33]

Despite these setbacks, the Alabama AFL-CIO continued to defy Wallace and resolutely stood by the national Democratic party. When the state council endorsed a loyalist slate for the Alabama Democratic party's executive committee in 1966, it overlooked the president of the Birmingham Building Trades Council, William Thrash, because he had supported independent electors in 1964. Weeks explained that the office required someone whose credentials with the Democratic party, not the union, were in order.[34] Speaker of the House Albert Brewer also forfeited the state council's support in his bid for lieutenant governor because of his past disloyalty to the party. The state council always had good relations with Brewer—it had even recommended him for his current post in the legislature—but now withheld its endorsement because Brewer had declared for independent electors in 1964.[35] Ruth Owens was endorsed for state treasurer because she was a loyal Democrat who had joined President Johnson's wife aboard the Lady Bird Special when it came through Alabama in 1964. In the 1966 Democratic gubernatorial primary, the COPE convention selected its loyal friend, former congressman Carl Elliot. Powell was particularly impressed by the preparation that secured the endorsement for Elliot over Lurleen Wallace, who ran in place of her husband because he could not succeed himself. But Powell also recognized the Elliot endorsement as a hollow victory because few members were likely to respect it. He reported to AFL-CIO COPE: "Indications are that a substantial portion of the rank-and-file membership . . . favor Mrs. Lurleen Wallace." He gave as an example the Hayes Aircraft local in Birmingham whose UAW representative and local union officers could not release money to Elliot from the local's citizenship fund because of the "strong Wallace sentiment among many of the rank-and-file members. Among many of the locals which are not affiliated," Powell continued, "the Wallace sentiment is even stronger."[36]

The 1966 COPE convention endorsements touched off a new wave of disaffiliations which the state council could ill afford. One member of the state council executive board broke ranks and charged that "the council meeting was turned into a National Democratic party meeting rather than a labor convention." Robert Lowe, president of the Mobile Building Trades Council, objected that the "endorsements definitely do not reflect those members of his council" and announced that the twenty-three locals in the Mobile council would disaffiliate. The Capital City Building Trades Council in Montgomery also repudiated the convention's endorsements and announced its locals would withdraw from the state council.[37] Hatters Local 122 and Electrical Workers Local 1998 followed suit and resigned from the state council over the Elliot endorsement. The labor movement in Birmingham was split, the Birmingham Building Trades Council defecting to Lurleen Wallace and the Birmingham Labor Council remaining loyal to Elliot. Conflict even erupted within local unions. Members of Rubber Workers Local 351 in Tuscaloosa ripped Elliot posters off the front door of the union hall on five different occasions.

Results from the 1966 Democratic primaries could not have been more disappointing. Every candidate the state council endorsed for statewide office lost. Despite the "most support ever given a candidate for public office by organized labor in Alabama," Elliot finished third behind Lurleen Wallace in a field of ten, with just 8 percent of the vote.[38] The Wallace vote attracted more white working class support with each new election.[39] The Alabama AFL-CIO found the alternatives in the November general election so objectionable that it did not endorse any candidate for governor, senator, or member of the House. Weeks wrote COPE research director Mary Zon to inform her that the state council planned to make no endorsements in November because it refused to endorse "the lesser of several evils."[40] The brevity of the state council's COPE program report on the 1966 elections could not hide the discouragement its officers felt: "Racial hatred stirred by Governor Wallace and the Klan have badly divided the ranks of Labor. . . . The state council conducts leadership week-end institutes in political and legislative action each year in a not-too-successful effort to unify the Labor Movement. State council is further weakened by the non-affiliation of most of the Steel locals."[41]

CONCLUSION

"In sum," George G. Kundahl concluded in his study of the state council, "the salience of race in Alabama, by alienating the rank and file from the leadership, has done more to damage the efficacy of organized labor as a political interest group than any other factor."[42] The Alabama state council suffered defections, lost revenue, closed offices, and laid off staff. Politically, the council was an outcast without influence. Candidates it endorsed were defeated, and members did not hesitate to repudiate it openly. Years later a UAW official confessed to Stanley Greenberg, "We couldn't get off the ground politically as long as that racial issue was there."[43] For Weeks and the other officers of the state council, the events of the period were draining and required them to draw on their reserves of courage and fortitude. The state council was so overwhelmed by Wallace's appeals to white supremacy that it had all it could do to maintain some organizational coherence.

There are many reasons why the Alabama AFL-CIO persevered instead of succumbing to the institutional and political pressures it encountered. First, leadership was a determining factor. At the very top of the labor hierarchy in Alabama were people with a commitment to civil rights. Alabama AFL-CIO president Barney Weeks believed in the justice of black demands. Weeks, of course, framed his civil rights position in indirect, muted tones out of political necessity, but he was no less courageous for doing so. Even Weeks's support of the national Democratic party and his denunciation of segregationists stretched the endurance and tolerance of his members.

Moreover, Weeks tangled not only with a popular but a pro-labor governor when he defied Wallace. Weeks could not simply attack Wallace as another southern demagogue who used race as a popular disguise to hide his anti-labor agenda because Wallace had a good record on labor issues. Norrell is accurate when he suggests that Wallace's "great popularity among white unionists was based on more than a simple appeal to racial fear. On almost all issues important to labor, Wallace took the correct position."[44] That Weeks was willing to oppose a governor with a solid labor record underscores even more his strong feelings on the racial question.

The state council also hoped that black enfranchisement would increase the influence of liberals inside the state legislature and the Alabama Democratic party. But the state council was after bigger game than simply a change in the relation of forces within the terms of southern Democracy. The Alabama AFL-CIO sought nothing less than party realignment, the creation of a two-party system that could offer voters in Alabama a choice between conservative Republicans and liberal Democrats. It sought to replace political coalitions in Alabama that were personalized, transitory, and built on friends-and-neighbors effects with a responsible, polarized two-party system.[45] The state council remained loyal to the policies and candidates of the national Democratic party, even endorsing candidates on the basis of whether they met this test, in pursuit of its larger vision. After the 1964 election, Weeks spoke to another group that had remained loyal to the national Democratic party, the Young Democrats of Alabama, and requested that they join him in creating the party realignment that Alabama politics required. Weeks argued that politics in Alabama could be changed

> only if right-thinking, forward-looking, progressive people within the state join together in one party and welcome others of like mind into that party. The greatest change of all must be a change in the thinking of Democratic leaders and Democratic office-holders. They ought to . . . run either as Democrats or Republicans; and if they run as Democrats, it ought to be plain that they support the Democratic platform and principles, or if they run as a Republican, they support Republican platforms and principles. We must not let them kid us ever again by adopting such hyphenated titles as Alabama Democrats, Southern Democrats, Conservative Democrats, Goldwater Democrats, or any other such camouflaged name for the Republican Party.[46]

But fewer and fewer white union members in Alabama cared whether candidates ran as Democrats, regardless of how they were classified. By 1968 only 39 percent of this group identified themselves as Democrats; fully half now claimed to be independents. They had defected so much from either party or union recommendations that 83 percent of all white union members in Alabama voted for Wallace in his third-party presidential bid in 1968, while AFL-CIO-endorsed Democratic presidential candidate Hubert Humphrey received a paltry 6 percent of their vote.[47]

As disheartening as this outcome was and as courageous as the Alabama AFL-CIO's efforts were to prevent it, Alabama was still more fortunate than its neighbor to the west. Mississippi was the last frontier of the Old South and its people defended segregation with the determination of zealots who knew they were making their last stand. Key observed that northerners tend to regard the South as one large Mississippi, but southerners, "with their eye for distinction, place Mississippi in a class by itself." Regardless of how poor other states' constituents were, or how illiterate they were, or how badly blacks were treated there, the rest of the South could always "fall back on the soul-satisfying exclamation, 'Thank God for Mississippi!' " But Mississippi cannot be dismissed as a caricature so easily because, as Key perceptively noted, "Mississippi only manifests in accentuated form the darker political strains that run throughout the South."[48]

6

Claude Ramsay,
the Mississippi AFL-CIO,
and the Civil Rights Movement

I am taking every precaution and stay armed at all times.

—Claude Ramsay, Mississippi AFL-CIO president

T HE FIRST NATIONAL holiday to honor Martin Luther King, Jr.,
should have been a day of joy and celebration for the civil rights
community in Mississippi. Instead, it was in mourning. On January 20, 1986, Aaron Henry, president of the Mississippi NAACP, Robert
Walker, former NAACP field secretary for Mississippi, and Robert Clark,
the first black elected to the Mississippi state legislature since 1890,
entered the Baldwin-Lee Funeral Home in Jackson. Already inside were
150 other guests, including former Mississippi governor William Winter,
lieutenant governor Brad Dye, and a rising young politician, Ray Mabus,
who would later become governor. The two Mississippis, one black and
one white, converged momentarily to pay tribute to a man who had fought
tirelessly for black equality, the national Democratic party, and labor
unions in a state that reviled all three. As mourners entered the room
where the body of Claude E. Ramsay lay in state, they were struck by the
flowers nearby. In the center of a dozen arrangements was one with a white
ribbon and red letters that read simply "AFL-CIO."

Claude Ramsay was president of the Mississippi AFL-CIO for twenty-six
years, and if he could have attended his own funeral he would have felt
satisfied, even vindicated. He would have been proud that black leaders in
Mississippi recognized his contributions by their attendance and that his
funeral was racially integrated, a principle he fought for throughout his
career. And he would have been pleased that so many politicians felt

obligated to make an appearance. When Ramsay first took over the Mississippi AFL-CIO in 1959, politicians did not even bother to solicit its endorsement. The Mississippi legislature, which had censured Ramsay during his career, passed a resolution upon his death commending him for his "early commitment to civil rights when it was not a popular thing to do." Ramsay also would have thought it appropriate that his funeral should coincide with a day reserved to honor Martin Luther King. Ramsay's support for the civil rights movement was the source of his notoriety, and he did not escape its shadow even in death. Finally, he no doubt would have been amused at the response of Mississippi's foremost newspaper, the *Clarion-Ledger*. The *Ledger* was a Citizens' Councils organ that excoriated Ramsay mercilessly for his civil rights activity during the 1960s. At his death, the *Ledger* hailed him as a "prophet," recognized him as "among the earliest of white Mississippi leaders to fully espouse and fight for civil rights," and acknowledged in an editorial that "Mississippi is a better state because of his life, his dreams, and his uphill fight." All these symbols from his funeral were evidence that Mississippi had learned from its native son.[1] Unfortunately, Ramsay paid with his life for Mississippi's education. He died in his sleep from apparent heart failure at the age of sixty-nine, just one month after retiring as president of the Mississippi AFL-CIO.[2]

Ramsay fought a battle on three fronts during his tenure as president of the Mississippi AFL-CIO. First, he struggled with his membership over racial policy. Ramsay used the power of his office to support civil rights for blacks. But many of his members supported segregation, and some even joined the Ku Klux Klan, the Citizens' Councils, and other white supremacist groups to defend it. Local unions censured Ramsay for his views on civil rights and disaffiliated in protest to his policies. This conflict not only damaged the state council but wounded Ramsay personally. He was isolated and unloved by the very members he tried to serve.

Ramsay also engaged in conflict with the Regulars, the conservative segregationists who controlled the Mississippi Democratic party. The Regulars were openly disloyal to the national Democratic party's candidates and repudiated its liberal policies. The Mississippi Democratic party supported a slate of unpledged presidential electors instead of the Democratic ticket in 1960, refused to campaign for President Johnson in 1964, and renounced the national party in 1968. Ramsay struggled against the apostasy and betrayal of the Regulars in favor of a Democratic party in Mississippi that would defend the national party.

Finally, Ramsay participated in the factional disputes that divided civil rights groups in Mississippi. Ramsay supported the NAACP in its bitter

124   *Conflict of Interests*

rivalry with the Mississippi Freedom Democratic party (MFDP) for influence over the state's newly enfranchised black voters. As a result of his alliance with the NAACP, the MFDP was contemptuous of Ramsay, who did not hesitate to return its vitriol in kind.

Ramsay fought on all three fronts because, like other labor leaders with political responsibilities, he recognized that black enfranchisement could rescue labor from its political impotence. Black enfranchisement, Ramsay believed, would initiate a realignment that would liberalize the Mississippi Democratic party and realign the state's party system. Ramsay struggled valiantly to fulfill this vision, and it was in homage to these efforts that mourners paid their respects to him when he died.

THE INITIATION

Claude Ramsay was born in 1916 in Ocean Springs, Mississippi, a little town on the Gulf Coast across the bay from Biloxi. Ramsay's father could trace his lineage to Mississippi's early settlers who arrived before it became a state. His mother was a Bilbo, a distant relative to the famous race-baiter, former Mississippi governor, and senator Theodore G. Bilbo. Despite her lineage, Ramsay remembered his mother as compassionate, religious, and considerate toward blacks. He gave his mother credit for his liberal racial views and held his father responsible for his obstinacy.[3]

Ramsay grew up on a farm near Fort Bayou, eight miles inland from Pascagoula on the Gulf Coast. The area was depressed, undeveloped, and, like the rest of Mississippi, thoroughly segregated. Upon graduation from Vancleave Consolidated High School, Ramsay attended Perkinston Junior College. His taste of higher education lasted only one year. He quit school in 1936 and spent two years at a Civilian Conservation Corps camp for the unemployed in Louisiana. He returned to the Mississippi Gulf Coast in 1939 when friends procured him a job at the International Paper plant in Moss Point. The paper mill provided some of the best-paying jobs in the state and was in the process of being organized by the United Paperworkers of the AFL when Ramsay started work.

World War II permitted Ramsay to fill new jobs that opened up when workers were drafted into the armed forces. Ramsay himself was inducted in 1942. He arrived in Germany when the war was all but over and consequently saw little combat. But the war made an indelible impression on Ramsay's racial views. It drove home to him the irrationality of segregation: that bullets do not discriminate and that blacks who risked their lives in Europe would not accept being treated like second-class citizens when they returned home.[4]

Ramsay began to take an interest in public affairs when he returned to the United States. He supported President Harry Truman in 1948 when the rest of Mississippi defected to the Dixiecrats. He became active in his union and was elected shop steward and then president of Paperworkers Local 203, a segregated local of 350 members, in 1951. The following year Ramsay was elected president of the Jackson County AFL Central Labor Council.

Ramsay's first foray into racial politics occurred at the 1954 Mississippi state AFL convention. He introduced a resolution that rejected massive resistance to *Brown* in favor of maintaining free public education. When Ramsay returned to his local, he recalled, "All hell broke loose," and he was accused of "pushing integration."[5]

In 1956, as a member of the Mississippi AFL Executive Board, he advocated merger with the Mississippi CIO, acknowledging that even united "we would still have a weak organization." But opposition from the building trades scuttled these efforts in 1957 and delayed merger of the two state councils for a year. When the newly merged Mississippi AFL-CIO suffered from weak leadership during its first year, Ramsay was approached by concerned officials from both former AFL and CIO unions to seek the state council presidency. That Ramsay had the skill for the job was evident from his work as chair of the Sixth District COPE in Mississippi. Ramsay's COPE program had the reputation as the most active in the state, even catching the attention of COPE officials at AFL-CIO headquarters in Washington.[6]

Ramsay's COPE activity and the fact that he enjoyed the confidence of CIO unions because he was reconciled to the merger convinced his sponsors that Ramsay could invigorate the state council. Ramsay obliged and was nominated for president at the 1959 Mississippi AFL-CIO convention. The incumbent, Ray Bryant, withdrew two days before the election and threw his support to Marvin Taylor from the Carpenters, whom Ramsay defeated by a two-to-one margin. COPE area director Daniel Powell observed the convention and in his report to AFL-CIO headquarters described the new president of the Mississippi AFL-CIO as "able, militant, tenacious, and deeply committed to the labor movement."[7] But Ramsay's new post was so insecure and paid so little that he continued to hold his $150 per week job at the paper plant and attended to his new responsibilities as head of the Mississippi labor movement in his spare time.[8]

Ramsay's first test as president was the 1959 Democratic primary. The Mississippi AFL-CIO Executive Board met on June 11 to hear a report from a screening committee that had interviewed the gubernatorial candidates.

Among the four candidates, Lieutenant Governor Carroll Gartin received the highest grade of ten points, and Ross Barnett finished second with eight. Both candidates supported right-to-work, both were members of the Citizens' Councils, both pledged to defend segregation, and both made clear that they viewed labor's endorsement more as a liability than an asset because, while they welcomed labor's support, each requested that it not be made public.[9] Gartin, however, was judged the lesser of the two evils because Barnett lacked experience in public office and had chosen the executive vice-president of the Mississippi Manufacturers Association as his campaign manager.[10]

When the COPE convention confirmed its executive board's choice and recommended Gartin for governor, Barnett, as expected, chided his opponent for selling out to the labor bosses. Gartin replied that Barnett had met with the same labor representatives that he had and, unable to get their support, now was attempting to smear them.[11] But as the campaign proceeded and Gartin found himself on the defensive, he tried to portray himself as being as anti-labor as his opponent. Gartin congratulated every member of the Mississippi congressional delegation for voting in favor of Landrum-Griffin, and in his stump speeches he proudly displayed the pen he used to sign Mississippi's right-to-work law. Ramsay's postelection report reveals the frustration that support for the lesser of two evils caused him over the course of the Gartin campaign: "Most of our natural allies were in the other camp. . . . Gartin's source of strength centered chiefly around the Chamber of Commerce crowd, the Miss. Economic Council— people we are constantly doing battle with. Many of them resented us and many of our people rebelled at the thought of going to bed with them. In truth, it was a hell of an alignment. Most of the County Chairmen [for Gartin] were people despised by our Union members, which didn't make our job any easier. . . . There can be no question but that a number of our people became disgusted to the point of either not voting or voting for Barnett."[12]

Barnett defeated Gartin by three thousand votes in the primary and then increased his margin in the runoff, which guaranteed his election. His administration defended white supremacy with all the gusto Barnett's Citizens' Councils connections would permit.[13] But the Citizens' Councils' influence on Governor Barnett went beyond racial matters to affect economic policy as well. At the same time the Barnett administration reduced rights for blacks, it proposed to enhance those of industry through an "Industrial Bill of Rights for Industry and Business." The governor's program lowered Mississippi's income tax, raised its sales tax, offered tax incentives to encourage low-wage industry to locate in the state, and weakened the workers' compensation law. The final blow occurred the day after the 1960 Mississippi AFL-CIO convention adjourned. The state legislature proposed amending the state constitution to include Mississippi's right-to-work law. Any amendment to the state constitution, however, required the approval of voters in a referendum.

Barnett's deference to business interests posed a challenge to the state council, which finally forced Ramsay's hand. Working full-time at International Paper and doing justice to his new post as Mississippi AFL-CIO president had become a "nightmare," according to Ramsay. He took a leave of absence from his job to become a temporary organizer for the United Papermakers and Paperworkers (UPP) in the hope of relieving the strain so he could spend more time on state council affairs. His assignment with the UPP went well until a strike occurred in his jurisdiction. Ramsay found he had even less time for state council matters than when he worked at his old job.[14] The right-to-work referendum, however, finally forced Ramsay to choose between his old job with International Paper and his new post with the state council. When International Paper refused to extend Ramsay's leave of absence so he could devote himself to the right-to-work campaign, he resigned to work full-time for the Mississippi AFL-CIO. Ramsay gave up twenty-one years of seniority and took a cut in pay in moving to his new job.[15]

The task Ramsay confronted was daunting. Daniel Powell believed the state council would receive no more than twenty thousand friendly votes from the entire state against the right-to-work amendment. As Powell explained to James McDevitt, "In the face of almost certain defeat, to their everlasting credit, the leaders of the Mississippi Labor Council are attempting to launch a state-wide campaign against the 'Right-to-Work' amendment, but they have not the time, money, or strength with which to make an effective fight."[16]

Ramsay took the state council's case against right-to-work to the public. He argued that the law, which the legislature passed in 1954, had failed to deliver on its promise of prosperity and putting it in the state constitution would only make it harder to repeal. Right-to-work had not lifted Mississippi from last place as the state with the lowest per capita income, the lowest average hourly wage rate, and the lowest average weekly earnings in the nation. In addition, Mississippi continued to lag behind the rest of the South in industrial development. Right-to-work, charged Ramsay, was fool's gold, and now, "in spite of the damage which right-to-work has done . . . in spite of the money it has taken out of your pocketbook . . . the sponsors of this proposition are now asking you to perpetuate all of this BACKWARDNESS into the basic law of the sovereign State of Mississippi."[17] In just three weeks, the Mississippi AFL-CIO raised $26,000 for use in its campaign against the amendment. But it was not enough. The right-to-work amendment passed eighty-seven thousand to forty-two thousand.

No defeat was ever more gratifying. The number of votes against the amendment was much larger than anticipated, and the two-to-one margin by which it passed much smaller than expected. The *Laurel Leader-Call* admitted that the number of votes against the amendment was "surprising." Ramsay crowed that the "unprecedented vote in our favor lends added support to our resolve," and he thanked "every voter who made this upset possible." Daniel Powell wrote Ramsay to offer his "belated congratulations. . . . Barnett and other politicians in the state . . . are not going to forget that there are 42,000 votes in Mississippi which can be mobilized against an Anti-Labor candidate or issue." The vote convinced Powell that "the money, time, and effort that went into the fight against the 'Right-to-Work' Amendment was wisely and profitably spent."[18]

Following the right-to-work fight, Ramsay prepared for the 1960 election and again ran headlong into Governor Barnett. Barnett returned from the national Democratic party convention in Los Angeles irate that the party had enacted the strongest civil rights plank in its history. He condemned the platform as "horrible," "repulsive," "obnoxious," and "contrary to our form of government."[19] The governor reconvened the state's Democratic party, which proceeded to break ranks and put up a slate of unpledged electors to challenge both the Republican and Democratic tickets in Mississippi.[20] Ramsay accused Barnett of trying to deliver Mississippi to the Republicans by this ploy. Ramsay then alerted the Democratic National Committee to other renegades loose in Mississippi. He collected newspaper articles to show that Mississippi congressmen John Bell Williams and William Colmer had campaigned for the unpledged elector slate rather than the Democratic ticket. Ramsay submitted these clippings as evidence of their apostasy and recommended that the Democrats punish both congressmen by stripping them of patronage, seniority, and committee assignments when Congress reconvened.[21]

In addition to the presidential contest, the 1960 Mississippi ballot included five constitutional amendments, three of which were intended to defend white supremacy. One amendment provided yet another weapon to reduce black voter registration by permitting registrars to judge whether citizens were of sufficiently good moral character to vote. A second amendment was designed to limit the number of blacks who served on juries by permitting the legislature to fix the qualifications of jurors. The third gave control over public schools to the Mississippi legislature, which could abolish them if necessary to prevent integration.

The Mississippi AFL-CIO publicly opposed all three measures. The state council contributed money for television spots to campaign against the amendments and notified its affiliated locals of the danger these measures posed to their members. But regrettably, as Mississippi AFL-CIO secretary-treasurer Tom Knight confessed to McDevitt, the state council had neither the time nor the money to conduct a credible campaign. Ramsay knew it would be impossible to defeat the amendments but felt "we should take a position for the sake of the record, if nothing else." When Ramsay spoke against the amendments, he avoided their obvious racial intent. He preferred to oppose them on the basis of the democratic principles they violated rather than the civil rights for blacks they were meant to abridge. Ramsay argued that if the legislature was permitted to set the qualifications for jurors "the haves will sit in judgment of the have-nots," and he warned that to give the legislature control over public schools would jeopardize free public education. Finally, Mississippi needed to liberalize its registration laws, not restrict them further, as the amendment giving registrars discretion to judge the fitness of voters would do.[22]

The outcome of the referenda was a foregone conclusion, as Ramsay well knew. Consequently, the Mississippi AFL-CIO devoted its attention in the 1960 election to defeating Barnett's slate of unpledged electors and holding Mississippi for the Democratic ticket. Ramsay and Knight appeared at local central bodies in Clarksdale, Tupelo, Greenville, and Columbus to discuss election issues and urge members to support the Kennedy-Johnson ticket. They also distributed literature produced by the state council that provided the voting records of candidates John F. Kennedy and Richard M. Nixon but omitted their civil rights votes. To give the Democratic ticket a further boost, the state council allied with the Loyal Democrats of Mississippi, led by Senator James Eastland. This group was formed to support the Kennedy-Johnson ticket when the Mississippi Democratic party defected to support Governor Barnett's unpledged slate. The irony of labor's cooperation with the Loyal Democrats was not lost on the labor leadership. Knight wrote McDevitt: "We find ourselves, so to speak, in bed with some politicians who have not been too favorable to labor in the past. But if it takes such as that to get the job done, it is not all in vain."[23] The campaign included other surprises. Ramsay was invited to ride on the Johnson train when it came through Mississippi. Previously, politicians avoided him, but now they openly courted his support. Ramsay attributed the new respect he received to labor's vote against right-to-work the previous year.[24]

But labor's horse came up short again. The three amendments were ratified by a three-to-one margin and the unpledged electors defeated the Democratic slate 116,000 to 108,000, with Republicans polling another 73,000 votes. Ramsay attributed the defeat of the Democratic ticket in Mississippi to the religious issue, Kennedy's Catholicism, which, he admitted, affected his own members. Although the unpledged slate was defeated in Jackson County, Ramsay conceded that in Adams and Hinds counties "our enemies did a better job with our members in these areas than we did."[25]

The Mississippi AFL-CIO emerged from the 1960 election politically ennobled but financially bankrupt. Ramsay's frequent attacks on Governor Barnett, who enjoyed considerable support from the rank and file, began to take a toll.[26] When Ramsay first took office in 1959, he promised to increase the membership, which stood at twenty-four thousand. Two years later, membership had declined to twenty thousand, less than one-half of all AFL-CIO members in the state. Consequently, the state council ran a $900 a month deficit, was unable to cover Knight's salary and expenses, and survived only by virtue of a subsidy it received from the AFL-CIO.[27]

Ramsay worked with COPE area director Daniel Powell throughout 1960 to solve the state council's financial problems. Their proposal, called the Mississippi Program of Progress, included an eighteen-point legislative agenda the state council would pursue and a special $1.50 per capita tax on affiliates—over and above their normal assessment—to pay for it. Routine COPE expenses that normally were charged against the state council's general fund would now come out of this assessment for political work. The legislative program enumerated in the Program of Progress included no civil rights measures because Ramsay and Powell thought they might endanger passage of the program. But civil rights threatened passage anyway. Freedom Riders were headed for Mississippi. Not the violence of Anniston, the beatings in Birmingham, or the savagery of Montgomery could stop them.

The first bus carrying Freedom Riders arrived in Jackson on May 25, 1961. The following day the AFL-CIO Industrial Unions Department announced it would contribute $5,000 to CORE to help defray expenses incurred by the Freedom Rides. Union members in the South who were hostile to the Freedom Riders were irate over the contribution. H. L. Woods, president of the Mississippi State Council of Carpenters Unions, complained to Ramsay about using money from Mississippi members to recruit Freedom Riders.[28] J. M. Franklin, a member of CWA Local 3519 in Gulfport, wrote Ramsay demanding to know why he and "other state heads of labor have not voiced an opposition to union money being sent to Mississippi to aid the Freedom Riders who have broken our laws." Franklin challenged Ramsay to condemn the IUD contribution in the same way he condemned the Mississippi State Sovereignty Commission for contributing money to the Citizens' Councils. Ramsay assured Franklin that he too was "disturbed" by the IUD contribution and corrected him that he had not publicly opposed the Sovereignty Commission's donation, though privately he thought it a mistake. Ramsay even received a protest to the IUD contribution from his old haunt, the Jackson County Central Labor Council, over which he had once presided. Knight feared that if the issue of the IUD contribution was raised at the 1961 special convention called to consider passage of the Program of Progress, "chances are that we would have a real battle and wind up with no program" at all. Local unions that previously suffered AFL-CIO support for civil rights in silence wanted to punish someone for the IUD contribution, and Ramsay found himself in the path of their spitefulness. Ramsay wrote AFL-CIO president George Meany to express the dilemma the IUD contribution posed to him: "The AFL-CIO can take only one position, and that is against racial discrimination. . . . Unfortunately, a wide segment of our membership doesn't know these things or don't give a damn, for today a lot of turmoil exists because of this contribution. . . . The thing boils down to this, we can overcome everything but the contribution of union funds. No explanation will satisfy these people in this respect."[29]

The Program of Progress escaped the IUD incident unscathed but was unable to stanch the flow of red ink. In February 1962, Ramsay sent AFL-CIO coordinator of state and central bodies Stanton Smith a copy of the state council's recent audit. "As you will note," Ramsay informed Smith, "we have just about reached the bottom of the barrel and it is becoming rather obvious that I will be compelled to resign and seek employment elsewhere unless the situation improves soon." Smith reassured Ramsay and indicated that he would ask Meany to increase Mississippi's subsidy to get the state council "over the hump." In the meantime, Smith suggested that the council prune its expenses. In March, Smith informed Ramsay that Meany had approved additional aid, and for the moment, Ramsay buried his thoughts of resigning.[30]

While Ramsay was trying to keep the state council afloat, James Meredith, the grandson of a slave and a former staff sergeant in the air force, prepared to enter the University of Mississippi at Oxford. After Mississippi officials rebuffed four previous attempts by Meredith to register and their judicial appeals were exhausted, Meredith entered the campus guarded by three hundred federal marshals. The National Guard was ready to assist if needed, and the 503d unit of the U.S. Army remained on alert in Memphis. On September 30 President Kennedy appeared on television to assure the nation that the rule of law had prevailed and Meredith was safely on campus. But even as the president spoke, a riot erupted at Ole Miss. A menacing crowd threw bricks, rocks, and bottles at federal marshals who protected Meredith. The violence escalated when pistol and rifle fire was directed at the marshals, who retaliated with tear gas in a vain attempt to disperse the mob. The crowd grew and threatened to overwhelm the marshals before the National Guard and army arrived to relieve them. The riot lasted fifteen hours, leaving two men dead and more than three hundred injured. By Monday night there were five thousand National Guardsmen and soldiers in Oxford to patrol the streets.[31]

The closest Ramsay came to Oxford during the Meredith affair was when he commuted from his home in Pascagoula to the state council's office in Jackson. Other citizens from Pascagoula, however, felt they needed to be closer to the conflict. The county sheriff organized a posse called the Jackson County Emergency Unit to travel to Oxford and defend the university from integration. The Emergency Unit participated in the riot at Ole Miss and returned to Pascagoula determined to root out more local threats to white supremacy. It quickly turned its attention to the *Chronicle*, Ramsay's hometown newspaper, which editorialized against Governor Barnett's defiance of the law. The *Chronicle* suffered an advertising boycott, had its windows shot out, and crosses were burned in front of the home of its publisher, Ira Harkey. Ramsay knew that many union members who worked in the Pascagoula shipyards were officers and members of the Emergency Unit responsible for this reign of terror. Ramsay demanded an audience with the Pascagoula Metal Trades Council, a coalition of unions in the shipyards, to warn them of the danger posed by the Emergency Unit. He argued that racial disturbances endangered federal contracts upon which the shipyard depended. Ramsay cautioned: "It is important that we come to the defense of the *Chronicle*. It is even more important that we do everything possible to keep this shipyard in operation."[32]

When Harkey was informed of Ramsay's speech he asked him for a copy of it. Ramsay delivered a transcript that he typed up from his notes, which Harkey ran as a front-page editorial. Intimidation by the Jackson County Emergency Unit ceased. Harkey later received the Sidney Hillman Prize from the Amalgamated Clothing Workers of America (ACWA) and a Pulitzer Prize for his editorials. He remembered Ramsay in his memoirs as "the most irrepressible and courageous civil libertarian in Mississippi" and the "only one of Jackson County's 54,317 persons who came publicly to the defense of the *Chronicle*."[33]

The state council continued to be dogged by political defeat. In 1962 it supported Frank E. Smith in his unsuccessful bid to retain his seat in Congress. Smith was a loyal Democrat who was defeated by Jamie Whitten, an unrepentant Dixiecrat, when their districts were combined by redistricting.[34] Smith's defeat was dispiriting, but the state council was looking ahead to the 1963 Democratic primary. Lieutenant Governor Paul Johnson would carry the mantle of the Barnett administration into the election. One of Johnson's rivals was former governor James Coleman, who was a loyal Democrat and a racial moderate. The COPE committee listed Coleman first in its order of preference but asked the COPE convention only to ratify the preference list rather than issue a recommendation or endorsement for Coleman. Coleman already suffered from his past association with the Kennedys and did not want the added burden of a labor endorsement. In addition, it was doubtful that Coleman could obtain the two-thirds majority needed for endorsement even if the COPE committee recommended him. Powell estimated that Coleman could depend on no more than 45 percent of the labor vote; Johnson, the Citizens' Councils' candidate, would receive 35 percent, and a third candidate, Charles Sullivan, would capture the rest.[35]

When the Mississippi COPE convention met in June 1963, Powell challenged the delegates to decide whether "we're living in 1863 or . . . in 1963," and whether their allegiance was to their unions or to the Citizens' Councils. Powell urged them not to be deceived by the race issue. Not only was it a ruse to deflect them from more important issues, but it was a matter over which state government had little control. "The real issues in this campaign," Powell explained, "are things that candidates for governor can do something about," such as increases in unemployment insurance, workers' compensation, and easing the tax burden on working people. Nor should members be deceived by attacks on the federal government, Powell warned. If members were upset that President Kennedy sent troops to Mississippi, they should also keep in mind that the federal government provided Mississippi with such benefits as highways, hospitals, public works, minimum wage laws, social security, and unemployment insurance.[36] Following more speeches, the COPE convention ratified the preference list that the executive board had recommended, with Coleman's name at the top.

Both Johnson and Coleman survived the primary to create a rematch of their 1955 contest in the runoff. Eight years before, Coleman upset Johnson to win the Democratic nomination and become governor. But now, with troops still on the University of Mississippi campus, the results were reversed. Coleman's promise to defend segregation, but without the strife that had occurred under Barnett, was simply no match for Johnson. The lieutenant governor reminded voters how he had personally blocked Meredith's first attempt to enter Ole Miss, and was still under a contempt citation for his effort to prevent Meredith's matriculation.[37]

When Coleman defeated Johnson in the 1955 runoff, that was tantamount to election because Coleman faced no Republican opposition in the November general election. This was not the case in 1963. Rubel Phillips, a former chair of the public service commission, switched parties to run for governor as a Republican.[38] The COPE screening committee was impressed with Phillips's "commendable record" as public service commissioner and his demands for educational and civil service reform.[39] But Phillips was an attractive candidate for reasons other than his record or his program. His greatest asset, the COPE screening committee believed, was that he was a Republican whose candidacy would contribute to the development of a two-party system in Mississippi. In October, the screening committee gave a slight nod to Phillips, which the Mississippi COPE committee promptly ratified. The state council announced that both Johnson and Phillips had been judged on their records, not their parties, and labor decided that "Phillips would serve the best interest of the people of Mississippi."[40]

Johnson used the announcement to attack Phillips through Ramsay. He reminded voters that Ramsay had a "tendency toward integration" and predicted that the rank and file would "not follow this false prophet or the false prophets he represents."[41] Phillips received only 38 percent of the vote, but his candidacy had its intended effect from the state council's point of view. It marked the first sign of serious two-party competition for statewide office in Mississippi since 1876.

Ramsay was disappointed by this latest defeat, which jaundiced his views when he turned to the state council's recurring problem with affiliations. Knight complained to Barkan, "If the leadership of the unaffiliated—local and national—unions would only realize that we must have the full affiliation and participation of every AFL-CIO local union in this state if we are to do the job in the manner that it must be done."[42] The affiliation problem was aggravated further by differences that arose between the state council and ACWA state director James Jackson. Jackson opposed the high dues structure mandated by the Program of Progress and accused the state council of being wasteful and extravagant, undeserving of the dues increase it requested. Unable to roll back the dues increase that the Program of Progress required, Jackson pulled all the ACWA locals out of the state council. AFL-CIO headquarters responded with fervent efforts to restore the ACWA locals to good standing. Stanton Smith, along with McDevitt and Al Barkan from COPE, met with ACWA assistant to the president Howard Samuel to work out a solution to the dispute between the state council and the union. No compromise could be reached.[43] Consequently, the second largest union in Mississippi—but the largest one in the state council—dropped out and would not reaffiliate until December 1964.

The affiliation problem, combined with the state council's unbroken record of political defeat, left Ramsay discouraged and dejected as 1963 ended. When Ramsay returned to his office after the New Year he delivered an ultimatum to the AFL-CIO. He explained that "the financial condition of the Labor Council and our apparent inability to correct the affiliation problem" forced him to consider other alternatives. Unless the situation improved considerably by May 1964, when the next Mississippi AFL-CIO convention was scheduled, Ramsay would not stand for reelection and would instead take a staff position with his old union, the UPP. In conclusion, he suggested that he could still be persuaded otherwise, but he also alluded to the discouragement that led him to make this threat: "I hope it will be possible to review this matter in its entirety with the four of you during the COPE conference at Little Rock. The frustration and disappointments are too many to go into detail at this time."[44]

In a frank discussion at the Little Rock COPE area conference in March, Ramsay told Smith and the COPE staff that he could no longer afford the luxury of his office. Ramsay wanted a pay raise at a time when the state council was so much in arrears that it could not afford two full-time officers, much less salary increases for them. The AFL-CIO representatives assured Ramsay that when they returned to Washington they would request additional aid for the Mississippi AFL-CIO to cover salary increases for its officers. But this offer did little to assuage Ramsay's melancholy. In February, Ramsay wrote Meany to inform him that he would resign if the affiliation situation did not improve. He told Meany that he could understand why local unions that disagreed with him over civil rights should disaffiliate but not why locals that agreed with him should remain unaffiliated as well. Ramsay complained:

> On several occasions during the past few years it has been necessary for
> me to speak out on matters relating to the "race question" in Missis-
> sippi. . . . As a result of my actions a number of local unions, apparently
> dominated by the "white citizens council," have disaffiliated with the
> Mississippi AFL-CIO. On the other hand, we have a rather large num-
> ber of local unions in the state which are predominantly Negro in
> membership who are not now affiliated. As a result of this unholy situa-
> tion the State Labor Council is in grave financial difficulty. . . . It is
> most difficult for me to understand why these locals which are predomi-
> nantly Negro in membership are willing to sit idly by and allow the
> "white councils" to destroy the one organization that is trying to bring a
> little sense and reason into the all-important field of race relations.

Ramsay appealed to Meany to contact those internationals with unaffiliated black locals to try to rectify the situation. He concluded: "I will not
stand for reelection at our next convention unless this affiliation problem is
licked. This, of course, will be a victory for the 'white citizens council' and
one that I would like to avoid if at all possible."[45]

Ramsay sent a copy of his letter to Stanton Smith, who was miffed that
Ramsay continued to threaten to resign despite the assurance of more aid
given at Little Rock. He wrote: "To the best of my memory, the only
condition you ever placed on running again was the financial one. It will
not make much sense for me to appeal to President Meany for a subsidy in
order to keep the operation in Mississippi going if you are going to back
away from the election unless the affiliation problem is licked." Smith told
Ramsay that both of them were aware the affiliation problem could not be
resolved "in a short period of time," and then he responded to Ramsay's
threat with a threat of his own—he would not recommend a subsidy for
the state council unless Ramsay agreed to stand for reelection. Ramsay
blinked. He assured Smith that the main purpose of his letter was to enlist
Meany's help in affiliating black locals because "I am damn well fed up with
being shot at continually by the White Councils while these people sit on
the side lines." Ramsay pleaded innocently that there must have been a
"misunderstanding" about the Little Rock meeting. He confided that he
was even more pessimistic than Smith about ever resolving the affiliation
problem, but if "the AFL-CIO is willing to further subsidize the organization for what appears to be a rather lengthy period . . . then certainly I
want to stay with the ship."[46]

The financial basis of the state council shifted as a result of these
arrangements. Dependence on per capita taxes from local unions was
reduced while subsidies from the AFL-CIO accounted for a larger propor-

tion of the state council's income. The AFL-CIO stake meant that the state council did not have to worry as much that its bank account would suffer every time it took a political position that offended local unions. The promise of AFL-CIO financial support and the independence from local union censure it permitted were crucial as Ramsay entered the most turbulent period of his career.[47]

A Lack of Labor and Party Discipline

If the labor movement could claim few victories in Mississippi, efforts to register black voters could claim even fewer. After being beaten, jailed, shot, and pursued, civil rights workers registered only five percent of all eligible blacks in Mississippi. In November 1963, the Voter Education Project confirmed this lack of progress when it withdrew financial support from the Council of Federated Organizations (COFO), which coordinated black voter registration efforts in the state. VEP director Wiley Branton concluded that Mississippi was too hostile and forbidding and that until the federal government intervened there VEP could get better results elsewhere.[48]

This blow led COFO to adopt a new strategy called the Mississippi Summer Project that it hoped would finally crack open the state. Freedom Summer planned to use white students from the North to register blacks in Mississippi. At the same time as plans for Freedom Summer were taking shape, civil rights groups mounted a challenge to the state's political institutions. In April 1964, the Mississippi Freedom Democratic party (MFDP) was organized to contest the Mississippi Democratic party for recognition at the 1964 national convention. With an invading army of northern students headed toward Mississippi and its political institutions being challenged, the state seethed with defiance. As racial violence escalated, Ramsay courageously joined civil rights groups in petitioning the Federal Communications Commission (FCC) to deny television station WLBT in Jackson, a semiofficial organ of the Citizens' Councils, a renewal of its broadcast license.

WLBT was not unique in its use of television to defend white supremacy, but it was more dedicated to that purpose than rival stations. In 1955, when NAACP general counsel Thurgood Marshall was scheduled to appear on an NBC network broadcast, WLBT told its viewers that it was experiencing cable trouble. Two years later it denied NAACP Mississippi field secretary Medgar Evers equal time to respond to Mississippi officials who defended Governor Faubus during the Little Rock school crisis. WLBT's news coverage was so biased against blacks that in 1958 the FCC delayed the station's license renewal for a year and then granted it only after directing the station to ensure that "authorized facilities are not used to misinform the viewing public." But WLBT was unmoved by such warnings. In 1962, the station's anti-Meredith editorials and its reports on the crisis at Ole Miss drew so many complaints from viewers that the FCC launched a special inquiry into the station's coverage of the events.[49]

WLBT's record of hostility toward blacks made it a target of civil rights activists. In April 1964, the United Church of Christ, joined by Aaron Henry, president of the Mississippi NAACP, and Reverend Robert L. T. Smith of the MFDP, petitioned the FCC to deny WLBT a license renewal. Their suit charged that WLBT's programming and that of another, less culpable television station, WJTV, did not serve black viewers and that both stations' news coverage was biased against blacks.

Unaware of the specific objections the church filed or that representatives of the NAACP and MFDP were included in the petition, Ramsay informed the FCC that the Mississippi AFL-CIO would like to join the suit. At this point, Ramsay recounted later to an interviewer, "all hell broke loose." Ramsay was attacked in the press as a Communist sympathizer and denounced in the Mississippi House of Representatives. The state senate adopted a resolution supporting WLBT's license renewal. But these official condemnations were not as depressing to Ramsay as the criticisms he received from his own constituents. The state officer of the Mississippi AFL-CIO Musicians Organization wrote the FCC: "This action was taken by Mr. Ramsay without consulting Mississippi AFL-CIO local unions and along with many other of these local unions, we are in absolute disagreement and are highly incensed at his unmerited and unauthorized action in this matter. . . . Many AFL-CIO locals are holding meetings and refuting the attack by Mr. Ramsay and I am sure you will receive numerous communications regarding this fact." Cement Workers locals and eleven locals from the Pascagoula Metal Trades Council disaffiliated, adding to the state council's woes in this regard. The Laurel Labor Council passed a resolution condemning Ramsay, and the Jackson County Building and Construction Trades Council furnished WLBT with a letter in support of its license renewal to offset Ramsay's protest. A CWA official wrote the FCC that "the only discrimination on the local television stations of which he was aware was 'the National shows are becoming overloaded with Negro entertainers.'" Ramsay was both resigned to and disheartened by this outcry from local unions. He wrote Stanton Smith,

"Believe you me it's hell when 'Birchites' take your own people and kick your teeth out."[50]

An emergency meeting of the state council's executive committee decided that, given the backlash Ramsay's action evoked, it would be prudent to withdraw from the United Church of Christ suit. The participation of NAACP and MFDP officials in the suit and the argument that the licenses should be revoked because of racial discrimination were just too difficult to explain or defend to the membership. But Ramsay and the executive committee were unwilling to capitulate completely. They decided to prepare their own petition to the FCC that would set forth their reasons for protest.[51] The state council suit differed from the church challenge in two respects. First, it protested license renewal for WLBT only, not WJTV, which was included in the United Church of Christ suit. Second, it avoided the racial basis of the previous protest and instead charged WLBT with using its facilities to encourage "opposition to organized labor" and to present right-wing news analyses to the exclusion of other viewpoints.[52] This retreat did not mollify local unions, nor did Ramsay have the luxury of waiting for the controversy to blow over. The 1964 Mississippi AFL-CIO convention was scheduled to open in just three weeks, on May 25, in Jackson.

Ramsay recalled it as "the most important convention . . . I ever presided over." He took the offensive at the outset to deny his opponents time to work on the delegates. In his opening address he challenged the delegates to decide "whether or not the John Birchers, the White Citizens' Council, the NAACP, or any other pressure groups are going to take over and run this organization . . . [or whether] we're going . . . to get back to sound trade union principles." He then warned that "if the Birchers take it over, if they've got control of this organization, I don't want to be President of it. I want you to know that." The first order of business, which Ramsay would interpret as a vote of confidence in his leadership, was the protest of WLBT's license renewal that the state council had prepared. Before the vote on this measure, Ramsay reviewed how in April the state council had decided to take some action against WLBT, how Ramsay had joined the United Church of Christ suit when he heard of it on the radio, how he then withdrew from it when he learned of the racial basis of its objections, and how the state council then prepared its own case for denying WLBT a renewal. The decision to proceed with the suit was ratified by a voice vote of the delegates. But this did not conclude the matter. The next day, the *Clarion-Ledger* reported that Ramsay had ignored demands for a division of the house when he ruled that the motion had passed. Bitter over the story,

Ramsay interrupted the convention to return the motion to the floor for a standing vote. Just twelve votes were cast against proceeding with the state council's suit.[53]

For the first (and last) time in his career, Ramsay faced an opponent for state council president at the 1964 convention. He was unsure whether he could withstand this challenge and included integrationists on the convention program so as to leave the delegates "something to remember me by."[54] Among those invited to address the convention was Hazel Brannon Smith. Smith published three weekly newspapers in Mississippi and was a target of the Radical Right for her editorials condemning defiance and urging readers to comply with the law. Two years earlier, Ramsay had raised money from union sources to rescue this Pulitzer Prize–winning publisher from a Citizens' Councils campaign that threatened to drive her into bankruptcy.[55] Smith was followed by Father Louis Twomey, head of the industrial relations program at Loyola University in New Orleans and an outspoken opponent of segregation. Smith, Twomey, and every other speaker invited to the convention hit the same notes: defiance was a doomed strategy, the Radical Right was a threat to organized labor, the race issue was a subterfuge, and union leaders should not be diverted by these false issues.

Ramsay's opponent for president of the state council was R. N. Thomas, president of International Union of Electrical Workers (IUE) Local 792 in Jackson. Thomas offered a choice, not an echo, on racial policy. In 1963, Thomas's local contributed money for the defense of Byron de la Beckwith, Medgar Evers's accused murderer. It also participated in the recent controversy over WLBT. The local's officers notified the FCC that they condemned Ramsay's "arbitrary action" and assured the commissioners that Ramsay "did not represent our views or the views of the members with whom we have talked."[56]

Ramsay defeated Thomas handily, 12,870 to 3,004, but this vote did not indicate that the rank and file approved of Ramsay's racial views or that his office was secure. Daniel Powell, who attended the convention, attributed Ramsay's victory to the opposition's inability to find a strong candidate to oppose him. "If Ramsay continues to follow the policies of the AFL-CIO," Powell warned COPE headquarters in Washington, "he will probably be defeated in the next convention."[57] Ramsay survived this electoral challenge because he had the advantages of incumbency. For instance, Ramsay knew who controlled the vote of delegates from particular unions. In addition, delegates were often union activists who were more likely to adopt AFL-CIO positions than were the rank-and-file members they represented. Finally, Ramsay benefited from a mistaken strategy employed by his opponents. The Radical Right had instructed allied locals to disaffiliate in protest against the state council's racial policies. This certainly hurt the state council financially and, if not for subsidies from the AFL-CIO, would have been fatal. But at the same time disaffiliation weakened the state council financially, it strengthened Ramsay's political control over it. Since local unions that disaffiliated could not vote in state council elections, this strategy deprived Ramsay's opponents of the votes to defeat him. Ironically, the Radical Right's strategy to disrupt the state council by disaffiliation was too successful; not enough locals opposed to Ramsay's policies remained inside the council to vote him out of office. By the end of the year there would be even fewer.

Ramsay gained notoriety as a result of the WLBT imbroglio. He received death threats and was denounced as a traitor to his race at Ku Klux Klan rallies. Friends concerned about his safety stood guard over him during the 1964 convention.[58] Even though they had an unlisted number, Ramsay's family was harassed on the phone. This was not the first time Ramsay was menaced. He first received threats when he came to the defense of the *Chronicle* in 1962. But the *Chronicle* episode was a Gulf Coast matter that earned him only the attention of local vigilantes. The WLBT struggle was of statewide interest, and Ramsay rose accordingly in the Klan's demonology. After a member of the Mississippi Council of Human Relations was shot, Ramsay was warned that he was next. To discourage such attempts, Ramsay let it be known that he kept a shotgun in his car and went armed at all times.[59] He taught his teenage sons how to use firearms and instructed them to shoot first and ask questions later if prowlers came around the house.[60] The Mississippi State Sovereignty Commission kept a file on Ramsay, and he was the target of surveillance. When Ramsay was visited by representatives of Public Radio, they noted that a man outside the office wrote down their license plate when they left.[61]

Ramsay was fortunate that he was never harmed and escaped the fate of Ottis Mathews, an official of Woodworkers Local 5443 in Laurel. After the local agreed with the Masonite Corporation to end discrimination inside the plant, Mathews was dragged from his car at gunpoint by Klansmen, tied, whipped, and had corrosive liquids poured on his wounds.[62] In the 1970s, after Ramsay was no longer in danger, a former Klansman admitted to him that he had been assigned to kill Ramsay. Ramsay replied that he was happy the Klansman never attempted his mission because Ramsay would have taken him out if he had.[63]

Reaction to the convention's decision to proceed with a suit against WLBT came quickly. E. B. Johnson, Jr., president of Commercial Telegraphers Union Local 19 in West Jackson, criticized the 1964 convention as an "unadulterated integration rally." Johnson complained that Hazel Brannon Smith and Father Twomey failed to mention organized labor in their speeches but spoke only of integration, and he condemned Ramsay for attacking "several white organizations" while "Communist infiltrated Negro groups . . . are planning the downfall of this Nation." Ramsay replied that he had worked tirelessly defending the interests of Johnson and his local in the state legislature, but "after reading a letter such as yours, I can't help but wonder if it's not wasted effort." One member told Secretary-Treasurer Tom Knight he regretted "that one cent of my money goes to support people like you," and another member informed Knight that he and Ramsay could serve organized labor best if they both resigned. Ramsay preferred these letters in which members vented their anger to others he received in which no criticism was made or challenge offered: just a simple note was included whose significance threatened to bring the state council to its knees. "I am enclosing another letter of disaffiliation," Ramsay wrote to Stanton Smith. "As you will note no explanation is given. . . . Frankly, I'm rather disturbed over the fact that we may lose several more before this thing is over. . . . As you know our budget was figured on an affiliation of 18,000 plus the subsidies. We are now below the 17,000 mark which means we are in serious trouble. If you have any ideas about coping with the situation I'll be glad to hear from you."[64]

Ramsay received no respite as spring turned to summer. On July 15, the Republican party nominated Senator Barry Goldwater for president. The AFL-CIO was appalled at Goldwater's nomination and did not even wait for the Democrats to convene before condemning the Republican platform as "an insult to the intelligence of the voters" that merited "not mere rejection but outright disdain." Five weeks later, on August 26, the Democrats nominated President Lyndon Johnson for reelection. The 1964 Democratic party convention had barely concluded when the AFL-CIO praised its platform and formally endorsed Johnson for president.[65]

It was Ramsay's task to carry this message into Mississippi, which seethed with feelings of betrayal and vengeance toward the national Democratic party. First, President Kennedy humiliated the state when he sent troops to desegregate the University of Mississippi in 1962. Then at the 1964 Democratic convention, the party insulted Mississippi when it legitimated the MFDP's challenge to the state's delegation by granting it two at-large convention seats. Now, encouraged by President Johnson's support for civil rights, the state was overrun with white students from the North trying to register blacks to vote. Holding the national Democratic party responsible for its distress, the state fought back to preserve white supremacy. Students and civil rights workers who participated in Freedom Summer were beaten, harassed, and jailed. Racial violence reached a deadly crescendo in August, when the disfigured bodies of three civil rights workers, Andrew Goodman, Mickey Schwerner, and James Chaney, were pulled from an earthen dam near Philadelphia, Mississippi. The high idealism with which Freedom Summer began was buried in the grisly reaction it encountered. By October, the toll stood at thirty-seven black churches bombed, six civil rights workers murdered, eighty assaulted, and over a thousand arrested.[66]

With the state engulfed in a violent paroxysm of hate and determined to wreak vengeance upon the national Democratic party for its humiliation and betrayal, Ramsay began the hopeless task of convincing union members to vote for Johnson. On August 1, Knight wrote Barkan: "We in the labor movement here are perhaps in the toughest situation that we have ever faced. The Klan, the Citizens Council, and the John Birch Society, etc., have infiltrated and influenced the minds of so many of our members it is the next thing to impossible to talk to so many of them." Two weeks later Knight described to Barkan how much the race issue overwhelmed appeals to economic self-interest when he noted how common it was to see old cars on the road, many barely running, some rusted out, but all of them with Goldwater stickers on their bumpers.[67]

In early September Ramsay and Knight began a tour of central labor councils across the state. They criticized Goldwater's voting record and emphasized the importance of defeating him in November. Later in the month, Louisiana state council president Victor Bussie sent Ramsay a flyer that was returned to his office by a member whose name and address Ramsay had given Bussie earlier. This member sent back the flyer, which announced labor's endorsement of President Johnson, with instructions for Bussie to "keep this bunch of junk for there is not a chance in one million of me ever voting for that s.o.b. nor any one else that I know of will either [sic]." Ramsay thanked Bussie for sharing the member's opinions with him and replied sarcastically, "Evidently this character is a member of the Americans for the Preservation of White Trash. I understand they have about taken over the Natchez-Vidalia area." Ramsay then reassured Bussie and probably deflated him a bit when he informed his colleague from Louisiana that "the note this character penned to you is rather mild compared to some I've received out of that section."[68] The Natchez

Central Labor Council confirmed this judgment later in the year when it passed a resolution demanding that Ramsay resign. The resolution accused Ramsay of pledging the Mississippi AFL-CIO to help secure voting rights for blacks although the state council had not adopted any such policy. Ramsay replied that he was stunned to find that some locals that were not even affiliated with the state council had signed the resolution. "These locals aren't helping pay the freight," he fired back in dismay, "yet they want to set policy for this organization." Ramsay defended himself by reminding the central labor council that support for black voting rights was AFL-CIO policy. The charter of any state or central council could be revoked, Ramsay warned, if this policy was defied.[69]

As the election approached, evidence of the growing rebellion within union ranks accumulated. The *New York Times* noted that workers across the South were prepared to bolt the national Democratic ticket but none more so than in Alabama and Mississippi. The *Times* reported that the Mississippi AFL-CIO "had been reduced by the intensity of the anti-Negro animus to a defensive holding operation." In October the *Clarion-Ledger* printed a letter from the steward of CWA Local 3950 that reassured its readers "Mississippi Labor will again repudiate" the attempts of Ramsay and CWA state director W. O. Stanley "to tell us how to vote."[70] CWA Local 3511 notified Ramsay that its members voted sixty-one to twenty-seven not to support the national Democratic ticket. CWA Local 3507 informed the state council it would disaffiliate, as did Glass Bottle Blowers Local 230. More disconcerting was a letter Ramsay received from Local 602 of his own union, the Paperworkers. The local informed Ramsay it had decided to "Withdraw From The State Labor Council," because "We Do Not Feel the State Labor Council Stands For The Same Principles And Ideals As We Do."[71] Ramsay contacted the Paperworkers' state director and members he knew inside the local to get this decision reversed, but to no avail.[72]

Goldwater carried Mississippi with a remarkable 87 percent of the vote, a gauge of how disaffected the state was from the national Democratic party. Following the election, Knight admitted to Barkan that "the Klan gained considerably in some of our locals." He reminded Barkan of Ottis Mathews's fate and informed him of other attempts physically to intimidate union leaders. Despite these threats, Knight lamented, union members remained hostile toward blacks although both groups were targets and victims of the Radical Right. "Well," Knight concluded disconsolately, "it looks very much like Hitler has come to Mississippi."[73]

The influence of radical right-wing groups among union members first became evident in 1963, when some locals in Mississippi contributed money to help defend Medgar Evers's accused murderer, Byron de la Beckwith. This generosity even extended across the border into Tennessee, where an IUE local voted to donate $500 to the Beckwith Defense Fund. When the international ordered the local to recover the money, it proceeded to solicit voluntary contributions from its members for Beckwith's defense.[74] According to Ramsay, the John Birch Society had taken over the Metal Trades unions in the Pascagoula shipyards, the Citizens' Councils were influential among local unions in Jackson, and the Americans for the Preservation of the White Race had infiltrated Paperworkers and Pulp, Sulphite and Paper Mill Workers locals in Natchez, as well as railroad locals in McComb. Daniel Powell confirmed the Radical Right's influence within local unions and offered a bleak postelection assessment when he recommended that COPE continue to subsidize the state council:

> The Mississippi situation is the most discouraging in the nation. The fear that blankets the state is almost unbelievable. . . . Despite the discouraging and dismal situation they face both inside and outside the Labor Movement in Mississippi, State AFL-CIO President Claude Ramsay and State COPE Director Tom Knight still have hope and are still trying to build COPE organization.
>
> If the Matching Grant for Mississippi is discontinued, there will be no full-time COPE Director and very little COPE activity in the State. If the Matching Grant is discontinued and Tom Knight is terminated, then I believe that Claude Ramsay will resign as President, because I doubt that even Ramsay has the fortitude to fight the Mississippi climate alone. Without Ramsay and Knight, the Mississippi State Council would be almost certain to collapse in a few months, and all the effort we have made in the state for the past nine years will have been wasted.[75]

Ramsay resigned himself to Johnson's defeat statewide but not to the disloyalty of Mississippi Democrats who contributed to it. During the campaign, Ramsay accused Bidwell Adam, chair of the Mississippi Democratic party, of apologizing for the Democratic ticket instead of defending it. Ramsay closed his letter to Adam by challenging him to "put on your fighting clothes and start swinging or throw in the towel and allow someone else to carry the ball."[76] When it became clear that the Johnson-Humphrey ticket would receive no help from the statewide Democratic party, Ramsay tried to create an organization of loyal Democrats to act in its place.[77] But this attempt to form an ad hoc group to support the Democratic ticket in Mississippi was less successful than a similar effort four years before. In 1960, when the Mississippi Democratic party threw its weight behind unpledged electors, Senator James Eastland rallied Demo-cratic loyalists for Kennedy. Now, in 1964, not one statewide officeholder or member of Congress—Democrats all—would support such a loyalist group or even endorse President Johnson publicly. Fifty percent of the state legislature joined Democrats for Goldwater organized by state senator Ellis Bodron from Vicksburg. Congressman John Bell Williams defected and announced he would vote for Goldwater, and his colleague Representative Arthur Winstead told his constituents that he could not in good con-science vote for President Johnson. This act of conscience, however, did not save Winstead from the Goldwater juggernaut that rolled across the state. He was defeated by Prentiss Walker, the first Republican elected to Congress from Mississippi since 1882.[78]

After the election, Ramsay confided to Barkan, "I never worked harder and accomplished less in my life." The disloyalty of Mississippi Democrats confirmed to Ramsay the need to build a "bona fide Democratic party" in Mississippi. In December, Ramsay and other state council officials from southern states that polled for Goldwater convened at AFL-CIO headquar-ters to review with AFL-CIO leaders the reasons for Goldwater's strength in the South. They described how influential right-wing organizations were among their members, how the race issue drowned out all other appeals, and how little cooperation the Johnson campaign received from the Democratic party in their states. They then went with COPE director Al Barkan to National Democratic Committee headquarters to inquire if it would support Loyalists who stood by President Johnson for control of the Democratic party in their states. Ramsay left Washington without a firm commitment from the Democrats, but he did receive $5,000 from the AFL-CIO to help build a loyal Democratic party in Mississippi.[79]

RAMSAY AND THE CIVIL RIGHTS MOVEMENT

Surprisingly, until 1965 Ramsay had little personal contact with the civil rights movement he was so vilified for supporting. The Mississippi AFL-CIO paralleled the statewide civil rights movement but rarely intersected with it. Ramsay's first contact with a civil rights leader occurred in 1959, when Mississippi AFL-CIO secretary-treasurer Ray Smithhart introduced him to Medgar Evers. Smithhart had worked closely with Evers and other black leaders on a campaign to fill a vacancy for city commissioner in Jackson. When the COPE-endorsed candidate won because of the large majorities he received in black districts, Smithhart sensed the potential of the black vote and asked McDevitt to send either COPE minorities director Philip Weightman or his associate Earl Davis to Mississippi. "We have several areas," Smithhart told McDevitt, "where a lot of good can be done if we make the right contacts. Some of the Negro leaders ask me if I would be able to send someone from the AFL-CIO to work with them and that is the reason I suggested this to you."[80] A year later, when Evers's group, the Community Improvement Association, needed a new mimeograph machine, Smithhart suggested that Evers apply to AFL-CIO COPE for the money. COPE responded with more money than Evers requested.[81] When Ramsay took office, he inherited the relationship with Medgar Evers that Smithhart had started. Ramsay and Evers soon developed a working relationship that blossomed into friendship between the two men.[82] But Evers's murder in 1963 left Ramsay without contacts to civil rights leaders in his state. It was not until the following year that Ramsay met Aaron Henry, president of the NAACP Mississippi chapter, at a COPE convention in Little Rock. Nor did Ramsay have much contact with COFO, SNCC, or SCLC, which also operated in Mississippi. It is unlikely that Ramsay ever met Robert Moses, and he was only a sympathetic observer of Freedom Summer.[83]

But the opportunities created by the 1965 Voting Rights Act and the reluctance of the statewide Democratic party to take advantage of it led Ramsay to seek working alliances with civil rights groups. Together they would act in place of a Democratic party that was so identified with white supremacy that it would make no effort to attract newly enfranchised black voters. Ramsay believed it was essential to register and mobilize these new voters to defeat anti-labor legislators from agricultural black-belt counties who controlled the state government. For Ramsay, a black-labor coalition was a case of simple arithmetic: "Twenty-six counties in Mississippi have a Negro popular majority. Many of labor's worst enemies in the Mississippi state legislature live in these counties: if these people are to be removed from office it will have to be with the Negro vote. To a large degree our legislative program is dependent on our ability to form alliances with these people and this we are trying to do."[84]

Black enfranchisement would not only remove labor's enemies from the state legislature but would realign the party system in Mississippi. Conservatives and upper-class whites would flee the Mississippi Democratic party for the GOP. The departure of these Dixiecrats would liberalize the Mississippi Democratic party, which would now be based on a biracial coalition of blacks and working-class whites. This would contribute to the development of two-party competition in Mississippi that finally would permit the emergence of liberal Democratic candidates whom the Mississippi AFL-CIO could support in good faith.

But Ramsay's participation in the civil rights movement also ensnared him in the ruthless factionalism that divided it. The NAACP and MFDP competed furiously to win the loyalty of newly enfranchised blacks in Mississippi. Ramsay's first taste of this bitter rivalry occurred in the struggle over the Young Democrats of Mississippi. Its charter had lapsed in 1963, and recognition from the Young Democratic Clubs of America (YDCA) was available. In August 1964, just three days before the MFDP challenge at the 1964 national Democratic convention, a group called the Young Democratic Clubs of Mississippi (YDCM) applied for a charter from YDCA. YDCM was led by Melvin Whitfield and was connected with MFDP, SNCC, and a black youth group called the Mississippi Student Union. YDCA denied this application for a charter but encouraged YDCM to reapply at the YDCA National Committee meeting in April.[85]

Although YDCM claimed to have advertised its founding convention, to have local chapters, and to have campaigned for the Johnson-Humphrey ticket in November, Ramsay had not heard of it. Ramsay and Robert Oswald, former president of the Young Democrats of Mississippi, were suspicious that YDCM was a paper organization, a MFDP and SNCC front that would do civil rights, not political, work under the Democratic party label. The effect of this, both men feared, would be to drive whites out of the Democratic party.

Ramsay's relationship with MFDP had not always been so testy. In 1964 he declined an invitation to be part of the challenging delegation that MFDP sent to the national Democratic convention in Atlantic City. But Ramsay was skeptical that MFDP could win elections in Mississippi, and he increasingly perceived it as an obstruction to building an organization that could. Ramsay's experience with the 1965 Delta Farm Strike confirmed his dismissive impression that MFDP created issues and then left them for others to resolve. Finally, if MFDP was detested by whites, there was little evidence that it was supported by blacks in Mississippi either. MFDP was a staff-led rather than membership-based organization that enjoyed a higher profile out of state than it did in Mississippi. After its spectacular appearance in 1964, it had "dwindled to little more than a spiritual union" a year later and "existed, for the most part, in name only," according to Hanes Walton, Jr.[86] Thus in the factional war between civil rights groups in Mississippi, Ramsay sided with the NAACP because it could attract broader support than the MFDP, which was as evanescent as it was effervescent.[87]

Suspicious of the YDCM, Oswald appealed to the National Democratic Committee and the YDCA to investigate Whitfield's group. A delegation led by Spenser Oliver, an aide to Senator Carl Hayden of Arizona, arrived in Mississippi. On April 4, just one week before the YDCA National Committee was to convene in Kansas City, a meeting was held in Ramsay's office. Among those present were Ramsay, Oswald, Oliver, Whitfield, and Charles Evers, NAACP field secretary for Mississippi. Oliver asked Whitfield to delay his request for a charter until the YDCA convention in October and to work with an integrated Young Democrats group that had since formed at the University of Mississippi. Whitfield replied that his group had waited long enough and was intent on being recognized as the official statewide chapter.

A showdown was now unavoidable, and all those who met in Ramsay's office the previous week were in Kansas City for the YDCA National Committee meeting. Evers, Ramsay, and Oswald spoke with delegates about the destructive consequences recognizing YDCM would have for Democrats in Mississippi and recommended the Ole Miss group as a more appropriate base around which to rebuild the state chapter. Oliver's report was openly hostile to YDCM and expressed doubt that it existed except on paper. After hearing appeals by both sides, the YDCA National Committee rejected YDCM's request for a charter by a three-to-one margin. It then passed a resolution instructing Young Democrats in Mississippi to hold a unity convention to elect officers who could apply for a charter at the next YDCA convention in October.[88]

But rival factions were in no mood to conciliate their differences when they returned to Mississippi. The convention to form a Young Democrats of Mississippi chapter took place on August 14 at the Heidelberg Hotel in Jackson. Conflicts aired at the Kansas City meeting resurfaced to mar this attempt at unity. The convention began well enough with Hunter Morey, SNCC field secretary, in the chair. Rules of procedure and an agenda were adopted. The first order of business was the election of convention officers. The faction supported by Ramsay won this contest when John Frazier of the NAACP and Bob Boyd of the Young Democrats group at Ole Miss were elected as chair and executive secretary of the convention, respectively. Recognizing its advantage, the NAACP faction made a motion to suspend the agenda temporarily and proceed directly to the election of officers. The motion passed, and in the elections that followed Cleveland Donald, another delegate from the Ole Miss group, and Hodding Carter III were elected cochairs of the new organization. The quick vote on officers caught MFDP supporters who backed YDCM by surprise.[89] They tried to delay the proceedings with countless points of order until reinforcements could arrive to provide them a majority. Shouts and pandemonium broke loose on the convention floor while, befitting the confusion, a United Klans of America organizer passed out KKK cards in the back of the room. By the time the convention recessed for lunch, the balance of power between factions in the room had shifted. When the delegates returned, Charles Morgan, Jr., a civil rights lawyer from Alabama, delivered the keynote address in which he pleaded with the delegates "to work together. . . . The enemy is outside, not in here."[90] But immediately following Morgan's appearance, MFDP supporters passed a motion to censure the convention chair and called for a new election to replace him. Hodding Carter denounced the vote as a mockery of democratic procedure and of everything that had taken place that morning. He then urged all those who repudiated the censure vote to walk out and join him in founding a loyal Young Democrats chapter. Consequently, separate factions met in separate rooms of the Heidelberg Hotel and selected separate slates of officers.[91] The attempt to transform the Democratic party in Mississippi by reviving its youth group had failed. "Frankly," Tom Knight wrote Daniel Powell, "I think we can forget all about the Young Democrats in Mississippi."[92]

While Ramsay tried to revive the Young Democrats, he was also involved in organizing the Mississippi Democratic Conference (MDC). The origin of the MDC can be traced back to the MFDP challenge at the 1964 Democratic party convention. The MFDP argued that the convention should recognize its delegates, instead of the segregated delegation sent by the Regulars, as the official representatives from Mississippi. The MFDP charged that the Regulars forfeited their seats because they had systematically excluded blacks from party deliberations and would not unconditionally support the party's platform or its ticket. The convention labored to arrive at a compromise that acknowledged both the justice of MFDP's claims and the need to placate southern sensibilities. At last a compromise was offered that granted MFDP two at-large seats but also seated Mississippi's segregated delegation with the proviso that future delegations would be integrated. But when the Regulars returned to Mississippi, they made no attempt to satisfy this requirement. They continued to deny blacks access to party meetings, and the disloyalty they displayed in the 1964 election further reduced their standing. It appeared more and more as if the national party would recognize MFDP because the Regulars would not comply with the 1964 convention agreement. Into this breach stepped MDC. MDC was created as an alternative to both the lily-white Regulars, who controlled the Mississippi Democratic party, and the MFDP, which could not attract white voters. Dismissing both the Regulars and the

MFDP, Ramsay told the founding convention of the MDC, "We feel there is no Democratic Party in Mississippi and we will fill the void."[93]

The rivalry between the NAACP and MFDP that disrupted the Young Democrats' convention now threatened to rend the MDC. The dispute between the two groups had become fierce. Not only did the NAACP and MFDP compete for recognition from the Democratic party, but passage of the Voting Rights Act had increased the stakes enormously. The act would enfranchise hundreds of thousands of new black voters whom the NAACP and MFDP each hoped to lead. Suspicious of each other before the Voting Rights Act, they were locked in mortal combat following its passage.[94] Consequently, when Ramsay and the NAACP made up the guest list for the MDC founding convention, they pointedly omitted SNCC and MFDP activists.

In July 1965, 125 delegates arrived in Jackson to help build "a Loyalist Mississippi Democratic group" that would "restore relations with the national party."[95] The immediate goal of the MDC was to create local chapters that would participate in Democratic party precinct meetings. These meetings were the first step in selecting Mississippi's delegation to the 1968 Democratic national convention.

The meeting in Jackson was notable for the MDC's self-conscious pursuit of integration. In the election of officers whites and blacks were alternated. A good portent for the future was the appearance of Donald Ellinger from the National Democratic Committee. His encouraging words gave the new organization a public semblance of national support.[96] Powell watched the proceedings and reported to COPE that the MDC convention was "the first time in nearly a hundred years that whites and Negroes publicly sat down to attempt to form a political coalition." But the convention drew a much less favorable review from MFDP and SNCC. They labeled the MDC a "labor and NAACP front" that was now opportunistically trying to harvest the crop MFDP first planted at the 1964 convention.[97]

The Democratic Conference, however, quickly ran aground. The National Democratic Committee never gave MDC the support it needed. In addition, the new organization could not distinguish between civil rights work, which some white members found repugnant, and liberalizing the statewide party. Finally, without help from the national party, the MDC was dependent on the Mississippi AFL-CIO, which could not sustain it financially.

The Democratic Conference received many promises from the national party, few of which ever materialized. After the founding convention,

Ramsay, NAACP Mississippi president Aaron Henry, and MDC vice-chair Charles Young went to Washington to discuss recognition and support with prominent Democrats. At Democratic party headquarters, Chris Carter, the president's personal representative to the national party, told them the party could not contribute money to MDC but would arrange for an "angel" to do so. Donald Ellinger then displayed to the group a memo indicating that the national party intended to recognize the MDC. The Mississippi delegation also visited the Office of Economic Opportunity, where its director, Sargeant Shriver, promised them veto power over the poverty program in Mississippi.[98] But no patronage or angel ever appeared.[99] President Johnson did not want to offend Mississippi's two powerful senators, James Eastland and John Stennis, by signaling support for the insurgent group. Eastland was chair of the Senate Judiciary Committee, which scrutinized the president's judicial appointments, and Stennis chaired the Defense Preparedness Subcommittee, which considered his Vietnam War effort. Tom Knight acknowledged the influence of Eastland particularly when he wrote Dan Powell, "I am convinced that as long as he is Chairman of the Judiciary Committee, we are not going to get anything out of LBJ and the National party."[100]

The Democratic Conference also suffered from a confusion of aims. Some viewed the MDC through the angle of Democratic party politics as an organization that would reestablish links between Mississippi and the national Democratic party. Others saw it as a vehicle to register and mobilize newly enfranchised blacks. After only two months, Oswald resigned as chair over such differences with the MDC executive board, explaining, "I accepted the chairmanship with the clear understanding this was to be a political organization affiliated with the national Democratic party and was not to be another civil rights movement or to be used for that purpose."[101]

The final blow was MDC's financial dependence on the Mississippi AFL-CIO, which could not even support itself financially. Disaffiliations continued to deplete state council coffers. Membership was down to sixteen thousand. In January 1966, Knight wrote Powell, "Our major problems are still poor affiliation and financial difficulties resulting from the radical right wing infiltration of our labor organizations." A month later Sheet Metal Workers Local 407 withdrew, a loss of another two hundred members that Ramsay attributed to "more Birchite work." By May, with the state council running a $300 per month deficit, its account was so depleted that Ramsay could not even cash his paycheck. He told Stanton Smith that "unless you or someone finds a golden goose for us in the near future we will have two unpaid state council officers at the end of the month."[102] Powell confirmed the state council's desperate plight when he reported to COPE headquarters in Washington, "The Radical Right-Wing's use of the racial issue to get local unions to withdraw has hurt the Mississippi Council more than it has anywhere in the South." Smith sent another letter to affiliated unions urging them to ensure that their locals were affiliated. One union president replied to Smith that he sympathized with Ramsay because his union faced a similar problem with its members in Mississippi: "Since the Civil Rights [sic], they have seceded from any AFL-CIO organization. We have had a hard time keeping them in our locals."[103]

The demise of the MDC did not prevent Ramsay from taking advantage of the new Voting Rights Act that Congress passed in 1965. The state council contributed $400 to keep a NAACP voter registration drive alive in Adams County. Ramsay then donated another $300 to assist a similar effort in adjacent Jefferson County, where a federal examiner was present. Ramsay told COPE director Al Barkan that he hoped to assist NAACP voter registration drives wherever proof of a viable organization existed and federal examiners were located. The state council received $5,000 from COPE and $1,000 from the UAW to defray the costs of these efforts.[104]

But the opportunities created by the Voting Rights Act called for a more comprehensive approach than these stopgap measures. In March 1966, Horace Sheffield from the UAW, Evers and Henry from the NAACP, Jessie Epps from the IUE, and Knight and Ramsay from the Mississippi AFL-CIO met with Voter Education Project director Vernon Jordan to form the Mississippi Voter Registration and Education League (MVREL). MVREL would "motivate, educate, and mobilize for a full-scale registration drive in Mississippi."[105] Jordan assured MVREL of VEP support, and a twelve-month budget of over $100,000 was prepared.

MVREL was a nonmembership umbrella organization that included representatives from the labor movement, the NAACP, the Negro Mississippi Teachers Association, the State Baptist Association, and the Prince Hall Masons. Even the MFDP attended, the first time it had cooperated politically with the NAACP since the demise of COFO in 1964. Aaron Henry was elected president, and each organization was guaranteed at least one seat on the board of directors. Ramsay was excited at the possibilities. Following MVREL's first meeting, he told COPE minorities director Philip Weightman, "I understand this was the first time some of these people had ever attended a meeting of this kind." He wrote Barkan that he was now more convinced than ever that "our political progress is dependent upon a large Negro voter registration."[106] But Ramsay's euphoria was short-lived. Revelations of his participation in MVREL led to another confrontation with the membership over racial policy.

Aaron Henry's letter inviting people to MVREL's first meeting could not have been more explicit about labor's involvement. "This noble endeavor," Henry wrote, "is encouraged by the AFL-CIO national leadership who will finance the campaign. I want, here and now, to acknowledge the support and assistance of Mr. Claude Ramsay and Mr. Tom Knight of the Mississippi State AFL-CIO who have been most helpful in getting the National Labor Leadership assistance in this brave and vital undertaking." On May 20, the *Delta Democrat-Times* revealed the contents of Henry's letter, thereby exposing Ramsay's involvement with MVREL.[107] Media reports connecting Ramsay with MVREL soon circulated throughout Mississippi. The response was sharp and prolonged. Klan rallies again denounced Ramsay, newspaper editorials were piercing in their criticism, and employers used the incident against unions in organizing campaigns. Local unions in Meridian issued a joint statement repudiating Ramsay's participation in MVREL and his leadership of the Mississippi AFL-CIO. Another local union reassured the public that "it lends no support either financially or otherwise to this newly formed voter registration group in which Mr. Ramsay is active."[108] Ramsay told Stanton Smith, "I understand the Klan has really given me hell in their last few rallies. Instead of one shotgun loaded, I am now keeping two."[109]

Ramsay defended his participation in MVREL to members by arguing that labor needed to ally with the black community before the business community did so. He argued that the Mississippi Economic Council was trying to entice black voters and that labor needed to reach them first.[110] He also challenged his critics to confront the facts of life in Mississippi: black votes were necessary to defeat anti-labor politicians. To placate his critics, however, Ramsay did not take a formal position with MVREL. But Ramsay was so identified with MVREL that local black registration groups appealed directly to him for funds or asked that Ramsay intervene on their behalf to obtain them from MVREL.

In spring 1967, MVREL hosted eight seminars to train people in voter registration. Mississippi NAACP assistant field secretary Reverend Allen Johnson served as Coordinator. He was joined by Ramsay and two members of Weightman's COPE staff, Fannie Neal and Earl Davis, who participated in all eight sessions. John Brooks, head of voter registration for the NAACP, and Horace Sheffield also contributed. The first meeting was in

Greenville, followed by workshops in Clarksdale, Yazoo City, and Meridian. Davis was impressed by Ramsay's commitment, reporting that he drove two hundred miles to attend one of the scheduled workshops. He wrote Weightman that "without the help of President Ramsay and Secretary Knight . . . we could not have made it."[111] More than 350 people attended the eight workshops, with requests for training coming from unserved areas.[112]

MVREL tried not only to increase black voter registration but to increase black influence within the Democratic party. In January 1968, MVREL, the Mississippi AFL-CIO, and Hodding Carter's Young Democrats group, which was now officially chartered, conducted eighteen workshops throughout Mississippi. In these sessions leaders explained how to participate in local Democratic party meetings, beginning at the precinct level, with the ultimate objective of sending a liberal, integrated delegation to the 1968 national Democratic party convention in Chicago. The Mississippi AFL-CIO paid the expenses for Reverend Johnson, who once again coordinated the workshops, and it prepared and paid for all of the material used in them.

When Democratic party precinct meetings were held in April 1968, the Regulars were not contrite and denied blacks participation in them. In some areas precinct meetings were not publicized; in other cases meeting times and places were changed without notice; in some locations blacks were locked out of the meetings; in still others no resolutions or nominations were permitted.[113] Aaron Henry told MVREL members who experienced discrimination that lawyers would be available to take their statements should a challenge to the Regulars be necessary in Chicago. Henry also wrote to Governor Richard Hughes, chair of the Special Equal Rights Committee of the national Democratic party, to inform him of the discrimination that had taken place. Following county conventions that showed no improvement over the precinct meetings, a coalition called the Loyal Democrats of Mississippi was formed to challenge the credentials of the Regulars in Chicago. The Loyal Democrats consisted of those groups already in MVREL but also included the MFDP and Hodding Carter's Young Democrats group. Ramsay and Knight were appointed to the Loyal Democrats Steering Committee but declined to serve. They wanted to avoid a repeat of the outcry from the rank and file that their participation in MVREL had provoked. Ramsay was chastened enough by recent criticisms to recognize that the rank and file would not tolerate his collusion with the MFDP or a challenge to the Mississippi Democratic party.[114] Indeed, the Mississippi AFL-CIO withdrew officially from the Loyal

Democrats once a firm decision to send a challenging delegation to Chicago had been made. But the state council continued to assist the Loyal Democrats behind the scenes, and two black labor officials, Wilson Evans of the International Longshoremen's Association and Robert Woodson of the Carpenters, served on its board. Ramsay continued to attend and even voted in meetings of the Loyal Democrats steering committee, although he was not officially a member.[115]

On July 21, the Mississippi Democratic state convention convened in Jackson to complete the selection of Mississippi's delegation to the national convention in Chicago. Twenty delegates, three of whom were black, had already been selected at the district level. The convention was to fill the remaining twenty-four posts. Despite protests from the Loyalists, not one black was selected as a delegate, nor were any blacks recruited to serve as alternates. Loyalist efforts to extract a loyalty pledge and nominate supporters to key party posts were also defeated resoundingly. According to one Regular, "The action of the Governor [John Bell Williams] was a dare to the Democratic party to throw us out."[116] It was clear that the Regulars were more concerned with maintaining the state party's ties to segregationists than with preserving its ties to the national party. Following the convention, the Loyal Democrats announced that they would challenge the credentials of the Mississippi Democratic party at the national convention.

Ever since Ramsay took office he had been at odds with the Mississippi Democratic party. Yet, surprisingly, Ramsay did not feel vindicated by the impending credentials challenge in Chicago. He sympathized with the Loyalists but felt that if they were recognized any chance the Democrats had of carrying Mississippi in November would be ruined. In addition, Ramsay had asked people to participate in the Mississippi Democratic party delegate selection process and could not now in good faith join a challenge to it. He tried to broker a compromise between the Loyalists and Regulars but was unable to resolve their differences. When the Loyalists were granted credentials, Mississippi was in the anomalous position of having two Democratic parties; the Loyalists were recognized by the national Democratic party while the Regulars retained title to the Democratic column on the state ballot. The Regulars could still select candidates who ran as Democrats but could not participate in the deliberations of their own party, while the Loyalists could participate in the drafting of the party's national platform but could not choose the candidates in Mississippi who ran under it. The breach between the two wings of the party in Mississippi would not be healed until 1976.[117]

Mississippi voted for third-party candidate George Wallace in the 1968 presidential election. In his report to COPE headquarters on the election, Tom Knight repeated the now standard refrain, "Racial prejudice in certain areas is responsible for 99% of our problem."[118] As the decade came to a close, the state council could point to little progress. Few of the legislative goals contained in the 1961 Program of Progress had been met eight years later. Those goals that had been achieved, such as abolition of the poll tax or reapportionment, were the result of changes in federal law, which the state council could not take credit for politically.

CONCLUSION

The 1960s were a decade of trial for Ramsay and the Mississippi AFL-CIO. He posed a threat to the conformity that sustained Mississippi as a closed society.[119] The defenders of the closed society found black resistance foolhardy and misguided, but they reserved a special loathing for whites such as Ramsay who renounced the privilege of color. There was no greater challenge to the closed society than to have it rejected by those it was meant to serve.

Although Ramsay was never challenged seriously for president of the state council, he took enough blows to make him consider quitting his office more than once. Perhaps Aaron Henry had Ramsay in mind when he told the U.S. Commission on Civil Rights: "It is political suicide for any white man in Mississippi to take a position that he believes that all Negroes should register to vote."[120] More important were the personal costs Ramsay suffered. He was married to the union and was remorseful later that he had neglected his family in favor of his work. Financially, Ramsay and his family suffered as well because his post with the state council did not pay as much as he could have earned if he had stayed with International Paper or joined the Paperworkers' staff. Moreover, Ramsay's heresy posed a constant threat to his physical safety. He received numerous death threats, his family was harassed, and he was denounced by name at Klan rallies. During the storm that broke over Ramsay's participation in MVREL, he wrote Philip Weightman to assure him that "I am taking every precaution and stay armed at all times."[121] When black garbage men in Jackson struck for union recognition in 1970, Ramsay received so many threats that he had floodlights placed around his home, police stood guard across from his house, and his children slept in the den rather than in their bedroom in the front.[122] When Ramsay persevered in the face of these threats, others found the courage to follow his example. Earl Davis recalled coming to

Mississippi for COPE and calling his wife to tell her that he was staying on Lynch Street in Jackson. She feared the street address was an omen and begged him to move. Davis himself was none too pleased with his assignment but stayed for the duration because of the example set by Ramsay.[123] The courage Ramsay displayed in the fight for civil rights was not overlooked by blacks. In 1981, the NAACP Mississippi State Conference presented Ramsay the Goodman-Schwerner-Chaney Award for his contributions to the field of race relations, and in 1983 the A. Philip Randolph Institute gave special recognition to Ramsay for his longtime advocacy of civil rights.

There are many reasons why Ramsay, a native Mississippian, never succumbed to the racism that surrounded him. Ramsay attributed his liberal racial views to his mother and the impression that World War II left on him. But Ramsay's racial views derived not so much from his life experience as from his position as president of the Mississippi AFL-CIO. The need for a black-labor alliance was compelling to anyone who occupied the office.[124]

But the risks of a black-labor coalition were as great as the rewards. Yet Ramsay persevered not only because of his personal beliefs or because a black-labor coalition was the only way labor could escape the debilitating confines of southern Democracy. The decisive factor was the support provided by the AFL-CIO in Washington. The AFL-CIO subsidized the Mississippi AFL-CIO, permitting Ramsay to hire staff and enjoy salary increases the state council could not afford on its own. But more telling was the safety net it held for Ramsay personally. The AFL-CIO even promised Ramsay a staff position should his policies ever cost him his job. Years later Ramsay told an interviewer that he would not have been as bold as he was without the support and guarantees the AFL-CIO provided him.[125]

Ramsay and the Mississippi AFL-CIO staggered out of the 1960s. The AFL-CIO could provide a parachute if Ramsay was pushed from his job, but it could not completely mitigate the damage Ramsay's views cost him. As a result of Ramsay's civil rights activity, the state council lost one-third of its membership in the first six years of his tenure, dropping from twenty-four thousand to sixteen thousand members between 1959 and 1965. Even though the Mississippi AFL-CIO received the largest subsidy of any state council from the AFL-CIO, it did not offset the revenue lost from disaffiliations. Consequently, the state council often operated at a deficit, and Ramsay had to make several pleas to the AFL-CIO and affiliated unions to keep it afloat. What was even more discouraging was that members continued to repudiate Ramsay's leadership publicly and failed to support

COPE-endorsed candidates. Union members, like other Mississippians, remained unreconciled to civil rights for blacks. At the end of the decade, the state council was as politically isolated and impotent as ever. In 1969, Powell admitted to Barkan: "The tragedy in Mississippi is that no matter how hard they may work on COPE there is little chance of winning major offices in the near future. For COPE activity, Mississippi is the most frustrating state in the whole nation."[126]

Still, all was not bleak. There were already signs that black enfranchisement would realign Mississippi politics, just as Ramsay had hoped. Republican successes in Mississippi federal elections indicated the demise of one-party Democracy and the arrival of a competitive two-party system. Whites of higher socioeconomic status and self-identified conservatives were defecting to the Republican party, leaving behind a more liberal Democratic party composed of blacks and working-class whites.[127]

A variety of small incidents also indicated that Ramsay would be vindicated.[128] After a decade of disappointment and ridicule, the rock against which Ramsay had been pushing began to move. Al Kehrer, southern director for the AFL-CIO Civil Rights Department, recalled a meeting he and Ramsay attended in 1969 with members from the Metal Trades Council in the Ingalls shipyards. In 1962, these union members had participated in the Emergency Unit that rioted at Ole Miss, and the John Birch Society later had success organizing among them. Locals in the Metal Trades Council subsequently disaffiliated in protest against the state council's racial policies, and the Boilermakers even barred Ramsay from their union hall. But the Metal Trades Council was threatened when Litton Industries built a new shipyard across the river and hired a predominantly black work force for it. Black workers were well aware of the racist reputation of the unions across the river and were warned by Litton not to join them. Kehrer and Ramsay quickly arranged a meeting between black workers and Metal Trades representatives to reconcile differences between the two groups. Unsure how the meeting would turn out, nervous that it would deteriorate, Kehrer arranged chairs in a circle to prevent blacks and whites from separating to different sides of the room. The air filled with tension as participants filed into the meeting. In one corner a heavyset black woman took a seat next to the male business agent of the Sheet Metal Workers. She looked at him and said, "Brother . . . you don't remember me do you?" After failing to get a response, she repeated her question a bit more insistently: "I'm a Boiler Maker now, and you really don't remember me do you?" The business agent looked over to her at last and said, "No, I don't know you." She replied quickly, "I used to be your wife's maid." Kehrer heard the exchange and feared the business agent would erupt and ruin the meeting before it had begun. Kehrer could feel a racial history marked by mastery and subordination closing in on the two speakers and feared the worst. It appeared as if the business agent was now glaring at her as his eyes searched her suspiciously. Finally, as if a past had been reconciled, he responded, "Sister, you've put some weight on since then."[129]

Conclusion
An American Dilemma

We're in the business of organizing, not bettering race relations.

—A CIO official

I N 1948 SOUTHERNERS bolted the Democratic party convention in protest over its civil rights platform. These Dixiecrats later convened in Birmingham to form the States' Rights party and nominate South Carolina governor J. Strom Thurmond for president. In the ensuing campaign Loyal Democrats and Dixiecrats clashed over who was responsible for the split in Democratic ranks. Loyal Democrats pleaded with voters not to desert their party. Thurmond replied that the South had not deserted the Democrats, but the Democrats had betrayed the South when they adopted a strong civil rights plank.[1] In this conflict between party loyalists and States' Rights bolters, no group in the South was more loyal to the Democratic ticket led by President Harry S. Truman than union field representatives and state council officials. Union officials fought a heroic but doomed campaign for the Democratic ticket in Mississippi, and in Alabama they worked with Governor Folsom to keep Truman's name on the ballot.[2]

A generation later, southern union leaders would again defend the national Democratic party against a South that was once more in revolt over civil rights. In the 1964 presidential contest, Mississippi cast 87 percent of its vote for Republican presidential candidate Senator Barry Goldwater, Alabama gave Goldwater 69 percent of its vote, and Louisiana and South Carolina went to Goldwater as well. Not only did the southern electorate defect to the Republican party, but so did the Democratic party leadership in the region. South Carolina senator J. Strom Thurmond led the exodus when he switched his registration from Democrat to Republican. In Alabama, President Johnson could not even get his name on the ballot. In Louisiana, thirty members of the state's Democratic party central committee signed a petition for Goldwater, who was publicly endorsed by such state officials as the lieutenant governor, the secretary of state, and the public service commissioner. In Mississippi, not a single state officeholder or member of its congressional delegation—Democrats all—publicly supported the Democratic ticket. The marriage between the Democratic party and the South dissolved finally and permanently in 1964. Yet even as the solid South shattered, unions in Dixie remained loyal to the national Democratic party, just as they had in 1948.

Although President Johnson defeated Goldwater easily without the South's vote, the loss of the South threatened future Democratic presidential majorities. Worried about the South's political future, COPE director Al Barkan asked area director Daniel Powell how the Democratic party could be rebuilt in those states that defected to Goldwater. Powell advised Barkan that black votes were essential to resurrect the Democratic party in the South: "Any effort to rebuild the Democratic party in Alabama without substantially increasing Negro registration may be like constructing a house on a foundation of quicksand." The situation was little different in Louisiana, where "the potential Negro vote offers a major source of new strength for the Democratic Party," or in Mississippi, where "any effort to rebuild and strengthen the state party must necessarily include encouragement and facilitation of Negro registration." Powell's suggestions for the other states Goldwater carried in 1964 reflected this same view. Black voters were indispensable for rebuilding the Democratic party in the South.[3]

This strategy was given a boost in 1965 by passage of the Voting Rights Act. Union leaders in the South who were skeptical previously now became confident in the potential of black enfranchisement once Congress removed obstacles to it. The Voting Rights Act provoked a union offensive across the South to register black voters. The AFL-CIO approved a $50,000 grant for that purpose. State council officials were urged to conduct voter registration drives among blacks, and delegates to labor conventions were exhorted to take advantage of the opportunity Congress had created. At the 1965 Virginia AFL-CIO convention, the president of the District of Columbia AFL-CIO, J. C. Turner, implored the delegates to register blacks because they were the most loyal supporters of COPE-endorsed candidates. Al Barkan was characteristically blunt about what needed to be done. Barkan urged the delegates to ensure that black voters across the South were registered. "The only way for us in the South," he pleaded, "the only way we can form a political majority, is to join with the minorities."[4]

Labor contributed money and other forms of assistance to increase black registration through such groups as VEP, local voter registration organizations, and its own state councils in the South. But it never delivered fully in ways that its own strategy required. Powell advised Barkan that attracting blacks required an alternative to existing Democratic parties in the South because these parties refused to recruit black voters. Democratic politicians were so caught in the web of their segregationist voting records that survival required them to oppose any attempt to rebuild the Democratic party by increasing black participation in it. But attempts to create parallel organizations that could serve as alternatives to the Regulars languished. In Georgia, union officials were among the founders of the Georgia Democratic Party Forum, which was created as an alternative to the Georgia Democratic party led by segregationist governor Lester Maddox.[5] In Texas, the state council participated in the Democratic Coalition, which opposed the Regulars, and in Arkansas the state council participated in the Democrats for Arkansas, which took aim at the Faubus machine. In still other states Young Democrats clubs were revived to serve as a base from which to challenge the Regulars. Except for Texas, however, these efforts were not sustained. Sometimes differences among the insurgents themselves scuttled such efforts. This certainly was the case in Mississippi, where ugly conflict between the MFDP and the NAACP-Ramsay faction divided the Loyalists. Loyalist groups supported by labor also suffered when the national Democratic party gave them little encouragement or support. Finally, labor itself failed to give Loyalist organizations the support they required. Southern labor leaders feared that challenging the Regulars would irrevocably sunder ties with legislators who voted on bills vital to labor's immediate workplace interests. Consequently, union leaders were reluctant to provoke them or to cut their ties to powerful legislators that ran through their states' Democratic party.

CONFLICT AND STABILITY

The AFL-CIO and southern state councils received the most support for their realignment strategy from those locals whose internationals were sympathetic to civil rights and had business agents that closely supervised their locals. Needle trades unions stand out in this regard. But labor's political strategy was more notable for the opposition it provoked than for the support it received. Southern white union members were unimpressed by the vision of class-based politics peddled by their state council leaders to redeem labor. Instead, the rank and file believed their interests were served best by defending their racial privileges. No group within labor was more determined or outspoken in defense of their racial privileges than craft local unions. According to Stanley Greenberg, craft unions that "daily emphasize skill scarcity and exclusions find racial lines both congenial and functional." But Greenberg then argues that craft unions' opposition to civil rights was motivated more by their concern "for the inviolability of their apprenticeships than for the framework that kept blacks voteless and impoverished."[6] Unfortunately, this economic explanation belittles craft union support for the entire edifice of Jim Crow. No local unions were more opposed to school desegregation or more apt to disaffiliate in protest from their state councils than craft local unions. Nor did civil rights pose a greater threat to apprenticeship programs that shielded skilled workers than it did to separate job and seniority lines that protected white unskilled workers. Civil rights, in short, did not pose a special challenge to the economic privileges of white skilled workers that it did not pose to white unskilled workers as well. Contrary to Greenberg, craft union locals in the South were more shrill and defiant in defense of segregation because these locals enjoyed more autonomy from their international and could act with more impunity than industrial locals.[7] Not only were southern craft locals freer to contravene international policy, but given the indifference, at best, of their international leaderships, it was unlikely they would.

Another source of opposition came from unions in the timber and lumber industry, such as the United Papermakers and Paperworkers, the Pulp and Sulphite Workers, and the Woodworkers. This is somewhat curious because of the relatively high proportion of blacks in the industry. The Woodworkers, for instance, had a particularly high proportion of black members. But segregated white locals from these unions were particularly susceptible to Klan and other right-wing influences because of their rural location in the Piney Woods section of the South and the black-belt origin of their members. Finally, unions that were located in areas of significant civil rights activity, such as Birmingham, were also outspoken in their opposition to labor's political strategy. Whites in these areas were mobilized to defend local institutions from desegregation, and local unions were summoned to do their part.

The passions stirred by the civil rights struggle could also divide work forces along racial lines with portentous results for organizing. In 1961 the

Retail Workers lost an election at a Coca-Cola plant in Selma, Alabama, when blacks voted as a block against the union. Four years later, another election was held and the Retail Workers lost again, this time because every white voted against the union.[8] Although it is hard to isolate the effects of civil rights on union recruitment, there is little doubt that southern employers made greater use of racial propaganda after the *Brown* decision. The 1957 Jewish Labor Committee survey of union responses to *Brown* reported that "the race issue was . . . playing a more important role in organizing problems than prior to the Supreme Court decision."[9] In 1957 SRC labor consultant Emory Via confirmed this view when he informed Benjamin Segal at the Fund for the Republic: "The place at which organized labor is hurt the most by the raising of racial issues is in its endeavors to organize the unorganized. Again and again, either the employer or some anti-union group in the community will raise some racial issue with devastating effect in order to stymie a union organizing campaign." *Business Week* supported these impressions in its report from the South. It declared, "Many southern workers are refusing to join locals because they firmly reject the federation leaders' strong pro-integration stand."[10] But these accounts tend to be impressed with the increased use of racial propaganda in organizing campaigns and to then presume its influence by its mere presence. Certainly there were times when such propaganda was decisive. But one study of the effectiveness of racial propaganda in defeating unions found that the use of such tactics "does not seem to be more significant than other forms of propaganda in defeating union organizing drives."[11] That is, racial propaganda was probably of some use in preventing workers from organizing, but it was no magic elixir that immunized southern employers from unions.

Despite increased use of racial propaganda by employers, labor's support for civil rights did not hurt organizing in the South. In fact, unions were more successful in recruiting new members in the South during the turmoil over civil rights than they were outside the region. Between 1953 and 1966, from just before *Brown* to just after Selma, unions gained 142,000 new members in the South while they lost 815,000 members outside of it.[12] These gains in membership for the South were most likely the result of the spectacular increase in nonagricultural employment that occurred there between 1953 and 1966. This increase was so great that despite a rise in absolute membership for the South and a decline outside of it, union density actually decreased faster in the South than in the rest of the United States.

NLRB election statistics provide no more evidence of retribution against labor for its support of civil rights than do union membership figures. Between 1953 and 1966 unions experienced a steeper decline in their rate of representation election victories outside the South than in Dixie. While the proportion of union election victories in the South dropped from 65 percent in 1953 to 58 percent in 1966, it declined almost twice as fast outside the South, from 73 percent in 1953 to 61 percent thirteen years later.[13]

The case of Mississippi, the South's most defiant state, also reveals the imperturbable nature of southern unionism during the tumultuous period of civil rights activism. Even Claude Ramsay's civil rights activity did not have a perceptible effect on organizing in the Magnolia State. To the contrary, unions grew even while they were being pilloried for the state's humiliation. Twice as many representation elections were held in Mississippi between 1961 and 1965 — at the height of civil rights turmoil — than in the preceding five-year period. And unions won a higher percentage of these elections in Mississippi than they did nationally.[14]

The stability of southern unionism, as measured by such gross indicators as membership and NLRB elections, is a mystery given the hostility to AFL-CIO support for civil rights. The equanimity these figures suggest is in marked contrast to the conflict and strife over civil rights that shook the labor movement. Perhaps southern workers were unwilling to jeopardize the economic benefits they derived from union membership over civil rights. They were willing to endure and dismiss union policy, make their own separate peace with it, to retain the economic benefits of membership. But this portrait of a southern working class that stoically accepted the loss of its racial privileges is at variance with much of what I described in this book. In fact, civil rights created tumult within the southern labor movement. Southern white trade unionists were not willing to tolerate a policy they disagreed with, nor were they shy about expressing their opinions to their leaders. Another possibility is that people are more capable of managing ambiguity, keeping their antagonistic commitments distinct, than we imagine. Bartley suggests that southern "union members could rely upon the Councils to protect their caste position and upon the unions for their class position."[15] Thus, by applying their values selectively, white workers could reconcile their support of segregation with their union membership. It might also be that the equanimity with which southern unionism withstood the storm of civil rights is only apparent. Beneath the raw figures that indicate stability might have been changes in the racial composition of southern unionism. Perhaps white members who resigned in disgust or were lost by attrition were replaced by newly empowered blacks who now eagerly joined unions. There are no data to check whether the racial composition of southern unionism changed in the 1960s, but it is clear that some unions had spectacular success recruiting southern blacks in the wake of the civil rights movement.[16]

A more likely solution to the puzzle of why southern union membership remained stable in the midst of conflict over civil rights lies in the decentralized structure of the American labor movement and its local autonomy. As the 1957 Jewish Labor Committee survey revealed, southern members retained a great deal of loyalty to their local unions and directed their rage elsewhere, particularly at their internationals and the AFL-CIO.[17] Southern unionists located their union identity at the local level, which was either silent on civil rights or reflected the disapproval of the surrounding community. This absolved southern local unions from the sins committed elsewhere within organized labor. Local union autonomy permitted southern unions to retain their southernness and protected them from the conflicts civil rights created by providing a "free space" in which disaffected members could thrive. While decentralization undermined labor's realignment strategy because it permitted local unions to avoid participating in it, local autonomy also permitted unions to escape the full effect of its fallout.

The South, Politics, and Civil Rights

Labor contributed financially to the civil rights movement, and black organizations showed their appreciation when they supported organizing drives among blacks.[18] Less appreciated, because the results were barely discernible, were the attempts made to wean union members from Jim Crow. Some union leaders fought with racial demagogues for the hearts and minds of the rank and file. They did so as much out of self-defense as out of conviction or sense of justice for blacks. These union leaders feared their members would fall prey to conservatives who used racial demagoguery to disguise their anti-labor agenda. These leaders identified with the struggle for black equality not because they held a broader social vision of unions—they came from unions that practiced the most conservative business unionism—but because they held organizational positions that permitted them to appreciate the political potential of the civil rights movement. State council officers and the AFL-CIO are supposed to defend labor's political interests. Those interests were threatened by southern Democracy, which elected politicians who voted for restrictive labor legislation, prevented the Democratic party from realizing its social democratic potential, and contributed to the irrationality of the American party system. Unable to challenge these politicians because the South remained unorganized, AFL-CIO and state council officials finally found their foil to defeat them in the civil rights movement. Black enfranchisement, union leaders hoped, would undermine southern Democracy and initiate a realignment the South desperately needed. Union leaders believed that as blacks allied with working-class whites to liberalize the Democratic party in the South, conservative upper-income whites would defect to the Republican party. This realignment would replace one-party rule in the South with two-party competition. In addition, southern politics would no longer be absorbed by race, which divided blacks from working-class whites, but would focus on class issues that united them. Finally, realignment would prevent the Democratic party in the South from dismissing liberals as irrelevant cranks. On the contrary, southern Democracy would now articulate progressive programs it previously had ignored. As the southern wing of the party came to reflect rather than oppose what the Democratic party stood for nationally, the American party system would become more responsible: organized into two parties that were disciplined, had distinctive class bases, and offered voters distinctive choices.

But leaders responsible for defending labor politically had difficulty convincing others who did not share their organizational perspective, their political responsibility, to embrace the civil rights movement. White rank-and-file members were reluctant to betray southern Democracy because it defended their racial privileges at work and outside of it. They were unwilling to exchange their racial privileges, a perception of their interests rooted in Jim Crow, for a vision of their interests based on racial coalition presented by their union political leaders.

Although white local union officers and business agents in the South enjoyed the same racial privileges as their members, they tended to respond more circumspectly. They tried to deflect the issue or insulate themselves from it by consigning civil rights to an area that was outside their domain, beyond the scope of union business. A Marine and Shipbuilding officer told Stanley Greenberg: "We tell the blacks to go to the NAACP, 'Take it to them.' Or tell the whites if they bring something up, 'You go to the Klan.' That was it. We are here to deal with working conditions."[19] As a CIO official once confessed to sociologist William Kornhauser: "Quite frankly, we aren't crusaders. We do our best to steer away from the race question whenever we can. We're in the business of organizing, not bettering race relations."[20]

But circumstances compelled AFL-CIO and southern state council officials to act like crusaders and support the struggle for black equality.

The civil rights movement created an opportunity to defeat southern Democracy that those responsible for political action inside the labor movement could not afford to ignore. Black voters could realign the South, rescue labor from its political impotence regionally, and usher in an ideologically coherent party system nationally. Delivering this message to reluctant, if not antagonistic local union officials upon whom state council officials were politically and financially dependent was another matter. The political wing of the labor movement had to use indirection even to get a hearing from the troops below. State council and AFL-CIO officials argued that members did not have to agree with new civil rights legislation but should obey and respect it as the law. They tried to create a parallel between the two movements by drawing attention to how the struggle for black equality appropriated such labor tactics as sit-downs. They warned that southern defiance was a ploy to disguise a new attack on union security. They portrayed the most vociferous opponents of desegregation as vigorous opponents of unions as well. Finally, they tried to redefine issues such as school desegregation by draining them of their racial implications. None of these arguments, in the end, were particularly persuasive to the rank and file. But the evasive and defensive way these arguments were presented reveals what state council and AFL-CIO officials had to contend with when they appealed to their members on civil rights.

RACE AND CLASS: BEYOND THE 1965 VOTING RIGHTS ACT

The politics of the South changed as a result of the civil rights movement but in ways unanticipated by labor's strategists.[21] Labor was deceived by its own economism into believing that a black-white working-class coalition would emerge spontaneously in the South. It did not acknowledge that white antagonism toward blacks runs deep and is easily triggered by politicians interested in exploiting it. Labor strategists failed to appreciate that their members enjoyed racial privileges that might be more attractive than the benefits of racial coalition. But all of this is moot today because the South is not the problem for labor it once was. The power of the South in Congress, both within the Democratic caucus and in committees, has declined. Nor is the South any longer a drag on the Democratic party. Its ability to hold the Democratic party hostage in return for policy concessions is not what it once was.

But even as the South loses influence in Congress and the Democratic party and, from labor's perspective, no longer casts the long, dark shadow over American politics it once did, race still does. Racial issues continue to bedevil American politics even without the South as their vehicle. What was once an issue that consumed a particular region now reverberates nationally. Indeed, a startling reversal has taken place in which race is more likely to prevail over class outside the South than within the old Confederacy. Southern Democrats are more successful at forging victorious biracial coalitions than their colleagues outside the South. While no more than the apparition of the New Deal coalition has appeared in the South, its real, corporeal form is dissolving outside of it because of racial acrimony. Robert Huckfeldt and Carol Weitzel Kohfeld argue that race first began to drive out class in 1964, when the Democrats sponsored civil rights legislation and programs to address urban black poverty. These initiatives led voters to distinguish the parties on race for the first time since the New Deal. The Democrats were perceived as more favorable to blacks than Republicans and were rewarded for their trouble with solid black support and white working-class defections.[22]

Some white workers defected from the Democratic party because they were racists. The more the Democrats supported black demands, the more unappealing the party became to these voters. But more significant than unalloyed racism in explaining why white workers defected from the Democratic party was a shift that occurred in how these voters viewed government, a shift that was propelled by race and worked to the disadvantage of the Democratic party. Previously, white working-class voters gave the Democratic party credit and felt gratitude to it for what they took from government. Now, however, they resent the party and hold it responsible for what government takes from them.[23] Whereas once white workers rewarded the Democrats because they perceived themselves as government's beneficiaries, now they punish the Democrats because they perceive themselves as government's victims. They blame the Democratic party for policies that confiscate their money and redistribute it to minorities who, they believe, are undeserving. Working-class whites perceive blacks as a threat to not only their economic interests but to their cultural values as well.[24] White working-class resentment over domestic policies as diverse as welfare, the size of the public sector, crime, affirmative action, schools, and housing is laden with racial overtones that rend the Democratic coalition. In addition, white workers harbor class resentment toward the Democratic party because the burdens of the racial revolution it legislated have fallen unfairly on them. White workers are more likely than upper-class whites to live in neighborhoods that adjoin black ghettos, have children who "attend schools most likely to fall under busing orders," and are more likely than upper-class whites to compete with blacks for jobs and status.[25]

The way the Democratic party integrated blacks into its coalition, failed to design programs for blacks that white workers had a stake in defending, or, worse, designed programs that pitted one group against another, left white workers with a sense that black gains came at their expense.[26] The Democrats conceded to the part of the civil rights movement that asked for a seat on the bus, but ignored the part of it that asked where the bus was going. They were willing to grant blacks a share of the pie, but not to embrace a more social democratic critique of American society that the civil rights movement offered. Martin Luther King articulated this social democratic vision toward the end of his career when he called for a redistribution of economic and political power.[27] Contrary to this vision, however, the results of the civil rights movement were limited to mere pluralistic inclusion.

Even though the race issue has been decoupled from the political role of the South, it has lost none of its power to prevent the emergence of a black-white working-class coalition through the Democratic party. In 1944 Gunnar Myrdal described race as "an American dilemma."[28] Much to the chagrin of labor's political leadership, it remains so today.

Notes

INTRODUCTION

1. See especially F. Ray Marshall, *Labor in the South* (Cambridge, Mass.: Harvard University Press, 1967), and *The Negro and Organized Labor* (New York: Wiley, 1965).

2. Michael Honey, "Industrial Unionism and Racial Justice in Memphis," in Robert H. Zieger, ed., *Organized Labor in the Twentieth Century South* (Knoxville: University of Tennessee Press, 1991), p. 153.

3. Herbert Hill, "The AFL-CIO and the Black Worker: Twenty-five Years after the Merger," *Journal of Intergroup Relations* 10 (Spring 1982): 12.

4. The AFL-CIO Executive Council statement on the march posed the question, "What role shall the AFL-CIO play in the civil rights struggle this summer? Our answer is to continue our own twin major efforts—on the legislative front and at the grassroots level. We are convinced that the AFL-CIO can make its major contribution to victory by continuing its all-out legislative activity on Capitol Hill and . . . in the local communities of America." The complete text can be found in Gary M. Fink, ed., *AFL-CIO Executive Council Statements and Reports, 1960–1963* (Westport, Conn.: Greenwood Press, 1975), p. 1027–28.

5. Jervis Anderson, *A. Philip Randolph: A Biographical Portrait* (New York: Harcourt Brace Jovanovich, 1973), p. 327.

6. Thomas Gentile, *March on Washington: August 28, 1963* (Washington, D.C.: New Day Publications, 1983), p. 37.

7. Robert Zieger, *American Workers, American Unions, 1920–1985* (Baltimore: Johns Hopkins University Press, 1986), pp. 158–59.

8. Press Conference, May 14, 1968, Reel 4, Bayard Rustin Collection, Library of Congress, Manuscripts Division, Washington, D.C.

9. Labor News Conference, "Transcript of Task Force for Civil Rights," Sunday, December 8, 1963, Program 32, Series 3, Box A180, Folder "Labor AFL-CIO 1963," NAACP Collection, Library of Congress, Manuscripts Division, Washington, D.C. In his chronicle of the march, Gentile agrees with Randolph's assessment that Meany's misgivings were purely tactical (*March on Washington*, pp. 57–59). It is noteworthy that Meany approved the AFL-CIO's first contribution for

$10,000 to the Leadership Conference on Civil Rights immediately after the march. It is not clear whether the AFL-CIO was trying to redeem itself through this contribution or prove the superiority of its lobbying tactics. See Denton L. Watson, *Lion in the Lobby: Clarence Mitchell, Jr.'s Struggle for the Passage of Civil Rights Laws* (New York: William Morrow, 1990), p. 567.

10. Philip Foner, *Organized Labor and the Black Worker, 1619 – 1973* (New York: International Publishers, 1974), p. 349.

11. For the Communist case see Donald T. Critchlow, "Communist Unions and Racism: A Comparative Study of the Responses of the United Electrical Radio and Machine Workers and the National Maritime Union to the Black Question during World War II," *Labor History* 17 (Fall 1976): 230–44.

12. "Civil Rights Committee, AFL-CIO," February 9–10, 1956, 5/1/2, William Schnitzler Collection, George Meany Memorial Archives, Silver Spring, Md.

13. Paul Christopher to William Schnitzler, ibid.

14. William B. Gould, *Black Workers and White Unions: Job Discrimination in the United States* (Ithaca, N.Y.: Cornell University Press, 1977); Herbert Hill, *Black Labor and the American Legal System: Race, Work and the Law* (Madison: University of Wisconsin Press, 1985).

15. John H. Bracey, Jr., and August Meier ("The NAACP and the Labor Movement: 1910-1964," unpublished manuscript in the author's possession) contend that this was part of an "extraordinarily clever and astute" two-pronged strategy by Wilkins. While NAACP labor secretary Herbert Hill held labor's feet to the fire on job discrimination, the more conciliatory Clarence Mitchell, the NAACP's lobbyist, played the good cop to ensure that the political alliance between the NAACP and the AFL-CIO remained intact. The impression from Bracey and Meier is that Wilkins manipulated this dual strategy to the NAACP's advantage. My own reading of the NAACP files that Bracey and Meier consulted is that Meany derived as much satisfaction from Wilkins as Wilkins did from him whenever they met to smooth over differences between their organizations. For example, see Roy Wilkins to Charles C. Webber, March 30, 1959, NAACP Administrative Files, Box A179, Folder "Labor, AFL-CIO 1959," NAACP Collection. There is reason to be skeptical of Bracey and Meier because they rely on the testimony of Herbert Hill and consequently present a very generous picture of the role Hill played in Wilkins's grand strategy. NAACP attempts to muzzle Hill were not simply staged to placate the AFL-CIO, as Bracey and Meier contend, but reflected Wilkins's own impatience with Hill's inability to restrain himself. After another tirade by Hill against the A. Philip Randolph Institute, Wilkins wrote an apology to its executive director, Bayard Rustin, in which he voiced his regret that "I once wrote that the late Adam Clayton Powell was Harlem's problem child. Herbert Hill is the problem child of the NAACP" (Roy Wilkins to Bayard Rustin, July 17, 1973, Reel 2, Rustin Collection). This is not meant as an aspersion on Hill's criticisms of AFL-CIO policy or on his professional writings. It is intended simply to confirm that the differences between Wilkins and Hill were more real than Bracey and Meier admit. For another, more balanced view of NAACP and AFL-CIO relations that ascribes their differences to the different institutional priority each accorded civil rights see James A. Gross, "The N.A.A.C.P., the

A.F.L.-C.I.O. and the Negro Worker" (Ph.D. dissertation, University of Wisconsin, 1962); and James A. Gross, "The NAACP and the AFL-CIO: An Overview," *Negro History Bulletin*, December 1962, pp. 111–12.

16. SNCC, for instance, asked the AFL-CIO to underwrite a conference it planned to hold in Atlanta. See William F. Schnitzler to A. Philip Randolph, September 26, 1960, Folder "Labor Correspondence, 1935–61, A. Philip Randolph," George Meany Collection, George Meany Memorial Archives, Silver Spring, Md. This was the infamous conference at which the AFL-CIO made its contribution conditional on SNCC dropping Bayard Rustin from its conference program. Robert Weisbrot contends that money for the conference came from the Packinghouse Workers union and not the AFL-CIO as many have believed. The Packinghouse Workers may have contributed money for the conference, but the record indicates that SNCC did approach the AFL-CIO for a donation. See Weisbrot, *Freedom Bound* (New York: Norton, 1990), p. 42.

17. Examples of this literature include Louis Hartz, *The Liberal Tradition in America: An Interpretation of American Political Thought since the Revolution* (New York: Harcourt, Brace, 1955); and Seymour Martin Lipset, *The First New Nation: The United States in Historical and Comparative Perspective* (New York: Norton, 1979).

18. My notes from Ira Katznelson's speech at St. Lawrence University, April, 15, 1990.

19. Goran Therborn, "The Role of Capital and the Rise of Democracy," *New Left Review*, May-June 1977, pp. 3–43.

20. Earl Black and Merle Black, *Politics and Society in the South* (Cambridge, Mass.: Harvard University Press, 1987).

21. This is a paraphrase from Alan Dawley, *Struggles for Justice: Social Responsibility and the Liberal State* (Cambridge, Mass.: Belknap Press of Harvard University Press, 1991), p. 46.

22. For the influence of the South on Congress and public policy see James T. Patterson, *Congressional Conservatism and the New Deal: The Growth of the Conservative Coalition* (Westport, Conn.: Greenwood Press, 1981); and Jill S. Quadagno, *The Transformation of Old Age Security: Class and Politics in the American Welfare State* (Chicago: University of Chicago Press, 1988).

23. V. O. Key, *Southern Politics in State and Nation* (New York: Knopf, 1949), p. 5.

24. Michael Goldfield, *The Decline of Organized Labor in the United States* (Chicago: University of Chicago Press, 1987), pp. 231–45; Michael Honey, "Labor and Civil Rights in the South: The Industrial Labor Movement and Black Workers in Memphis, 1929–1945" (Ph.D. dissertation, Northern Illinois University, 1987); Michael Honey, "Industrial Unionism and Racial Justice in Memphis"; Michael Honey, "Labor, the Left, and Civil Rights in the South: Memphis during the CIO Era, 1937–1955," in Judith Joel and Gerald M. Erickson, eds., *Anti-Communism: The Politics of Manipulation* (Minneapolis: MEP Publications, 1987), pp. 57–85; Michael Honey, "Labour Leadership and Civil Rights in the South: A Case Study of the CIO in Memphis, 1935-1955," *Studies in History and Politics* 6 (1986): 97–121; Robert Rogers Korstad, "Daybreak of Freedom: Tobacco Workers and the CIO, Winston-Salem, North Carolina, 1943–1950" (Ph.D. dissertation, University of North Carolina, Chapel Hill, 1987); Robert Korstad and Nelson Lichtenstein,

"Opportunities Found and Lost: Radicals and the Early Civil Rights Movement," *Journal of American History* (September 1988): 786–811; William Edward Regensburger, "Ground into Our Blood: The Origins of Working Class Consciousness and Organization in Durably Unionized Southern Industries, 1930–1946" (Ph.D. dissertation, University of California at Los Angeles, 1987).

25. F. Ray Marshall, "The Development of Organized Labor," *Monthly Labor Review*, March 1968, pp. 65–73; Barbara S. Griffith, *The Crisis of American Labor: Operation Dixie and the Defeat of the CIO* (Philadelphia: Temple University Press, 1988).

26. Michael Honey, "Operation Dixie: Two Points of View," *Labor History* (Summer 1990): 378.

27. George Sinclair Mitchell, "The Negro in Southern Trade Unionism," *Southern Economic Journal* (January 1936): 32.

28. Rick Halpern, "Interracial Unionism in the Southwest: Fort Worth's Packinghouse Workers, 1937-1954," in Zieger, ed., *Organized Labor in the Twentieth Century South*, pp. 158–82. With regard to the Packinghouse Workers, Halpern writes, "From the onset of organizing activity in the late 1930s, through the arrival at a racial accommodation in the 1940s, and up through the tumultuous period following the desegregation provisions, the weight of the international union was the determining factor in establishing the rights and relationships of white and black workers" (p. 176).

29. Honey, "Labor and Civil Rights in the South," pp. 392–96, 483.

30. Goldfield, *Decline of Organized Labor*, p. 240.

31. Both Griffith, *Crisis of Organized Labor*, p. 87, and Solomon Barkin, "Operation Dixie: Two Points of View," *Labor History* (Summer 1990): 383, are skeptical that labor failed to organize the South because its racial policy was "not liberal enough."

32. Bruce Nelson, "Class and Race in the Crescent City: The ILWU from San Francisco to New Orleans," in Steven Rosswurm, ed., *The CIO's Left-Led Unions* (New Brunswick, N.J.: Rutgers University Press, 1992), p. 40.

33. Moses Adedeji, "Crossing the Color Line: Three Decades of the United Packinghouse Workers of America's Crusade against Racism in the Trans-Mississippi West, 1936–1968" (Ph.D. dissertation, North Texas State University, 1978), pp. 53–55. Adedeji uses the adjective *disappointing* to describe the reaction of UPWA leaders to these results.

34. Honey, "Labor and Civil Rights in the South," p. 490. See also Horace R. Cayton and George S. Mitchell, *Black Workers and the New Unions* (Chapel Hill: University of North Carolina Press, 1939), pp. 354–55, 365.

35. See Korstad, "Daybreak of Freedom." Revealingly, Korstad does not acknowledge white working-class racism as one of the factors that contributed to the demise of Local 22 in his conclusion. See also Korstad and Lichtenstein, "Opportunities Found and Lost"; and Aingred Chislayne Dunston, "The Black Struggle for Equality in Winston-Salem, North Carolina, 1947–1977" (Ph.D. dissertation, University of North Carolina, 1981).

36. This issue is handled sensitively and sensibly in Halpern, "Interracial Unionism"; and Bruce Nelson, "Mobile during World War II: Organized Labor and the Struggle for Black Equality in a 'City That's Been Taken by Storm,'" paper

presented at the Seventh Southern Labor Studies Conference, October 1991, Atlanta, Ga., in possession of author.

37. Goldfield, *Decline of Organized Labor*.

38. Key, *Southern Politics*, pp. 298–311, 663–64.

39. Robert Huckfeldt and Carol Weitzel Kohfeld explain: "With regard to *national* politics, however, the South served as an impediment to the development of class based coalitions because, at least in congressional and presidential elections, all southerners were Democrats" (*Race and the Decline of Class in American Politics* [Urbana: University of Illinois Press, 1989], p. 76).

40. Samuel Lubell, *The Future of American Politics* (Garden City, N.Y.: Doubleday, 1956), p. 125.

41. Numan V. Bartley, *The Rise of Massive Resistance: Race and Politics in the South during the 1950s* (Baton Rouge: Louisiana State University Press, 1969), p. 293.

CHAPTER 1

1. The full text of the Court's opinion can be found in the Appendix to Richard Kluger, *Simple Justice: The History of Brown vs. Board of Education and Black America's Struggle for Equality* (New York: Vintage Books 1975). This book is a remarkable account of the litigation that preceded *Brown* and of the process by which the Supreme Court reached its decision in this landmark case.

2. For a vivid and superb account of black life in the Jim Crow South see Neil R. McMillen, *Dark Journey: Black Mississippians in the Age of Jim Crow* (Urbana: University of Illinois Press, 1989).

3. Bartley, *Rise of Massive Resistance*, pp. 190–237.

4. Adedeji, "Crossing the Color Line," p. 149.

5. Bartley, *Rise of Massive Resistance*, p. 192.

6. The best and most thorough account of the massive resistance movement is Bartley, *Rise of Massive Resistance*. Other books that cover the resistance movement in the South include Neil R. McMillen, *The Citizens' Councils: Organized Resistance to the Second Reconstruction, 1954 – 64* (Urbana: University of Illinois Press, 1971); Elizabeth Jacoway and David R. Colburn, eds., *Southern Businessmen and Desegregation* (Baton Rouge: Louisiana State University Press, 1982); Andrew Manis, *Southern Civil Religions in Conflict* (Athens: University of Georgia Press, 1987); and David M. Reimers, *White Protestantism and the Negro* (New York: Oxford University Press, 1965).

7. An example of this omission is Reed Sarratt, ed., *The Ordeal of Desegregation: The First Decade* (New York: Harper & Row, 1966). This volume examines the response to desegregation by such southern institutions as educational systems, the church, and the business community—all the usual suspects—except labor unions. What is included in this volume and what is left out typifies historical coverage of southern institutions as a whole.

8. The most outstanding though not singular example of a southern labor leader who believed that the fate of labor in the South depended on the success of the civil rights movement was Mississippi AFL-CIO president Claude Ramsay. See Robert S. McElvaine, "Claude Ramsay, Organized Labor, and the Civil Rights Movement in Mississippi, 1959–1966," in Merl E. Reed, Leslie S. Hough, and

Gary M. Fink, eds., *Southern Workers and Their Unions, 1880−1975* (Westport, Conn.: Greenwood Press, 1981), pp. 110–37.

9. AFL-CIO Convention Proceedings, 1955, pp. 109–10.

10. "Minutes of the Committee Meeting," February 9–10, 1956, AFL, AFL-CIO Office of the Secretary-Treasurer, Box 1, Folder 2, Schnitzler Collection.

11. H. L. Mitchell, "On the Rise of the White Citizens Council and Its Ties with Anti-Labor Forces in the South," January 30, 1956, marked Confidential and Not for Publication, Box 84, Folder 36, L. J. Twomey, S.J., Collection, Special Collections and Archives of the Loyola University Library, Loyola University, New Orleans, La. Mitchell reported that members of the Advisory Committee of the segregationist Federation for Constitutional Government for Louisiana included W. M. Rainach, who introduced the right-to-work measure that passed the Louisiana legislature in 1954; Joseph W. Pitts, who introduced a similar bill in 1946 and testified on behalf of the 1954 bill; John Garrett, who led the floor fight for right-to-work in the state legislature; Malcolm Daugherty, who urged the Louisiana legislature to adopt right-to-work on behalf of the Louisiana Farm Bureau Federation; T. M. Barker of the American Sugar Cane League, who took the lead in organizing right-to-work councils in parishes throughout the state; and the notorious bigot Leander H. Perez, district attorney from Plaquimines parish.

12. Statement by the Executive Council, AFL-CIO, "Report of the Civil Rights Committee," February 10, 1956, in Gary M. Fink, ed., *AFL-CIO Executive Council Statements and Reports, 1965−75* (Westport, Conn.: Greenwood Press, 1977), 1: 4.

13. Boris Shiskin, "Organized Labor and the Negro," p. 127, Series II, Box 18, Folder "Organized Labor and the Negro," Boris Shiskin Collection, George Meany Memorial Archives, Silver Spring, Md.

14. The AFL-CIO Civil Rights Committee analyzed these letters and claimed that they were planted or inspired by the segregationist Federation for Constitutional Government. But those letters still in AFL-CIO files show little evidence of being mass produced and differ stylistically from one another. The best indicator of their authenticity, however, is the seriousness with which the AFL-CIO responded to them. See "Progress Report on the Work of the Civil Rights Department AFL-CIO," February 9–July 14, 1956, marked Not for Publication, Box 18, Folder "Civil Rights−Correspondence and Reports 1956–1957," Shiskin Collection.

15. Jack W. Gager to George Meany, February 17, 1956, Box 4, Folder "White Citizens Councils, January–March, 1956," AFL-CIO Civil Rights Collection, George Meany Memorial Archives, Silver Spring, Md.

16. A. B. Blackwelder, Sr., to George Meany, February 13, 1956, ibid. A newspaper report on racial problems in southern unions also quotes an AFL old-timer who held the recent merger accountable for the labor movement's condemnation of the Citizens' Councils. This rank-and-filer deplored "Reuther's words put into Mr. Meany's mouth to placate C.I.O. unions which have a lot of Negro members" (Ed Townsend, *Christian Science Monitor*, April 27, 1956).

17. Addressed to George Meany, President, February 24, 1956, Box 4, Folder "White Citizens Councils, January–March, 1956," AFL-CIO Civil Rights Collection.

18. C. A. Cardwell to The Hon. George Meany, March 10, 1956, ibid.

19. Recording Secretary to George Meany, February 21, 1956, ibid.

20. For Meany's standard response to these letters see, for example, George Meany to A. B. Blackwelder, Sr., March 8, 1956, ibid.

21. *Chattanooga Times*, August 24, 28, 1955.

22. A full description of this episode, complete with documents as it was reported by the *Labor World*, the newspaper of the Chattanooga central labor council, is contained in Box 1278, Folder 21, Emory Via Papers, Southern Labor History Archives, Georgia State University, Atlanta, Ga. See also "Interviewers Summary," Box 4, Folder "Questionnaire: Tennessee, Chattanooga, 1956–57," AFL-CIO Civil Rights Collection. Secondary accounts can be found in Bartley, *Rise of Massive Resistance*, p. 307; F. Ray Marshall, "Union Racial Problems in the South," *Industrial Relations* (May 1962): 119; and Marshall, *The Negro and Organized Labor*, p. 178. For an account of the riots that occurred in Chattanooga after the school board announced its decision see "Chattanooga Story—What Happened?," *Southern School News*, June 1956.

23. For the strength of white supremacy groups such as the Citizens' Councils and Ku Klux Klan among southern trade unionists see McMillen, *Citizens' Councils*, p. 203; and Bartley, *Rise of Massive Resistance*, p. 309.

24. "Progress Report on the Work of the Civil Rights Department AFL-CIO," February 9–July 14, 1956, marked Not for Publication, Box 18, Folder "Correspondence and Reports 1956–1957," Shiskin Collection.

25. *Birmingham News*, February 23, 1956.

26. Robert Gaines Corley, "The Quest for Racial Harmony: Race Relations in Birmingham, Alabama, 1947–1963" (Ph.D. dissertation, University of Virginia, 1979), p. 106. For the working-class and petit-bourgeois backgrounds of Citizens' Council and Klan members see ibid., pp. 120–22; and James W. Vander Zander, "The Klan Revival," *American Journal of Sociology* (March 1960): 458.

27. Corley, "Quest for Racial Harmony," pp. 161–63.

28. *New York Times*, February 26, 1956.

29. Quote from Englehart in Robert J. Norrell, "Labor Trouble: George Wallace and Union Politics in Alabama," in Zieger, ed., *Organized Labor in the Twentieth Century South*, p. 258.

30. H. L. Mitchell to Boris Shiskin, March 7, 12, 1956, Box 4, Folder "National Agricultural Workers Union, 1956 & 1960," AFL-CIO Civil Rights Collection. See also George G. Kundahl, "Organized Labor in Alabama" (Ph.D. dissertation, University of Alabama, 1967), p. 47, for Citizens' Councils influence among Birmingham steelworkers.

31. This incident has been fully covered in the secondary literature. For instance, see Marshall, "Union Racial Problems in the South." See also Kundahl, "Organized Labor in Alabama," p. 47; and Henry L. Trewitt, "Southern Unions and the Integration Issue," *Reporter*, October 4, 1956, pp. 25–28. The *Birmingham Post-Herald*, May 28, 1956, covers the election of officers to the secessionist group. For an internal report to the Southern Regional Council that refers to these events see Morton T. Elder, "Labor and Race Relations in the South," October 1956, Fund for the Republic Collection, Box 108, Princeton University Library, Princeton, N.J.

32. Quoted in Stanley B. Greenberg, *Race and State in Capitalist Development: Comparative Perspectives* (New Haven: Yale University Press, 1980), p. 354.

33. *Birmingham Post-Herald*, May 21, 1956; see also Elder, "Labor and Race Relations," p. 3. Brock was subsequently expelled from the Painters union for "engaging in acts tending to bring . . . the Brotherhood into disrepute." See *Labor's Daily*, August 11, 1956.

34. *Birmingham Post-Herald*, July 23, 1956.

35. On the United Southern Employees Association see Marshall, "Union Racial Problems in the South," pp. 121–23, and *Southern School News*, November 1956, p. 13. For information on the Southern Crafts, Inc., see the *Birmingham Post-Herald*, August 2, 1956.

36. Elder, "Labor and Race Relations," p. 3; Bartley, *Rise of Massive Resistance*, pp. 307–9.

37. "Southern Tension Seizes Labor," *Business Week*, April 14, 1956, pp. 47–50.

38. Bartley, *Rise of Massive Resistance*, p. 310.

39. "A Survey of the Resistance Groups in Alabama," n.d., 41.1.6.2.10., Southern Regional Council Collection, Birmingham Public Library, Birmingham, Alabama. This report is unsigned but was probably written by Paul Anthony.

40. Emory Via to Ben Segal, n.d., Box 1278, Folder 14, Emory Via Collection.

41. Boyd E. Payton to Administrative Staff, August 24, 1956, Box 4, Folder "Questionnaire: T.W.U.A. 1956-57," AFL-CIO Civil Rights Collection. See also the responses to Payton's request for information from Charles Auslander, August 27, 1956, and Wayne L. Dernoncourt, September 12, 1956, ibid.

42. Granite Local 1113, Haw River, N.C., Box 4, Folder "Questionnaire: North Carolina–South Carolina, 1956-57," AFL-CIO Civil Rights Collection.

43. "Proposals for Trade Union Education Program," Box 51, Fund for the Republic Collection. For background on Benjamin Segal see his unpublished autobiography that was kindly made available to me by his widow, Elizabeth Segal, Washington, D.C.

44. "Three Year Review," May 8, 1956, pp. 110–11, Box 51, Fund for the Republic Collection. See also the photocopy of Mitchell's report that Segal sent to the fund with a note at the top that the survey was "financed by our program" in Benjamin Segal's Personal Papers, in possession of Elizabeth Segal, Washington, D.C. Segal also mentions financing Mitchell's study in his autobiography, p. 9. Mitchell mistakenly attributes financing of his study to Walter Reuther in his autobiography. See H. L. Mitchell, *Mean Things Happening in This Land: The Life and Times of H. L. Mitchell, Co-Founder of the Southern Tenant Farmers Union* (Montclair, N.J.: Allenheld, Osmun, 1979), p. 243.

45. William Clifton Allred, Jr., "The Southern Regional Council, 1943–1961" (M.A. thesis, Emory University, 1963), pp. 124–27, describes Mitchell's labor education activities for the SRC. See also "Three Year Review," May 8, 1956, Box 51, Fund for the Republic Collection, for the fund's reimbursement of Mitchell's expenses.

46. George S. Mitchell to Benjamin Segal, October 21, 1955, Box 51, Fund for the Republic Collection. A short resumè of Via's experience before joining the Southern Regional Council is provided in "Recommendations to the Board," May 1, 1957, Box 109, ibid.

47. Ben Segal to David F. Freeman and Frank Loescher, October 25, 1955, Box 51, ibid.

48. For details of how Via's salary and office at the SRC were funded see Burke to Elmo Roper, March 22, 1957, and "Memorandum on the Work of the Trade Union Consultant to the Fund for the Republic," n.d., ibid.

49. Emanuel Muravchik, "Emergency Survey of Civil Rights Situation and Trade Unions in the South," May 23, 1956, I-66, Box 62, Folder "Advance Preparations," Jewish Labor Committee Collection, Robert F. Wagner Labor Archives, New York University, New York, N.Y. See also "Covering Letter to Questionnaire on Impact of Race Relations on Labor Unions in the South," NAACP Administrative Files, Group III, Box A206, Folder "Jewish Labor Committee 1956–64," NAACP Collection.

50. Emanuel Muravchik, "Report on Current Status of Survey," August 8, 1952, I-66, Box 62, Folder "National Contacts and Reports," Jewish Labor Committee Collection.

51. Lloyd Bailer, "The Negro in the Automobile Industry" (Ph.D. dissertation, University of Michigan, 1943), p. 49, quoted in William Kornhauser, "Ideology and Interests: The Determinants of Union Actions," *Journal of Social Issues* 9, no. 2 (1953): 54.

52. *Atlanta Journal*, April 17, 1956.

53. Local Union Questionnaire, Box 4, Folder "Questionnaire: Georgia 1957–57," AFL-CIO Civil Rights Collection.

54. Kevin Gerard Boyle, "Politics and Principle: The United Automobile Workers and American Labor-Liberalism, 1948–1968" (Ph.D. dissertation, University of Michigan, 1990), p. 214.

55. See Elder, "Labor and Race Relations," p. 10. For reports of racial problems in this local following Via's survey see Marshall, *The Negro and Organized Labor*, p. 179.

56. Local 3204 CWA Atlanta, Georgia, supplement, Box 4, Folder "Questionnaire: Georgia Additional Material," AFL-CIO Civil Rights Collection.

57. Elder, "Labor and Race Relations," p. 30.

58. *Chattanooga Times*, April 7, 1956.

59. Local Union Questionnaire, Box 4, Folder "Questionnaire: Tennessee, Nashville, 1956–57," AFL-CIO Civil Rights Collection.

60. Steelworkers Local 3967, Box 4, Folder "Questionnaire: Tennessee, Chattanooga, 1956–57," AFL-CIO Civil Rights Collection.

61. Boyle, "Politics and Principle," p. 214.

62. Ibid.

63. *Memphis Commercial-Appeal*, March 14, 1956.

64. Ed Townsend, *Christian Science Monitor*, April 25, 1956. In 1960 this local was placed under trusteeship by the UAW for failing to comply with the union's racial policies.

65. Elder, "Labor and Race Relations," pp. 23–24. See also Marshall, "Union Racial Problems in the South," p. 120; Marshall, *The Negro and Organized Labor*, p. 188.

66. But the Carolinas also included the Durham central labor council, the one bright spot on the otherwise bleak southern landscape. The Durham labor council advised its members to respond to the racial issue with "calmness, maturity and

Christian good will." It asked its members "to study the issues and not fall into the clutches of big business. We cannot afford to lose the wages and working conditions we won under Roosevelt" ("Labor, the Negro and the South," *Durham Labor Journal*, March 22, 1956, in Box 4, Folder "Questionnaire: North Carolina–South Carolina, 1956–57," AFL-CIO Civil Rights Collection.)

67. Elder, "Labor and Race Relations," pp. 18–21; Local Union Questionnaire, Box 4, Folder "Questionnaire: North Carolina–South Carolina, 1956–57," AFL-CIO Civil Rights Collection.

68. Elder, "Labor and Race Relations," p. 17.

69. *Texas Observer*, August 9, 1957.

70. Texas AFL-CIO Convention Proceedings, 1957, p. 141. A report on the convention is also contained in *Southern School News*, September 1957.

71. "A Survey of the Resistance Groups in Alabama."

72. "Local Union Questionnaire #7," I-66, Box 62, Folder "Alabama," Jewish Labor Committee Collection.

73. Norrell, "Labor Trouble," p. 254.

74. "Local Union Questionaire #3," I-66, Box 62, Folder, "Alabama," Jewish Labor Committee Collection.

75. "A Survey of the Resistance Groups."

76. "Local Union Questionnaire #4," I-66, Box 62, Folder "Alabama," Jewish Labor Committee Collection.

77. *New York Times*, May 13, 1957.

78. "Interim Report on Survey of Southern Trade Unions and the Race Problem," May 10, 1957, Box 21-03, Folder "Labor–Civil Rights," Jewish Labor Committee Collection.

79. Emory F. Via to Ben Segal, "Various Aspects of Race Relations as They Affect Unions in the South," n.d., Box 1, Folder "Reports, etc.," Via Collection.

80. *Southern School News*, March 1957, p. 4. This local later voted to endorse every resolution passed at the 1957 Texas AFL-CIO unity convention except one supporting *Brown*. See Donna Sue Beasley, "A History of OCAW Local 4-228 Port Neches, Texas" (M.A. thesis, Lamar State College of Technology, 1970), p. 125.

81. Corley, "Quest for Racial Harmony," p. 175.

82. See Elder, "Labor and Race Relations," pp. 33–34; and questionnaires in Box 4, AFL-CIO Civil Rights Collection, for numerous expressions of these views.

83. Emory Via, "First Annual Report of the Southern Regional Council's Consultant, and of the 1957 Trade Union Program on Civil Liberties and Rights," Box 1278, Folder 13, Via Collection.

84. Louis J. Twomey to James C. O'Brien, April 3, 1957, Box 16, Folder 6, Twomey Collection.

85. John Robert Payne, "A Jesuit Search for Social Justice: The Public Career of Louis J. Twomey, S.J., 1947–1969" (Ph.D. dissertation, University of Texas, 1976), p. 214. Marshall's research, which was published as *The Negro and Organized Labor*, was financed by the Fund for the Republic.

86. James Wilfred Vander Zander, "The Southern White Resistance Movement to Integration" (Ph.D. dissertation, University of North Carolina, 1957), p. 136.

87. Louisiana state council convention proceedings, 1961, vol. 2, pp. 436–44.

88. For this reason, Bartley's judgment of the unions' response to the crisis *Brown* created appears a bit harsh to me. He indicts the unions for placing "institutional concerns above all else" and for functioning more as "observers than as movers of events." There is much truth in these remarks, but they fail to appreciate the courage it took for state labor leaders to take even the timorous actions they did and how even these jeopardized the "institutional concerns" they were so anxious to protect. See Bartley, *Rise of Massive Resistance*, p. 294. Zander gives the labor movement more credit than Bartley when he lists it among the "foes" of "the white resistance movement" ("Southern White Resistance Movement," p. 377).

89. Will Chasan, "American Labor Attacks Its Own Segregation Problem," *Reporter*, May 1, 1958, p. 29. See also Kornhauser, "Ideology and Interests," p. 56.

90. Oral History of Ruben Farr, pp. 39–40, Historical Collection and Labor Archives, Patee Library, Pennsylvania State University, University Park, Pa.

91. *Atlanta Constitution*, March 25, 1955.

92. *AFL-CIO News and Views*, June 1956. This article describes some efforts by affiliated unions to address the issue raised by *Brown* but it also acknowledges, "The progress being made should not be overrated for there are serious problems in some local unions."

93. Emory Via, "An Informal Report to Ben Segal," 1278/14, Via Collection.

94. Joseph Mire to Harold C. Fleming, July 13, 1959, 1277/2, ibid.

95. J. Harvie Wilkinson III, *From Brown to Bakke: The Supreme Court and School Integration, 1954 – 1978:* (New York: Oxford University Press, 1979), p. 72.

96. On the church's response to *Brown* see Francis M. Wilhoit, *Politics of Massive Resistance* (New York: Braziller, 1973); Andrew Manis, *Southern Civil Religions*; and Reimers, *White Protestantism*. For the response from the business community see Jacoway and Colburn, eds., *Southern Businessmen and Desegregation*.

97. Key, *Southern Politics*, pp. 663–64.

98. Numan V. Bartley and Hugh D. Graham, *Southern Politics and the Second Reconstruction* (Baltimore: Johns Hopkins Press, 1975), p. 186.

CHAPTER 2

1. Coverage of the massive resistance movement in Virginia is provided in Benjamin Muse, *Virginia's Massive Resistance* (Bloomington: Indiana University Press, 1961); Robbins L. Gates, *The Making of Massive Resistance: Virginia's Politics of Public School Desegregation, 1954 – 1956* (Chapel Hill: University of North Carolina Press, 1962); James W. Ely, Jr., *The Crisis of Conservative Virginia: The Byrd Organization and the Politics of Massive Resistance* (Knoxville: University of Tennessee Press, 1976).

2. Jacob Schlitt, "Draft of Confidential Memorandum to JLC Field Staff and Leadership," Box 4, Folder "Virginia, 1956–61," AFL-CIO Civil Rights Collection.

3. H. B. Boyd and Julian Carper to William F. Schnitzler, December 29, 1955, Box 4, Folder "Virginia 1955–61," ibid.

4. Gates, *Making of Massive Resistance*, p. 81.

5. Jacob Schlitt to Boris Shiskin, "Report on Virginia," September 2–6, 1958, Box 4, Folder "Virginia, 1956–57," AFL-CIO Civil Rights Collection.

6. H. B. Boyd and Julian Carper to William Schnitzler, January 25, 1956, Box 4, Folder "Virginia, 1955–56," ibid.

7. Joseph F. Heath to Boris Shiskin, January 11, 1956, Box 4, Folder "Virginia, 1956–57," ibid.

8. Tuck is quoted in Muse, *Virginia's Massive Resistance*, p. 23.

9. A copy of Boyd's testimony was sent to all affiliated locals in the state. See Harold B. Boyd, Julian F. Carper, and I. C. Welstead to All Virginia AFL-CIO Locals, September 17, 1956, Box 4, Folder "Virginia 1955–61," AFL-CIO Civil Rights Collection.

10. Virginia state AFL-CIO Convention Proceedings, 1957, p. 166.

11. Jacob Schlitt to Boris Shiskin, October 14, 1958, Box 4, Folder "Virginia 1955–61," AFL-CIO Civil Rights Collection. See also Virginia State Executive Board meeting, September 6, 1958, Virginia State AFL-CIO Collection, Southern Labor Archives, Georgia State University, Atlanta, Ga., where the leaflet is discussed. The article on which the leaflet was based was Charles Zimmerman, "Justice When It Counts Most," *I.U.D. Digest*, Summer 1958, pp. 87–95. At the time he wrote the article Zimmerman was chair of the AFL-CIO Committee on Civil Rights.

12. Ely, *Crisis of Conservative Virginia*, p. 25.

13. Jacob Schlitt to Boris Shiskin, "Report on Virginia," September 2–6, 1958, Box 45, Folder "Virginia, 1956–57," AFL-CIO Civil Rights Collection.

14. *Washington Post*, May 23, 1960. Julian Carper, who was a member of Local 371 and served as its president for two years before becoming vice-president of the state council, drove from Richmond to address his old local when it met to consider a one dollar raise in union dues to support private schools. He remembers being the only one to speak against the resolution, which passed 281 to 83. Carper recalls the risks vividly: "The emotions were so high that for three years every time the phone rang in my Richmond office I would expect it to be that my home had been destroyed or my family injured. I lived in Middletown which was 10 miles west of Front Royal" (Carper to author, n.d., in possession of author). The original resolution had to be modified when the NAACP threatened to bring suit against American Viscose if it checked off an additional one dollar per member to finance private schools. The local then proposed to raise the money itself by dunning its members for voluntary contributions as opposed to raising union dues. See "Minutes of Regular Membership Meeting, Local 371" for October 15, 22, 29, 1958, in possession of author.

15. *Washington Post*, October 3, 1958.

16. George D. Butler to Theodore E. Brown, October 14, 1958, Box 4, Folder "Virginia 1955–61," AFL-CIO Civil Rights Collection. These allegations are made in Roy Wilkins to William Pollock, March 5, 1959. I am indebted to James Kilby, one of the black local union members who was reportedly threatened with dismissal, for supplying me with a copy of the letter and for the minutes from Local 371. Accounts of these charges appeared in *Washington Star*, February 22, 1959 and *Washington Post*, March 1, 1959.

17. Byrd is quoted in Ely, *Crisis of Conservative Virginia*, p. 25. Senator Byrd's quote is also interesting for what it indicates about how the state council's position was perceived. Contrary to Byrd, the state council never endorsed integration, but

labor's defense of public schools was widely interpreted as equivalent to an endorsement.

18. I thank Keir Jorgenson, research director for the Amalgamated Clothing and Textile Workers Union of America (ACTWU), for sending me "The Civil Rights Record of the Textile Workers Union of America, 1939–1976," which contains a full account of the Local 371 controversy. I also appreciate the newspaper reports on file at Local 371 made available by David Ramsey, office secretary for the local, that cover these events. In 1961, a follow-up report on Front Royal to the AFL-CIO Civil Rights Department found whites attending the integrated public high school. White enrollment at the public high school had increased because "funds for the private [school] are no longer available from the local union and thereby its financial existence must be that much more insecure." See Don Slaiman to Boris Shiskin, January 11, 1961, Box 4, Folder "Virginia 1955–61," AFL-CIO Civil Rights Collection. Muse also mentions the role of the union in the Front Royal controversy, *Virginia's Massive Resistance*, pp. 113–14.

19. H. B. Boyd, "Statement of Virginia State AFL-CIO Presented to the Governor's Education Commission," *Union News*, 1959, p. 21.

20. Report of the Officers of the Virginia State AFL-CIO to the Fourth Annual Convention, 1959, p. 7.

21. Virginia State AFL-CIO 1959 Convention Proceedings, p. 121. Southern moderates and resisters both tried to use the Cold War to their advantage. When resisters argued that the civil rights movement was part of the Communist conspiracy, moderates replied that massive resistance gave comfort to Communists by providing them with propaganda to embarrass the United States.

22. Ibid., p. 67. See also the Report of the Education Committee at the same convention for a similar sentiment, p. 121.

23. Julian Carper, "The Inevitable Cannot Be Escaped," *Union News*, 1959, p. 9.

24. Boyd, "Statement of Virginia State AFL-CIO Presented to the Governor's Education Commission."

25. Virginia State AFL-CIO 1959 Convention Proceedings, pp. 7, 14.

26. Ibid., pp. 43–47.

27. Gates, *Making of Massive Resistance*, pp. 97, 100.

28. Jacob Schlitt, "Draft of Confidential Memorandum," Box 4, Folder "Virginia 1955–61," AFL-CIO Civil Rights Collection.

29. Boyd, "Statement of Virginia State AFL-CIO," p. 21. A good description of the "freedom of choice" doctrine is found in Ely, *Crisis of Conservative Virginia*, p. 108.

30. Wilkinson, *From Brown to Bakke*, pp. 99–100.

31. Virginia State AFL-CIO 1961 Convention Proceedings, p. 124.

32. "Tuition Grants in Question," *News Hi-Lites*, July, 1964.

33. Morton T. Elder, "Labor and Race Relations," p. 5, Box 108, Fund for the Republic Collection. Arkansas AFL-CIO president Odell Smith also saw no reaction from locals in his state to *Brown* although the three founders of the segregationist White America in Arkansas were union members. For Smith's view of the response in Arkansas see *Arkansas Gazette*, July 1, 1956.

34. Arkansas State AFL-CIO 1956 Convention Proceedings, p. 55.

35. A good description of interposition can be found in Bartley, *Rise of Massive Resistance*, p. 132.

36. Executive Board Minutes, August 25, 1956, in the Arkansas AFL-CIO Files, Little Rock, Ark.

37. Wayne E. Glenn to Jim McDevitt, December 10, 1956, Lot 1, Box 2, Folder "Arkansas 1956," AFL-CIO COPE Research Department Collection, George Meany Memorial Archives, Silver Spring, Md. The Arkansas AFL-CIO endorsed Faubus because he supported abolition of the poll tax, a priority for the state council, and because his populism "assuaged a hunger for Arkansas labor as definite as its hunger for the cornbread and beans so many of its members had grown up on." This quote is from Victor K. Ray, "The Role of the Labor Union," in Leland DuVall, ed., *Arkansas: Colony and State* (Little Rock: Rose Publishers, 1973), p. 102.

38. Virgil T. Blossom, *It Has Happened Here* (New York: Harper & Row, 1959), p. 116.

39. Philip Foner says that the Executive Council was "hesitant" to act in Little Rock because members were part of the Ku Klux Klan and White Citizens' Councils. Although it is true that Klan and Citizens' Councils activity among the membership increased as a result of the school crisis, there is little evidence to support his statement that this made AFL-CIO leaders hesitant to comment on it. In the midst of the school crisis, Meany made two statements clarifying the position of the AFL-CIO. See Foner, *Organized Labor*, p. 317.

40. Untitled, September 12, 1957, Box 4, Folder "Little Rock, 1957," AFL-CIO Civil Rights Collection.

41. Statement of the AFL-CIO Executive Council, September 25, 1957, Box 4, Folder "Little Rock, 1957–59," ibid.

42. Statement attached by the Arkansas State Federated Labor Council, AFL-CIO, September 1, 1957, Box 4, Folder "Arkansas Little Rock Incident 1957," ibid. See also *New York Times*, September 1, 1957, for an account of Odell's statement.

43. E. V. Williams to Benjamin D. Segal, October 11, 1957, Box 4, Folder "Little Rock 1957," AFL-CIO Civil Rights Collection. See also Benjamin D. Segal, "Racism Stymies Unions in the South," *New Leader*, November 11, 1957, pp. 14–18.

44. Field Report, November 30, 1957, Folder 42, Daniel Powell Collection, Southern Historical Collection, University of North Carolina Library, University of North Carolina, Chapel Hill, N.C.

45. Arkansas state council executive board minutes, January 18, 1958, Arkansas AFL-CIO Files.

46. Field Report, March 17, 1958, Folder 42, Powell Collection.

47. Field Report, April 25, 1958, ibid.

48. Field Report, June 16, 1958, ibid. See also *Arkansas Gazette*, May 25, 1958.

49. Field Report, July 27, 1958, Folder 42, Powell Collection.

50. Don Slaiman to Boris Shiskin, September 30, 1958, Box 4, Folder "Arkansas Little Rock Incident 1958," AFL-CIO Civil Rights Collection.

51. George H. Ellison to Daniel A. Powell, October 14, 1961, Folder 30, Powell Collection.

52. See the minutes to the Arkansas AFL-CIO executive committee meetings of June 4 and August 27, 1960, where restoring the retainer to McMath's law firm is discussed, Arkansas AFL-CIO Files.

53. Don Slaiman to Emanuel Muravchik, "Summary Report on Arkansas," November 25, 1958, Box 21-03, Folder "Labor on Little Rock," Jewish Labor Committee Collection.

54. Odell Smith, "Let's Keep Free Public Education," *Arkansas Union Labor Bulletin*, September 26, 1958. See also the accompanying editorial. The *Bulletin* was the official newspaper of the Arkansas state council, and it too came under attack from pro-Faubus supporters within the labor movement.

55. Victor K. Ray to George T. Guernsey, October 15, 1958, Box 4, Folder "Arkansas Little Rock 1958," AFL-CIO Civil Rights Collection.

56. For a description of the recall election that underestimates labor's contribution to the STOP campaign see Henry M. Alexander, *The Little Rock Recall Election* (New Brunswick, N.J.: Eagleton Institute, 1960).

57. *Arkansas Gazette*, July 3, 1959.

58. George Ellison to Jim McDevitt, May 18, 1959, Lot 2, Box 2, Folder 37, AFL-CIO COPE Research Department Collection.

59. "Our Rights Are at Stake," *Arkansas Union Labor Bulletin*, May 22, 1959.

60. Field Report, May 23, 1959, Folder 42, Powell Collection.

61. Letter to the author from Victor Ray, July 21, 1989.

62. See Alexander, *Little Rock Recall Election*, pp. 30–33, for an analysis of the vote.

63. Victor K. Ray to George Guernsey, October 15, 1958, Box 4, Folder "Arkansas Little Rock 1958," AFL-CIO Civil Rights Collection.

64. Ernest Q. Campbell and Thomas F. Pettigrew, *Christians in Racial Crisis: A Study of Little Rock's Ministry* (Washington, D.C.: Public Affairs Press, 1959), quote on p. 130.

65. Daniel A. Powell to Jim McDevitt, December 18, 1961, Folder 196, Powell Collection.

66. See George H. Ellison to Daniel A. Powell, October 4, 1961, Folder 30, Powell Collection, in which Ellison describes the state council's affiliation problem.

67. Field Report, December 18, 1961, Folder 196, ibid.

68. Kornhauser, "Ideology and Interests," p. 54.

69. "Report of James L. McDevitt to the COPE Administrative Committee," August 20, 1958, Lot 1, Box 3, Folder 30, AFL-CIO COPE Research Department Collection.

CHAPTER 3

1. This episode is recounted in Peter B. Levy, "The New Left and Labor: The Early Years (1960–1963)," *Labor History* (Summer 1990): 314.

2. Oral History of Milton Webster, Oral History Collection, Columbia University, New York, N.Y.

3. Herbert Hill, "Racism within Organized Labor: A Report of Five Years of the AFL-CIO, 1955–1960," *Journal of Negro Education* (Spring 1961): 109–18.

4. Oral History of Fannie Neal, Oral History Collection, Bentley Library, University of Michigan, Ann Arbor, recounts the use of a rope to separate black and white delegates at union conventions in the South.

5. H. L. Mitchell to Boris Shiskin, March 12, 1956, Box 4, Folder "National Agricultural Workers Union," AFL-CIO Civil Rights Collection.

6. Ray L. Richard to Barney Weeks, October 23, 1958, Alabama AFL-CIO Files, Alabama AFL-CIO, Birmingham, Ala.

7. Quoted in Peter J. Rachleff, *Black Labor in the South: Richmond, Virginia, 1865–1890* (Philadelphia: Temple University Press, 1984), p. 72.

8. Ibid.; and Melton Alonzo McLaurin, *The Knights of Labor in the South* (Westport, Conn.: Greenwood Press, 1978).

9. See *Birmingham News*, May 16, 1950, for local newspaper story on CIO policy. See also R. E. Farr to Mr. Philip Murray, May 19, 1950, Philip Taft Collection, 49.1.2.1.20., Birmingham Public Library, Birmingham, Ala.

10. *Southern School News*, June 1959, November 1959.

11. Daniel A. Powell to Jim McDevitt, n.d., Folder 141, Powell Collection.

12. Jerry Holleman to Stanton Smith, June 11, 1959, 110-20-4-1, Texas AFL-CIO Collection, University of Texas at Arlington, Arlington, Texas.

13. Oral History of Claude Ramsay, Oral History Program of the University of Southern Mississippi, Hattiesburg, Miss., Vol. 215, p. 53.

14. "White Citizens Councils Plague Unions but Make Few Inroads," in Benjamin Segal Personal Papers.

15. Virginia State AFL-CIO Convention Proceedings, 1958, p. 94.

16. A. Philip Randolph to George Meany, June 21, 1961, Box 24, Folder "Virginia State AFL-CIO Convention, 1961," A. Philip Randolph Collection, Library of Congress, Manuscripts Division, Washington, D.C.

17. Boris Shiskin to President Meany, June 26, 1961, Series II, Chronological Files, Folder "Memos and Letters, 1961," AFL-CIO Civil Rights Collection.

18. In his biography of George Meany, Joseph Goulden alludes to Shiskin's defense of the Virginia state council at a meeting of the Executive Council without giving the substance of his remarks. I presume Shiskin offered the same defense to AFL-CIO Executive Council members that he gave to Meany privately. See Goulden, *Meany* (New York: Atheneum, 1972), pp. 315–19.

19. A. Philip Randolph to David D. Alston, August 10, 1961, Box 24, Folder "Virginia State AFL-CIO Convention, 1961," Randolph Collection. See also the story on this convention in the *AFL-CIO News*, July 22, 1961.

20. Virginia State AFL-CIO Executive Board Meeting, August 27, 1961, Virginia State AFL-CIO Collection.

21. Virginia State AFL-CIO Convention Proceedings, 1961, p. 52.

22. Don Slaiman to Boris Shiskin, August 10, 1962, Series II, Chronological Files, Folder "Memos and Letters, August–September, 1962," AFL-CIO Civil Rights Collection.

23. Boris Shiskin to President Meany, August 3, 1961, Series II, Chronological Files, Folder, "Memos and Letters, 1961," ibid.

24. Boris Shiskin to President Meany, October 18, 1961, ibid.

25. George Meany to All State and Local Central Bodies Affiliated with the AFL-CIO, February 6, 1962, 5-1-4, Schnitzler Collection.

26. H. S. Brown to George Meany, February 27, 1962, 5-1-4, Schnitzler Collection.

27. President to Edward J. Shea, July 22, 1963, 5-1-12, Schnitzler Collection.

28. "Housing Accommodations and Facilities for Delegates," March 1, 1962, Series II, Chronological Files, "Memos and Letters, March, 1962," AFL-CIO Civil Rights Collection. See also Boris Shiskin to Secretary-Treasurer William Schnitzler, April 17, 1962, Series II, Chronological Files, Folder "Memos and Letters, April–May, 1962," ibid.

29. William F. Schnitzler to J. O. Moore, October 25, 1962, Series II, Chronological Files, Folder "Memos and Letters, October–December, 1962," ibid.

30. "Rough Minutes: Civil Rights Committee Meeting," November 15, 1962, ibid.

31. *Journal of Labor*, May 3, 1963, in Box 23, Folder "Civil Rights: The CIO-AFL, General," Randolph Collection.

32. Interview with E. T. Kehrer, May 10, 1990, Atlanta, Ga. Kehrer was the southern representative for the AFL-CIO Civil Rights Department headquartered in Atlanta at the time.

33. George Meany to Leroy Lindsey, March 8, 1962, 1-0001-005, Schnitzler Collection.

34. Daniel Powell to Jim McDevitt, October 11, 1960, Folder 195, Powell Collection.

35. Edward Shanklin, Sr., to Ray Andrus, February 22, 1961, and Andrus's reply, February 23, 1961, Folder 87, Powell Collection.

36. Ray Andrus to Daniel Powell, October 8, 1963, Folder 199, ibid.

37. Emery O. Jackson, "The Tip-Off," *Birmingham World*, January 15, 1964, 15-06-14-22, Southern Regional Council Collection, Atlanta University Library Center, Special Collections, Atlanta University, Atlanta, Ga.

38. Interview with Emanuel Muravchik, June 28, 1989, New York, N.Y.

39. Emory Via, "Summary of Southern Regional Council's Labor Conference," marked Confidential: Not for Publication, n.d., in Benjamin Segal's Personal Papers.

40. "Comments by Emory Via," May 19–24, 1957, Box 1278, Folder 13, Via Collection.

41. Ibid.

42. *AFL-CIO News and Views*, July–August 1956.

43. *St. Louis Post-Dispatch*, May 24, 1959.

44. *AFL-CIO News and Views*, May, 1959, December 1956.

45. Benjamin D. Segal and Emory Via to B. Sexton et al., May 6, 1957, 75-05-15-04, Southern Regional Council Collection, Atlanta.

46. See Robert E. Hughes to Emory F. Via, May 13, 1957, Box 1, Folder "EFV," Via Collection; and Reverend Robert E. Hughes to Emory Via, June 28, 1957, 75-05-14-04, Southern Regional Council Collection, Atlanta. See also Corley, "Quest for Racial Harmony," 1979, p. 175.

47. *Chattanooga Free Press*, July 12, 1957, in Box 1278, Folder 20, Via Collection.

48. Daniel A. Powell to James L. McDevitt, August 4, 1957, Folder 168, Powell Collection.

49. Emory Via, "Things Which Southern Unions Can Do to Ease Racial Tension," n.d., Box 1278, Folder 14, Via Collection.

50. Interview with Barney Weeks, January 7, 1987, Montgomery, Ala. See also "Transcript of Comments by Barney Weeks" at the Southern Labor History Conference, May 4–6, 1978. I thank Robert Dinwiddie of the Southern Labor Archives for supplying me with this material.

51. Emory F. Via, "An Informal Report to Ben Segal," Box 1278, Folder 14, Via Collection.

52. Daniel Powell to Al Barkan, June 18, 1963, in possession of the author.

53. For a description of NILE see Joseph Mire, "The National Institute of Labor Education," in Box 2, Folder 4, National Institute of Labor Education Collection, Labor-Management Documentation Center, New York State School of Industrial and Labor Relations, Cornell University, Ithaca, N.Y.

54. "Proposal on Inter Group Relations," June 1959, Box 19, Folder 20, ibid.

55. Ibid.

56. "Report by Executive Director for Meeting of Board of Directors," May 2 and 3, 1962, Box 15, Folder 10, ibid.

57. Marc Karson to Joseph Mire, January 16, 1962, Box 8, Folder 18, ibid.

58. Ronald Donovan, "The Southern Union Staff Institute Training Institute," Box 1278, Folder 14, Via Collection.

59. Aaron E. Sloss to Alfred L. Wickman, April 13, 1963, Box 8, Folder 17, National Institute of Labor Education Collection.

60. Donovan, "Southern Union Staff Training Institute," pp. 18–20.

61. Ibid, p. 28.

62. Via resigned as director before the opening of the Texas institute as a result of the change in dates. Mire was then appointed co-director.

63. George T. Guernsey, "Comments on the 1965 Texas NILE Southern Staff Training Institute," n.d., Box 15, Folder 28; and "National Institute of Labor Education: Report by the Executive Director for Meeting of the Board of Directors," n.d., Box 20, Folder 58, National Institute of Labor Education Collection. See also a story on the North Carolina and Texas institutes, "Staff Training with a Southern Accent," *American Federationist*, September 1965, pp. 19–22.

64. Emory Via, "N.I.L.E. Southern Staff Institute Director's Report," n.d., pp. 41–45, Box 19, Folder 10, National Institute of Labor Education Collection. See also evaluations by two of the participants, Hugh Owen to A. F. Grospiron, March 14, 1966, and Frederick W. Cory, "Impressions of the Southern Staff Institute," n.d., ibid.

65. Shubel Morgan, "The Negro and the Union: A Dialogue," *American Socialist*, July–August 1958, p. 38.

66. Interview with Weeks.

67. Philip Foner claims that the educational effort by the AFL-CIO was "minimal" because of fear of repercussions. He mentions an educational effort in the North that seemed to have no more success than those that took place in the South. He says white liberal union leaders did make a "truly serious effort" in Chicago to approach their members on race but found "they could not speak for the racists in their organizations." Perhaps the problem was not, as Foner contends, lack of labor effort, but that union leaders in the South could not speak for

racists in their organizations any more than could the leaders Foner describes in Chicago. See Foner, *Organized Labor*, p. 364.

68. Marshall, "Union Racial Problems in the South," p. 128.

69. Donovan, "Southern Union Staff Training Institute," p. 32.

70. Emory Via, "Labor Project Report, January–June, 1967," n.d., Box 74, Folder 32, Southern Regional Council Collection, Atlanta.

71. Arnold Rose conducted a study in an attempt to assess the influence of a union on its members' attitudes toward civil rights. Rose interviewed members of Teamsters Local 688 in St. Louis, which actively tried to promote racial equality among its members. In addition to preventing discrimination by employers, the local union sponsored mixed dances, demanded the desegregation of recreational facilities in St. Louis, and sponsored a civil rights ordinance before the city council. Rose found that as a result of these efforts, union "influence can be expected to eliminate race prejudice completely in only a few members, but it can be expected to reduce hostile attitudes on matters that are perceived to fall within the union's direct interest for a great number of members (a majority in our case). In so far as the union's leaders can rationally demonstrate to its prejudiced members that union solidarity extends to matters hitherto perceived to be outside the union's baliwick, prejudice will decline in regard to these other matters" (Rose, "The Influence of a Border City Union on the Race Attitudes of Its Members," *Journal of Social Issues* 9:2 [1953]: 23). Rose's study did not reflect the impact of union education efforts, at least of the kind described here, and it predated the Supreme Court's *Brown* decision, which inflamed racial feelings among whites considerably.

72. Kornhauser arrived at a similar conclusion in his investigation of union attempts to improve race relations. Such efforts were often made through education programs, but these programs were perceived as peripheral to union activity and "not integrated with central trade union functions" (Kornhauser, "Ideology and Interests," p. 59).

CHAPTER 4

1. Irving Panken to Walter Lurie, February 28, 1961, 21-03, Jewish Labor Committee Collection.

2. Marshall, "Union Racial Problems in the South," pp. 127–28.

3. *Birmingham Post*, August 25, 1961.

4. Claude Ramsay to George Meany, June 9, 1961, 2186/8, Mississippi AFL-CIO Collection, Southern Labor Archives, Special Collections Department, Georgia State University, Atlanta, Ga.

5. "Report of the National Director to COPE Operating Committee," August 13, 1957, Lot 1, Box 3, Folder 31, AFL-CIO COPE Research Department Collection. For discussion of arrangements for COPE to assist ASCARV, see Box 1, Folders "Alabama-Local" and "Alabama-State," Philip Weightman Collection, Robert F. Wagner Labor Archives, Tamiment Library, New York University, New York, N.Y.

6. Earl W. Davis to Director James L. McDevitt, May 15, 1958, Folder 3, Powell Collection.

7. This incident is recounted in my book, *A Rope of Sand: The AFL-CIO Committee on Political Education, 1955–67* (New York: Praeger, 1989), p. 109.

8. An example of such a disclaimer appears in Jim McDevitt to Elliot Gage, July 15, 1963, Box 5, Folder "James L. McDevitt, 1961–1963," Weightman Collection.

9. George Ellison to Jim McDevitt, April 20, 1959, Folder 29, Powell Collection.

10. Paul E. Golson to Leroy Lindsey, June 22, 1961, Alabama AFL-CIO Files, Birmingham, Ala.

11. Wilbur Hobby to Walter Bartkin, n.d., Folder 29, Powell Collection.

12. George Ellison to Philip Weightman, July 17, 1961, Box 3, Folder "Arkansas State," Weightman Collection.

13. Ray Smithhart to Philip M. Weightman, September 3, 1959, 2148/4, Mississippi AFL-CIO Collection.

14. *AFL-CIO News*, September 10, 1966.

15. Henry Paley to Claude Ramsay, June 30, 1960, 2130/2, Mississippi AFL-CIO Collection. See also Mississippi AFL-CIO 1964 Convention Proceedings, p. 8.

16. Emory Via, "Rough Report on Emory Via's Trip to Montgomery, Alabama," May 3, 1957, 41.1.1.1.12, Southern Regional Council Collection, Birmingham.

17. See Black and Black, *Politics and Society in the South*, on the rural character of southern industrialization.

18. Donald C. Mosley, "The Labor Union Movement," in Richard Aubrey McLemore, ed., *A History of Mississippi* (Jackson: University and College Press of Mississippi, 1973), 2: 265.

19. *Birmingham News*, July 19, 1967, Alabama AFL-CIO Files.

20. Quoted in Kundahl, "Organized Labor in Alabama State Politics," p. 437.

21. *Arkansas Union Labor Bulletin*, July 6, 1962.

22. Ibid., August 3, 1962.

23. George Ellison to James McDevitt, August 21, 1962, Box 2, Folder "Arkansas 1962–63," AFL-CIO COPE Research Department Collection.

24. Arkansas AFL-CIO 1962 Convention Proceedings, p. 18.

25. *Arkansas Union Labor Bulletin*, May 8, 1964.

26. *Arkansas Gazette*, July 1, 1965.

27. *Arkansas Union Labor Bulletin*, May 21, 1965.

28. *Arkansas Gazette*, July 1, 1965.

29. Bill Becker to Daniel Powell, June 17, 1965, Arkansas AFL-CIO Files, Little Rock, Ark.

30. Arkansas AFL-CIO Executive Board Meeting, August 29, 1965, p. 60, ibid.

31. Bill Becker to Daniel Powell, October 20, 1965, ibid. See also *Arkansas Union Labor Bulletin*, October 22, 1965, for a report on the Young Democrats' national convention. For Powell's reporting of these events to COPE's office in Washington see Daniel Powell to Joseph Rourke, November 26, 1965, Folder 226, Powell Collection.

32. *Arkansas Union Labor Bulletin*, October 22, 1965, reprinted the *Arkansas Gazette* editorial.

33. George Ellison to Philip Weightman, March 3, 1961, Folder 30, Powell Collection.

34. George Ellison to Jim McDevitt, October 3, 1961, Box 3, Folder "Arkansas 1962–63," AFL-CIO COPE Research Department Collection.

35. George Ellison to Philip Weightman, August 7, 1961, Box 3, Folder "Arkansas-State," Weightman Collection.

36. George Ellison to Al Barkan, February 6, 1964, Folder 32, Powell Collection.

37. Jim Ranchino, *From Faubus to Bumpers: Arkansas Votes* (Arkadelphia: Action Research, 1972).

38. Union efforts to repeal the poll tax in Arkansas date back to 1937, when the Arkansas AFL state federation sponsored a constitutional amendment for repeal. Another union attempt at repeal was defeated in a 1956 referendum. See Frederick G. Ogden, *The Poll Tax in the South* (University Ala.: University of Alabama Press, 1958), for union efforts throughout the South to repeal the poll tax.

39. Arkansas Executive Committee Minutes, July 11, 1964, Arkansas AFL-CIO Files.

40. Daniel Powell to Helmuth Kern, May 15, 1964, Folder 201, Powell Collection; George Ellison to Al Barkan, March 5, 1964, and Bill Becker to Al Barkan, November 20, 1964, Lot 2, Box 2, Folder 40, AFL-CIO COPE Research Department Collection.

41. Bill Becker to Daniel Powell, August 6, 1964, Arkansas AFL-CIO Files.

42. *Arkansas Gazette*, August 11, 1964.

43. Bill Becker to Al Barkan, September 3, 1964, Lot 2, Box 2, Folder 40, AFL-CIO COPE Research Department Collection; Becker to Barkan, August 6, 1965, Arkansas AFL-CIO Files; *Pine Bluff Commercial*, August 13, 1964.

44. Dan Powell to Joseph Rourke, May 10, 1965, Folder 204, Powell Collection; *Arkansas Gazette*, June 20, 1965; Arkansas AFL-CIO 1965 Convention Proceedings, pp. 162–75.

45. Bill Becker to Daniel Powell, October 4, 1965, Arkansas AFL-CIO Files.

46. *Arkansas Union Labor Bulletin*, October 8, November 5, 1965; Bill Becker to Daniel Powell, November 19, 1965, Arkansas AFL-CIO Files.

47. *Arkansas Gazette*, June 20, 1965; Becker quoted ibid., August 2, 1966.

48. Daniel Powell to Al Barkan, May 16, 1968, Folder 227, Powell Collection.

49. *Dallas Morning News*, October 22, 1958.

50. *Southern School News*, November 1958.

51. Jerry Holleman to Stanton Smith, June 11, 1959, 110-20-4-1, Texas AFL-CIO Collection.

52. George Norris Green, *The Establishment in Texas Politics: The Primitive Years, 1938–1957* (Norman: University of Oklahoma Press, 1984); Chandler Davidson, *Race and Class in Texas Politics* (Princeton: Princeton University Press, 1990).

53. *Dallas Morning News*, June 1, 1958, 110-26-9-4, Texas AFL-CIO Collection.

54. W. Don Ellinger to Jim McDevitt, August 16, November 15, 1957, 110-9-1-4, Ellinger to McDevitt, January 15, 1958, 110-9-1-5, Texas AFL-CIO Collection.

55. Harry Holloway, *The Politics of the Southern Negro* (New York: Random House, 1969).

56. Philip M. Weightman to W. Don Ellinger, September 15, 1959, W. Don Ellinger to James L. McDevitt, December 5, 1959, 110-9-1-6, Texas AFL-CIO Collection.

57. Erma D. Leroy to Jerry R. Holleman, January 6, May 9, 1960, 110-1-12-1, ibid.

58. W. Don Ellinger to James L. McDevitt, October 21, November 21, 13, 1960, 110-9-1-7, Texas AFL-CIO COPE Collection, University of Texas at Arlington, Arlington, Tex.

59. *Dallas Times-Herald*, June 19, 1960, 110-26-9-4, Texas AFL-CIO Collection. See also W. Don Ellinger to James L. McDevitt, July 2, 1960, 110-9-1-7, ibid.

60. W. Don Ellinger to Jim McDevitt, April 4, 1961, "Memo: Texas Special Senate Election," 110-9-1-7, ibid.

61. James R. Soukup, Clifton McCleskey, and Harry Holloway, *Party and Factional Division in Texas* (Austin: University of Texas Press, 1964), p. 13.

62. "Summary of Coalition Action," July 9, 1961, 110-26-9-4, Texas AFL-CIO Collection.

63. *Houston Post*, October 22, 1961, ibid. See also Albert A. Pena, Jr., "The Texas Coalition Movement," *Labor Today*, December–January 1963–64, pp. 13–15.

64. "The Blockworker Program of the Texas Democratic Coalition," n.d., 110-26-9-5, Texas AFL-CIO Collection. This report is unsigned but was probably written by Larry Goodwyn, then executive secretary for the coalition.

65. H. S. Hank Brown to Al Barkan, May 13, 1964, 33-2-5, Texas AFL-CIO COPE Collection; Harry Hubbard, Jr., to Brown, August 15, 1963, 110-1-13-4, Texas AFL-CIO Collection; Brown to C. J. Haggerty, June 5, 1964, 33-2-5, Texas AFL-CIO COPE Collection.

66. Walter Davis to Don Slaiman, 1964, Box 5, Folder "Memos and Letters, November–December, 1964," AFL-CIO Civil Rights Collection.

67. Holloway, *Politics of the Southern Negro*, pp. 255–65.

68. H. S. Hank Brown to Al Barkan, May 13, 1964, 33-2-5, Texas AFL-CIO COPE Collection.

69. Walter F. Gray to Al Barkan, December 16, 1964, 33-3-6, H. S. Hank Brown to C. J. Haggerty, June 5, 1964, 33-2-5, Brown to Walter P. Reuther, May 26, 1964, 33-2-5, and Walter F. Gray to Al Barkan, December 16, 1964, 33-3-6, Texas AFL-CIO COPE Collection.

70. Davidson, *Race and Class in Texas Politics*, p. 25.

71. Jack Bass and Walter DeVries, *The Transformation of Southern Politics: Social Change and Political Consequences since 1945* (New York: Basic Books, 1976), p. 392.

72. Dan Powell to James L. McDevitt, May 19, 1959, Folder 226, Powell Collection.

73. Harry Fleishman, "Labor and the Civil Rights Revolution: Trade Union Civil Rights for Negroes Proceed Slowly, but AFL-CIO Speeds Progress," *New Leader*, April 18, 1960, pp. 16–20.

74. Daniel Powell to Al Barkan, July 5, 1961, Folder 171 Powell Collection, and Powell to Joseph Rourke, October 13, 1965, Folder 136, Powell Collection.

75. E. T. Kehrer to Don Slaiman, March 7, 1966, Box 1593, Folder 8, Southern Area Civil Rights Department, AFL-CIO Collection, Southern Labor Archives, Georgia State University, Atlanta, Ga.

76. W. M. Barbee to J. R. Fry, October 30, 1963, 2238/5, North Carolina AFL-CIO Collection, Southern Labor Archives, Georgia State University, Atlanta, Ga. See also G. E. Gill to Roger L. Bauguss and Coy M. Vance, May 15, 1964,

Folder 135, Powell Collection. Barbee's background would lead one to doubt his sensitivity to civil rights matters. Barbee was reportedly associated with a racist group that waged a bitter fight within the Tobacco Workers local of which he was a member before his election as state council president. See Emanuel Muravchik to Emory Via, November 13, 1956, Box 4, Folder "White Citizens' Councils, April-December, 1956," AFL-CIO Civil Rights Collection, which discusses Barbee's past.

77. Victor Bussie to Emory Via, April 20, 1966, Box 7, Folder 21, Southern Regional Council Collection, Birmingham.

78. Jerry Colburn, "Victor Bussie: Louisiana's Lord of Labor," *New Orleans Magazine*, August 1977, pp. 62–67. Bussie's role in the confrontation at Bogalusa is described in Vera Rony, "Bogalusa: The Economics of Tragedy," *Dissent*, May–June 1966, pp. 234–43.

79. Leaflets and mailings that the Louisiana state council produced and distributed during the Morrison campaign are available in the Louisiana AFL-CIO Files, Louisiana AFL-CIO, Baton Rouge, La.

80. See the letters from Davis to McDevitt on June 30 and July 15, 1959, for reports of this activity. These letters are in Box 3, Folder "Earl Davis #1," Weightman Collection.

81. For a description of the Virginia Democratic primary see Julian Carper to James L. McDevitt, "Virginia Democratic Primary," July 11, 1961. For an account of black voting in the primary see Earl Davis to McDevitt, July 31, 1961. Both are in Lot 2, Box 24, Folder 545, AFL-CIO COPE Research Department Collection.

82. Virginia State AFL-CIO 1963 Convention Proceedings, pp. 93–95.

CHAPTER 5

1. *Alabama Labor Council Newsletter*, May 26, 1958. For Wallace's remarks to the Alabama CIO see Philip Taft, *Organizing Dixie: Alabama Workers in the Industrial Era* (Westport, Conn.: Greenwood Press, 1981), p. 132.

2. Marshall Frady, *Wallace* (New York: World, 1968), p. 98.

3. Minutes of the Executive Board Meeting, March 9, 1962, p. 5, Alabama AFL-CIO Files.

4. Ibid.

5. Alabama State AFL-CIO COPE Convention Proceedings, 1962, p. 48.

6. Kundahl, "Organized Labor," p. 149.

7. "Minutes of the Executive Board Meeting," October 28, 1962, Alabama AFL-CIO Files.

8. Alabama AFL Convention Proceedings, 1956, p. 48. See also Taft, *Organizing Dixie*, p. 163. Before the merger, the Alabama CIO Industrial Union Council held three of its last five conventions in Mobile because of the city's relative racial tolerance.

9. Taft, *Organizing Dixie*, p. 163. The state council received a request from the AFL-CIO that it no longer distinguish its "Colored Vice-Presidents at Large" from the other vice-presidents on its official letterhead.

10. Emory Via, "Rough Report on Emory Via's Trip to Montgomery, Alabama," May 3, 1957, 41.1.1.1.12, Southern Regional Council Collection, Birmingham.

11. Newspaper accounts dated March 11, 1964, in Folder 5, Powell Collection. See also the letter from Barney Weeks to Al Barkan, March 13, 1964, Alabama AFL-CIO Files.

12. Barney Weeks to Daniel A. Powell, July 7, 1964, Alabama AFL-CIO Files; newspaper reports "Wallace's Labor Stand Defended," "Wisconsin Labor Criticism of Wallace Irks Leader Here," and *Birmingham News*, April 2, 1964, Folder 5, Powell Collection. See also Kundahl, "Organized Labor," p. 354, for more evidence of support for Wallace among the rank and file.

13. *Tuscaloosa News*, April 13, 1964, Alabama AFL-CIO Files.

14. Barney Weeks to Dallas W. Sells, April 21, 1964, ibid.

15. George C. Wallace to Delegates, March 11, 1964, Folder 5, Powell Collection.

16. William A. Nunnelley, *Bull Connor* (Tuscaloosa: University of Alabama Press, 1991), p. 14.

17. Daniel A. Powell to James L. McDevitt, May 17, 1957, Lot 1A, Box 1, Folder 3, AFL-CIO COPE Research Department Files. On labor's friendly relations with Connor see also Ben Segal, "The Educational Implications of Labor's Public Responsibility in Public Affairs: Civil Rights, Civil Liberties, and International Affairs," November 1959, p. 172, in Segal Personal Papers. Southern Regional Council ambassador Ben Muse reported on the conflict over the desegregation of Birmingham's parks in 1962: "The rank and file of organized labor seems to support the segregationist attitude of the city commission but the unions have taken no formal stand, with the exception of the Carpenters union supporting the city commission. Labor leaders like Mitch and Bruce Thrasher are associated with business leaders in the open parks movement" (Report, January 11, 1962, 41.1.3.2.8., Southern Regional Council Collection, Birmingham).

18. Alabama AFL-CIO COPE Convention Proceedings, 1964, pp. 23–31.

19. Ibid., pp. 37–38. For a description of this convention see Taft, *Organizing Dixie*, p. 174.

20. Barney Weeks to Al Barkan, March 13, 1964, Alabama AFL-CIO Files; Dan Powell to Al Barkan, July 12, 1964, Folder 201, Powell Collection; President to William Burnell, May 4, 1964, Alabama AFL-CIO Files; Barney Weeks to Daniel A. Powell, April 3, 1964, Folder 5, Powell Collection.

21. These membership figures are from Kundahl, "Organized Labor," pp. 90–105.

22. Barney Weeks to Al Barkan, April 3, 1964, Alabama AFL-CIO Files; Weeks to Barkan, May 6, 1964, Folder 5, Powell Collection.

23. Barney Weeks to Al Barkan, June 4, 5, 1964, Alabama AFL-CIO Files; Ben Albert to Daniel Powell, July 8, 1964, Folder 201, Powell Collection.

24. *New York Times*, June 14, September 29, 1964.

25. Kundahl, "Organized Labor," p. 77.

26. Daniel Powell to Al Barkan, July 12, 1964, Folder 201, Powell Collection. Taft mentions sympathy for the Klan among members of the old Alabama CIO that created problems for its leadership similar to those Weeks faced (*Organized Dixie*, p. 129).

27. Alabama AFL-CIO Convention Proceedings, 1964, pp. 29–41, 73–87, 109–117, 198–203. Taft describes this convention in *Organizing Dixie*, p. 175.

28. Barney Weeks to Al Barkan, December 2, 1964, Folder 5, Powell Collection.

29. Taft, *Organizing Dixie*, p. 176.

30. Fannie Neal to Philip Weightman, n.d., in possession of the author.

31. Norrell, "Labor Trouble," p. 264.

32. "Executive Board Minutes," September 9, 1965, Alabama AFL-CIO Files.

33. Barney Weeks to Stanton Smith, March 28, 1966, Alabama AFL-CIO Files.

34. The decision against endorsing Thrash was made at the executive council meeting that preceded the COPE convention where questions as to why Thrash was not being endorsed were raised. See "Executive Council Meeting," March 18, 1966, Alabama AFL-CIO Files.

35. See the debate on whether to endorse Brewer in the Alabama COPE Convention Proceedings, 1966, pp. 32–39.

36. "Field Report," April 20, 1966, Folder 12, Powell Papers.

37. Reactions from the building trades to the 1966 Alabama COPE convention are reported in the *Birmingham News*, March 27, 1966. See also Kundahl, "Organized Labor," pp. 134–74.

38. The quote is from Kundahl, "Organized Labor," p. 171. Voting patterns in the 1966 Alabama gubernatorial race are analyzed in Daniel A. Powell to Al Barkan, May 20, 1966, Folder 12, Powell Collection.

39. Earl Black and Merle Black, "The Wallace Vote in Alabama: A Multiple Regression Analysis," *Journal of Politics* 35 (1973):730–37.

40. Barney Weeks to Mary Zon, October 14, 1966, Lot 1A, Box 1, Folder 10, AFL-CIO COPE Research Department Collection.

41. "Alabama C.O.P.E. Program 1966," Folder 206, Powell Collection.

42. Kundahl, "Organized Labor," p. 397.

43. Quoted in Greenberg, *Race and State in Capitalist Development*, p. 340.

44. Norrell, "Labor Trouble," p. 263.

45. This description of Alabama politics is drawn from Key, *Southern Politics*, pp. 36–58.

46. Speech by Barney Weeks to the Young Democrats of Alabama, n.d., Alabama AFL-CIO Files.

47. David M. Kovenock, James W. Prothro, et al., *Explaining the Vote: Presidential Choices in Individual States* (Chapel Hill: Institute for Research in Social Sciences, 1973), pp. 483–87.

48. Key, *Southern Politics*, p. 229.

CHAPTER 6

1. On the anti-labor views of Mississippi's newspapers see John Ray Skates, Jr., "Fred Sullens and the Growth of Organized Labor," *Southern Quarterly* (Summer 1972): 341–51.

2. On Ramsay's funeral see the *Clarion-Ledger*, January 19, 20, 21, 1986, 2138-13, Mississippi AFL-CIO Collection; Carolyn Phillips, secretary for the Mississippi AFL-CIO, sent copies of these articles to friends of Claude Ramsay with a note saying, "Al Barkan, friend and former COPE Director, called this morning and after telling him of these things he made a very observant remark, 'Labor leaders never get good press until their death.' I think Claude would appreciate that and enjoy a chuckle about it" (Phillips to Friends of Claude Ramsay, January 21, 1986, in possession of author).

3. Oral History of Claude Ramsay, pp. 8–9.

4. Ibid., pp. 13–18.

5. McElvaine, "Claude Ramsay," pp. 110–37.

6. In 1958 Ramsay appealed successfully to COPE director James McDevitt for help in unseating Representative William Colmer in the Democratic primary. Ramsay argued that Colmer was the most vulnerable member of Mississippi's conservative delegation because his district included more union members, liberals, and registered black voters than any other in Mississippi. In addition, an attractive candidate, former state legislator Boyce Holleman, had emerged to challenge Colmer. COPE donated $1,200 and the Mississippi AFL-CIO contributed another $3,000 for Holleman's campaign. Colmer defeated Holleman by fourteen thousand votes, but this was the closest any opponent came to defeating Colmer in his twenty-six years in office. See Claude Ramsay to James McDevitt, May 20, 1958, 2147/1, and "Mississippi AFL-CIO Executive Board Report to 2nd Annual Convention," October 31, 1959, 2130/1, Mississippi AFL-CIO Collection.

7. Daniel Powell to James L. McDevitt, May 11, 1959, Folder 119, Powell Collection.

8. This background on Ramsay is drawn primarily from the Oral History of Claude Ramsay, pp. 1–30. See also "Claude E. Ramsay," in Gary M. Fink, ed., *The Biographical Dictionary of American Labor* (Westport, Conn.: Greenwood Press, 1984), pp. 476–77; Stan P. Haggerson, "The Life and Times of Claude Ramsay, President of the Mississippi AFL-CIO, 1959–86," 2138/10, Mississippi AFL-CIO Collection; and the short biography in the Finders Guide to the Mississippi AFL-CIO Collection produced by the Southern Labor Archives at Georgia State University. Where there were discrepancies among these sources I relied on the Ramsay entry in the *Biographical Dictionary*.

9. "Mississippi Labor Council, AFL-CIO Executive Board Meeting," June 11, 1959, 2155/11, Mississippi AFL-CIO Collection. For instance, at the bottom of Barnett's answer sheet to the questions posed by the state council was a message that he "would personally consider it an honor to have the endorsement of organized labor but in the small communities it would be detrimental to us. The objective is to get elected now and to help us . . . by just passing the word down the line. . . . I hope and believe you will go along with us rather than a public endorsement" ("Ross Barnett, Governor," n.d., 2184/14, ibid.).

10. "Report of State COPE Committee on Gubernatorial Candidates to Mississippi State COPE Convention, AFL-CIO," June 13, 1959, 2184/14, ibid. Gartin's campaign also received support from the business community. He was endorsed by the Mississippi Chamber of Commerce, whose members served as his county campaign chairs. See Ray Smithhart to James McDevitt, September 11, 1959, Lot 1A, Box 14, Folder 290, AFL-CIO COPE Collection.

11. "Statement of Carroll Gartin," June 16, 1959, 2184/14, Mississippi AFL-CIO Collection.

12. "A Report to the Executive Board," n.d., 2155/11, ibid.

13. McMillen, *Citizens' Council*, pp. 326–27.

14. "A Memorandum: The ACWA Affiliation Problem," 2139/7, Mississippi AFL-CIO Collection.

15. "Executive Board Meeting," May 21, 1960, 2156/1, Mississippi AFL-CIO Collection. The contract at International Paper permitted leaves of absence only for work with the Paperworkers and not for other organizations.

16. Daniel A. Powell to James L. McDevitt, May 2, 1960, Folder 111, Powell Collection.

17. "Statement by Claude Ramsay," May 25, 1960, 2220/2, Mississippi AFL-CIO Collection.

18. *Laurel Leader-Call*, June 8, 1960; "Statement by Claude Ramsay," June 9, 1960, 2220/14, and Daniel A. Powell to Claude E. Ramsay, June 27, 1960, 2130/2, Mississippi AFL-CIO Collection.

19. *New York Times*, July 20, 1960.

20. Guy Paul Lord, "Mississippi Republicanism and the 1960 Presidential Election," *Journal of Mississippi History* 40:1 (1978): 33–48.

21. Claude E. Ramsay to Senator John F. Kennedy, July 28, 1960, 2186/4, Ramsay to Honorable Chet Holifield, August 23, 1960, 2130/3, and Thomas Knight to James L. McDevitt, December 5, 1960, 2147/2, Mississippi AFL-CIO Collection.

22. "Report to the Mississippi Labor Council Executive Board," January 21, 1961, 2130/4; Thomas Knight to James L. McDevitt, December 5, 1960, 2147/2; and "Statement by Claude Ramsay," October 24, 1960, 2190/18, Mississippi AFL-CIO Collection.

23. "Executive Board Meeting," September 24, 1960, 2156/1, and Thomas Knight to James L. McDevitt, November 1, 1960, 2147/2, Mississippi AFL-CIO Collection.

24. "Report to the Mississippi Labor Council Executive Board," January 20, 1961, 2130/4, ibid.

25. Ibid.

26. Barnett's appeal was demonstrated when members pressured two union leaders to withdraw from a suit that challenged contributions a state agency, the Mississippi State Sovereignty Commission, made to the Citizens' Councils. CWA area director Lonnie B. Daniel removed his name from the suit after members tried to remove him from his post. He conceded that his withdrawal came "at the expressed wishes of some of our members." C. E. Shaffer, an Electrical Workers business agent, encountered similar pressure and admitted that he withdrew "at the request of some of the members of the two local unions of Electrical Workers with whom I work." See James W. Silver, *Mississippi: The Closed Society* (New York: Harcourt, Brace and World, 1964), pp. 79–80; *Southern School News*, February 1961; *Jackson Daily News*, January 9, 1961, and *Jackson State Times*, January 23, 1961, in 2224/1, Mississippi AFL-CIO Collection. See also McMillen, *Citizens' Council* p. 339.

27. Daniel Powell to James McDevitt, December 18, 1961, Folder 196, Powell Collection.

28. *Jackson Daily News*, June 13, 1961.

29. J. M. Franklin to Claude Ramsay, June 7, 1961, Ramsay to Franklin, June 9, 1961, and J. M. Holloway to Whom It May Concern, June 22, 1961, 2186/8, Thomas Knight to James A. McDevitt, 2147/2, Claude E. Ramsay to George Meany, June 9, 1961, 2186/8, Mississippi AFL-CIO Collection.

30. Claude E. Ramsay to Stanton E. Smith, February 7, 1962, Smith to Ramsay, February 13, and March 7, 1962, 2130/7, ibid.

31. For accounts of the Meredith incident see Walter Lord, *The Past That Would Not Die* (New York: Harper & Row, 1965); Anthony Lewis, *Portrait of a Decade: The Second American Revolution* (New York: Random House, 1964), pp. 204–38; and Taylor Branch, *Parting the Waters: America in the King Years, 1954 – 1963* (New York: Simon & Schuster, 1988), pp. 633–73.

32. Oral History of Claude Ramsay, p. 57.

33. Ira B. Harkey, Jr., *The Smell of Burning Crosses* (Jacksonville, Ill.: Harns-Wolfe, 1967), p. 17. See also the Oral History of Claude Ramsay for an account of this episode, pp. 55–65.

34. Ramsay tried to assist Smith by scheduling a meeting for the candidate to meet international representatives who serviced locals in the new district. The state council did other mundane campaign chores for Smith, but it is unlikely that they had much effect. Smith does not mention labor's support in his account of the campaign, *Congressman from Mississippi* (New York: Capricorn Books, 1964), pp. 278–301. Accounts of state council activity in the 1962 Democratic primaries are drawn from "Mississippi COPE Activities," Thomas Knight to James L. McDevitt, March 16–30, April 1–15, and June 1–15, 1962, 2147/3, Mississippi AFL-CIO Collection.

35. Daniel A. Powell to Al Barkan, August 5, 1963, Folder 119, Powell Collection.

36. Mississippi COPE Convention Proceedings, 1963, pp. 13–18.

37. Neil R. McMillen, "The Development of Civil Rights, 1956-1970," in McLemore, *History of Mississippi* 2:154–97.

38. Billy Burton Hathorn, "Challenging the Status Quo: Rubel Lex Phillips and the Mississippi Republican Party, 1963-1967," *Journal of Mississippi History* 47:4 (1985): 240–64.

39. Phillips had a fairly good record on race issues to recommend him to Mississippi COPE. He was lax by Mississippi standards in permitting blacks to register to vote when he served as Alcorn County clerk and, though a confirmed segregationist, he told the COPE screening committee that he would use all legal means to prevent school desegregation but would not close schools to prevent blacks from attending them. He also earned plaudits from labor because, when still a Democrat, he had supported the national ticket in 1956 and even in 1960, when Dixiecrats took the state.

40. The *Atlanta Constitution*, December 16, 1963, quotes Ramsay as admitting that labor backed Phillips "to help build a two party state" (Folder 199, Powell Collection). For details of the Mississippi AFL-CIO and the 1963 gubernatorial race see "Report by Mississippi COPE Director Thomas Knight," n.d., 2185/1; "Mississippi COPE Progress Report," September 16–September 30, 1963, October 1–October 15, 1963, October 15–October 31, 1963, November 1–November 15, 1963, 2147/3; and "Minutes of the Executive Board Meeting," September 21, October 5, 1963, 2156/2, Mississippi AFL-CIO Collection.

41. Hathorn, "Challenging the Status Quo," p. 250.

42. Thomas Knight to Al Barkan, August 9, 1963, 2147/3, Mississippi AFL-CIO Collection.

43. See "A Memorandum: The ACWA Affiliation Problem," 2139/7, ibid. See also Thomas Knight to Daniel A. Powell, August 29, 1962, and James E. Jackson to Howard D. Samuel, August 13, 1962, ibid. Beginning in 1964, a compromise was arranged in which the ACWA Mississippi Joint Board agreed to pay a portion of its dues with the international making up the difference through COPE. See Howard D. Samuel to Al Barkan, December 30, 1964, Folder 202, Powell Collection.

44. Claude Ramsay to Al Barkan, Stanton Smith, Phil Weightman, and Dan Powell, January 2, 1964, 2149/1, Mississippi AFL-CIO Collection.

45. Claude Ramsay to George Meany, February 4, 1964, 2150/1, ibid.

46. Stanton E. Smith to Claude Ramsay, February 10, 1964, and Ramsay to Smith, February 13, 1964, ibid.

47. Mississippi AFL-CIO secretary-treasurer Tom Knight estimated that at its peak the AFL-CIO subsidy accounted for almost one-third of the state council's budget (interview with Tom Knight, May 21, 1991, Jackson, Miss.).

48. Clayborne Carson, *In Struggle: SNCC and the Black Awakening of the 1960s* (Cambridge, Mass.: Harvard University Press, 1981), p. 97. See also the testimony of Wiley Branton in *Hearings before the U.S. Commission on Civil Rights*, Jackson, Miss., February 16–20, 1965, 1:153–76.

49. Walter Pincus, "Discriminating TV in Jackson, Mississippi," *New Republic*, June 5, 1965, pp. 7–8.

50. McElvain, "Claude Ramsay," p. 115; Wyatt Sharp to Federal Communications Commission, April 28, 1964, W. W. Thompson to Claude Ramsay, n.d., and "News Release," April 30, 1964, 2235/8, Mississippi AFL-CIO Collection; "Local Labor Supports WLBT," *Broadcasting*, August 24, 1964, pp. 66–67; Claude Ramsay to Stanton Smith, April 28, 1964, 2235/8, Mississippi AFL-CIO Collection. Ramsay did probably act impetuously, without authorization, in joining the United Church of Christ suit. He claimed that the state council executive committee decided to take some measure against WLBT at a meeting on April 3. According to Ramsay, the church suit occurred while he was preparing these objections. Unfortunately, I have been unable to locate a copy of the minutes from the executive committee's April 3 meeting to verify Ramsay's account, but it is unlikely that events occurred as coincidentally as he recalled. There is some evidence that Ramsay was concerned about right-wing use of the media before the WLBT imbroglio, but it is unlikely that this resulted in any official action by the state council on April 3. If it did, Ramsay would have referred to this decision in defending himself from local unions that accused him of acting in an unauthorized manner. But he never did so. Tom Knight also recalled Ramsay acting without authorization in joining the United Church of Christ suit (interview with Knight).

51. "Executive Committee Minutes," April 29, 1964, 2235/8, Mississippi AFL-CIO Collection. See also *Jackson Daily News*, May 1, 1964.

52. "Before the Federal Communications Commission," May 1964, 2235/9, Mississippi AFL-CIO Collection.

53. Oral History of Claude Ramsay, pp. 117, 121; Mississippi State AFL-CIO 1964 Convention Proceedings, p. 11.

54. Oral History of Claude Ramsay, p. 122.

55. After Ramsay made the AFL-CIO aware of Smith's dire circumstances, the AFL-CIO Civil Rights Department tried to raise money for her from affiliated

unions. Unions were urged to send contributions to the IUD which wired the publisher $1,500 to keep her afloat. See Boris Shiskin to David Sullivan, June 22, 1962, 0001-007, Schnitzler Collection; and James B. Carey to Claude E. Ramsay, June 22, 1962, 2130/8, Mississippi AFL-CIO Collection. The publishing career of Hazel Brannon Smith is also discussed in the Oral History of Claude Ramsay, p. 121; and Hodding Carter III, *The South Strikes Back* (Westport, Conn.: Negro Universities Press, 1959), pp. 148–56.

56. John T. McDaniel to the Federal Communications Commission, April 20, 1964, 2235/8, Mississippi AFL-CIO Collection.

57. Daniel A. Powell to Al Barkan, July 12, 1964, Folder 201, Powell Collection.

58. Oral History of Claude Ramsay, p. 123.

59. McElvain, "Claude Ramsay," p. 119–20.

60. Stan P. Haggerson, "Life and Times of Claude Ramsay," p. 17.

61. Frank A. Millspaugh to Claude Ramsay, October 21, 1965, 2181/8, Mississippi AFL-CIO Collection.

62. John Herling, "Poison in Laurel," *Washington Daily Times*, December 1, 1964. Two days after the attack on Mathews, the local took out a full-page advertisement in the *Laurel Leader-Call* to announce that it would not be intimidated and urged its members to arm themselves. The Mathews incident was precipitated by an order from the Equal Employment Opportunity Commission (EEOC) to desegregate the plant. Blacks could not bid for certain jobs, parts of the plant were segregated, and by prior agreement with the union, black employment was limited to one-third of all workers at Masonite. To comply with the EEOC order, management and local union officials agreed to let blacks apply for supervisory positions from which they had previously been excluded. See Mathews's testimony in *Hearings before the U.S. Commission on Civil Rights*, Jackson, Miss., February 16–20, 1965, 2:186–94.

63. Oral History of Claude Ramsay, pp. 124–25.

64. E. B. Johnson, Jr., to Claude Ramsay, July 25, 1964, Ramsay to Johnson, August 27, 1964, James A. Butler to Thomas Knight, July 7, 1964, and Logan R. Crouch to Knight, n.d., 2131/4, Mississippi AFL-CIO Collection; Claude Ramsay to Stanton E. Smith, July 8, 1964, 2150/1, ibid.

65. *New York Times*, August 4, September 2, 1964.

66. Carson, *In Struggle*, p. 302.

67. Thomas Knight to Al Barkan, August 1, 15, 1964, 2147/4, Mississippi AFL-CIO Collection.

68. Victor Bussie to Honorable Claude Ramsay, September 22, 1964, and Ramsay to Bussie, September 23, 1964, 2131/4, ibid.

69. Rayford Huff to Claude Ramsay, October 15, 1964, ibid.

70. *New York Times*, September 29, 1964; *Clarion-Ledger*, October 27, 1964.

71. J. B. Williams to Thomas Knight, October 3, 1964, 2131/5, Mississippi AFL-CIO Collection.

72. After the election, Ramsay alerted Paperworkers president Paul Philips that "a hell of a situation" had developed in which a right-wing group, Americans for the Preservation of the White Race, had taken over both Paperworkers locals in the Natchez area, that neither local was affiliated with the state council any

longer, and that both would "stay out as long as I am President" (Ramsay to Philips, December 30, 1964, 2131/4, ibid.).

73. Thomas Knight to Al Barkan, December 3, 1964, 2147/4, ibid.

74. See the *Memphis Commercial-Appeal*, July 10, 11, 1963, in Folder 199, Powell Papers.

75. Claude Ramsay to Stanton Smith, December 14, 1964, 2131/5, Mississippi AFL-CIO Collection; Daniel A. Powell to Joe Rourke, December 3, 1964, Folder 202, Powell Collection.

76. Claude Ramsay to Bidwell Adam, September 25, 1964, 2131/4, Mississippi AFL-CIO Collection.

77. Neil McMillen mistakenly claims that the MFDP was the only "discernible group in Mississippi" to support the Johnson-Humphrey ticket in 1964. In fact, the Mississippi AFL-CIO was responsible for whatever campaign occurred on behalf of the national Democratic ticket, although this may not have been discernible because these efforts were rejected by union members. See McMillen, "Development of Civil Rights," p. 170.

78. See Claude Ramsay, "A Memorandum and Summary of the Presidential Election in Mississippi," November 10, 1964, and Ramsay, "Supplement to Summary of Presidential Election," December 4, 1964, Folder 113, Powell Collection.

79. Claude Ramsay to Al Barkan, November 17, 1964, 2131/5, Mississippi AFL-CIO Collection; Ramsay, "A Memorandum and Summary of the Presidential Election"; Ramsay, "Supplement to Summary"; William Simpson, "The Birth of the Mississippi 'Loyalist Democrats' (1965–1968)," *Journal of Mississippi History* (February 1982):27–44.

80. Ray Smithhart to Jim McDevitt, October 16, 1959, Folder 110, Powell Collection.

81. Ray Smithhart to Philip Weightman, June 7, 1960, and Walter Bartkin to A. B. Britton, June 24, 1960, in Box 2, Folder "Mississippi, Local," Weightman Collection.

82. For Ramsay's relationship with Medgar Evers see Oral History of Claude Ramsay, p. 68. Ramsay's friendship with Evers is corroborated in interviews with Tom Knight; Ed King, May 22, 1991, Jackson, Miss.; and a letter to the author from John Salter, May 22, 1991.

83. Ever boastful, Ramsay portrayed himself as an elderly adviser to the participants of Freedom Summer in his oral history, p. 110. Ed King, however, confirms that Ramsay played little or no role in the planning or implementation of Freedom Summer. King recalled that Ramsay had sufficient problems of his own at the time without being part of Freedom Summer and that COFO was difficult enough to manage without including labor as well (King interview). Salter confirmed these impressions in his letter to the author, May 22, 1991.

84. *AFL-CIO News*, September 10, 1966.

85. A copy of the YDCM by-laws can be found in Box 10, Folder 199, Aaron Edd Henry Collection, Special Collections Department, Zenobia Coleman Library, Tougaloo College, Tougaloo, Miss.

86. Claude Ramsay, "Report on the Delta Farm Strike," August 16, 1965, 2132/7, Mississippi AFL-CIO Collection; Hanes Walton, Jr., *Black Political Parties: A Structural and Theoretical Analysis* (Philadelphia: Lippincott, 1971), p. 172. See

also Marion Symington, "Challenge to Mississippi" (B.A. Honors thesis, Harvard University, 1969), p. 67.

87. MFDP supporters harbored much bitterness toward Ramsay. They maligned him as a conservative and an opportunist. Ramsay returned the calumny in an even more vicious manner by red-baiting the MFDP and questioning its patriotism. The relationship was ugly because the MFDP attributed the ascendancy of the NAACP over itself to the support labor provided the NAACP. MFDP sympathizers complained that the Mississippi AFL-CIO "funded NAACP voter registration workers in areas around the state," while the MFDP was confined to the Delta because it lacked the resources to compete statewide. This is wrong on two counts. First, the NAACP benefited far more from VEP largess than it did from the Mississippi AFL-CIO's generosity. VEP director Vernon Jordan was the villain MFDP supporters should have defamed, not Claude Ramsay. Second, this MFDP perspective misconstrues the reason for its failure at the same time it conveniently absolves the MFDP from it. In fact, the NAACP's success over the MFDP is far more attributable to its firmer organizational base and the fact that Mississippi blacks did not find MFDP's radical rhetoric as appealing as white journalists did. For an analysis of the NAACP-MFDP conflict that is very critical of Ramsay see Gary H. Brooks, "Inter- and Intra-Group Conflict in Black Politics: A Case Study of the Mississippi Freedom Democratic Party" (M.A. thesis, Tulane University, 1970), pp. 100–110. See also Leslie Burl McLemore, "The Mississippi Freedom Democratic Party: A Case Study of Grass Roots Politics" (Ph.D. dissertation, University of Massachusetts, 1971), pp. 409–41.

88. For a report on the Kansas City meeting see the syndicated column by Rowland Evans and Robert Novak, "YD Group Rejects Snick Power Play," carried in the *Clarion-Ledger*, April 28, 1965. See also the material on this confusing episode in 2183/5, Mississippi AFL-CIO Collection. On the resolution passed at the YDCA meeting in Kansas City see *Kansas City Star*, April 11, 1965, 2183/6, ibid.

89. Ed King claimed that the quick vote on officers violated an agreement between MFDP and Carter that officers would not be elected until after the recess (King interview).

90. *New Orleans Times-Picayune*, August 15, 1965.

91. See Robert Oswald, "Summary of the Convention of Mississippi held in the Heidelberg Hotel," August 17, 1965, 2183/4, Mississippi AFL-CIO Collection. Another account is found in "COPE Report to Dan Powell from Thomas Knight," August 17, 1965, 2147/4, ibid.; as well as in the *New Orleans Times-Picayune*, August 15, 1965. Symington, "Challenge to Mississippi," pp. 55–65, and Paul Feldman, "Young Democrats' Convention Considers New Role," *New America*, September 30, 1965, also describe the attempt to build a Young Democrats chapter in Mississippi.

92. "COPE Report to Dan Powell from Thomas Knight," September 16, 1965, 2147/4, Mississippi AFL-CIO Collection.

93. *Memphis Commercial-Appeal*, July 19, 1965, 2182/11, ibid. See also *Delta Democrat-Times*, July 18, 1965, and *New York Times*, August 15, 1965.

94. For a similar interpretation of the NAACP and MFDP conflict in Mississippi see Walton, *Black Political Parties*, p. 171. Other interpretations stress political

and class differences that separated the two groups, the NAACP being less radical and more middle class than the MFDP. For instance, see McLemore, "Mississippi Freedom Democratic Party," and John Dittmer, "The Politics of the Mississippi Movement," in Charles W. Eagles, ed., *The Civil Rights Movement in America* (Jackson: University Press of Mississippi, 1986), pp. 65–93. These authors reiterate MFDP rhetoric that its differences with the NAACP were over principles and were not rooted in a competition for power. But the class and political differences these authors posit between the MFDP and NAACP are hard to reconcile with the two organizations' cooperation on various projects and their overlapping membership. For instance, NAACP leaders were among the founders of MFDP, MFDP invited NAACP field secretary Charles Evers to serve on its Executive Committee, MFDP worked for Evers when he ran for Congress in 1968, and the two organizations cooperated on various voter registration organizations and on the challenge at the 1968 Democratic convention in Chicago. These examples of cooperation between the MFDP and NAACP hardly typify organizations separated by irreconcilable class and ideological differences. For a better treatment of these matters see David C. Colby, "The Mississippi Freedom Democratic Party and the Democratization of the Democratic Party, " paper presented at the 1990 American Political Science Association Convention, San Francisco, in the author's possession.

95. Simpson, "Birth of the Mississippi 'Loyalist Democrats,' " p. 29.

96. Newspaper reports on the founding convention appear in the *Tylertown Times*, July 29, 1965, *Clarion-Ledger*, July 19, 1965, and *Memphis Commercial-Appeal*, July 19, 1965, all in 2182/11, Mississippi AFL-CIO Collection.

97. Dan Powell to Joseph Rourke, "Field Activities Report," August 6, 1965, Folder 119, Powell Collection. Reaction from SNCC and MFDP to MDC is found in the *Mobile Press Register* (Mississippi ed.), July 25, 1965, 2182/11, Mississippi AFL-CIO Collection.

98. "Minutes of Meeting of Mississippi Democratic Conference Executive Committee," October 10, 1965, 2183/4, ibid.

99. One exception was that Head Start money for Mississippi was funneled through MDC supporters. See Simpson, "Birth of the Mississippi 'Loyalist Democrats,' " p. 32.

100. Thomas Knight to Dan Powell, January 3, 1966, 2147/4, Mississippi AFL-CIO Collection.

101. *Memphis Commercial-Appeal*, November 25, 1965.

102. Tom Knight to Daniel Powell, "COPE Report January 1–15, 1965," 2147/4; Claude Ramsay to Stanton E. Smith, February 11, May 4, 1965, 2150/1, Mississippi AFL-CIO Collection.

103. Joseph N. De Paola to Stanton E. Smith, June 24, 1965, 2150/1, Mississippi AFL-CIO Collection.

104. Claude Ramsay to Alexander Barkan, November 15, 1965, 2148/9, ibid. For the UAW contribution see Roy L. Reuther to Claude Ramsay, November 24, 1965, 2132/2, ibid.

105. Claude Ramsay to Phil Weightman, March 22, 1966, Folder 114, Powell Collection. The quote is from "Proposal to Organize a Mississippi Voter Registration and Education League" in the same folder.

106. Claude Ramsay to Phil Weightman, April 22, 1966, Folder 114, Powell Collection; Ramsay to Al Barkan, March 22, 1966, 2234/1, Mississippi AFL-CIO Collection.

107. Aaron E. Henry to Friend, April 18, 1966, 2206/11, Mississippi AFL-CIO Collection; *Delta Democrat-Times*, May 20, 1965.

108. For responses from some local unions to Ramsay's association with MVREL see the *Hattiesburg American*, June 16, 1966; see also the *Laurel Leader-Call*, May 31, 1966.

109. Claude Ramsay to Stanton Smith, June 6, 1966, 2150/1, Mississippi AFL-CIO Collection.

110. *Jackson Daily News*, April 5, 1966.

111. Fannie Neal and Earl Davis to Philip Weightman, March 6, 1967, Box 3, Folder "Voter Registration—Mississippi," Weightman Collection.

112. Claude Ramsay to Al Barkan, April 19, 1967, Folder 114, Powell Collection.

113. Symington, "Challenge to Mississippi," p. 71.

114. For instance, see the letter Ramsay received from the president of IBEW Local 1209. After reading a list of groups that supported the Loyal Democrats, this local union officer complained to Ramsay that "at least one of these groups is a little too controversial even for Labor to form a coalition with" (M. A. Evans, Jr., to Claude Ramsay, August 3, 1968, 2182/9, Mississippi AFL-CIO Collection). See also Thomas Knight to Dan Powell, "COPE Progress Report," July 1–31, 1968, 2147/6, ibid., which discusses the Executive Board action on Ramsay's and Knight's participation in the Loyal Democrats.

115. See "Minutes of the District Leadership Steering Committee of the Loyal Democrats of Mississippi," July 15, 1968, which records Ramsay's remarks and votes. This was three weeks after Ramsay notified Aaron Henry that he would not take a position on the steering committee. For Ramsay's notice that he would not sit on the steering committee see Claude Ramsay to Aaron Henry, June 24, 1968. Both of these documents can be found in 2182/9, Mississippi AFL-CIO Collection.

116. For details on the 1968 Mississippi challenge see Simpson, "Birth of the Mississippi 'Loyalist Democrats,'" and Symington, "Challenge to Mississippi," pp. 66–76.

117. McLemore, "Mississippi Freedom Democratic Party," provides the most complete account of the credentials challenge by the Loyal Democrats and of the events leading up to it, pp. 409–86. Ramsay's role in the Loyalist-Regulars conflict is reported in Jan H. Lewis, "Mississippi's Experiment in Biracial Politics, 1960–1973: A Challenge to White Supremacy" (M.A. thesis, Mississippi State University, 1974).

118. Tom Knight to Al Barkan and Joseph Rourke, January 29, 1969, 2147/6, Mississippi AFL-CIO Collection.

119. Silver, *Mississippi*. Silver and Ramsay were familiar with each other. When Congressman John Bell Williams demanded that the University of Mississippi fire Professor Silver for defaming the state, Ramsay countered that the resignation of Williams would be of greater service to Mississippi ("Press Release," November 12, 1963, 2221/9, Mississippi AFL-CIO Collection).

120. *Hearings before the U.S. Commission on Civil Rights*, Jackson, Miss., February 16–20, 1965, 162.

121. Claude Ramsay to Philip Weightman, May 13, 1966, 2234/2, Mississippi AFL-CIO Collection. Tom Knight also suffered harassment and always traveled with a weapon. See Oral History of Thomas Knight, p. 319, Oral History Program of the University of Southern Mississippi, Hattiesburg.

122. Interview with Mae Helen Ramsay, May 22, 1991, Jackson, Miss.

123. Interview with Earl Davis, March 22, 1988, Richmond, Va.

124. Oral History of Claude Ramsay, pp. 8–9. Scholars have noted that black veterans who offered their lives for their country during World War II would not accept being treated like second-class citizens when they returned home. See James C. Cobb, "Federal Farm Policy and Welfare Policy and the Civil Rights Movement in the Mississippi Delta," *Journal of American History* (December 1990): 916. But scholars have not paid much attention to the impact the war had on the racial views of white southerners who fought in it. In addition to Ramsay, Ira Harkey, publisher of the *Chronicle*, who Ramsay defended from racist vigilantes in 1962, attributed his liberal racial views to his experience in World War II. See Harkey, *Smell of Burning Crosses*, pp. 205–7.

125. Interview with Claude Ramsay, December 27, 1985, "Inquiry," WLBT-TV, Channel 3, Jackson, Miss. See also History of Claude Ramsay, p. 49.

126. Dan Powell to Joseph Rourke, April 30, 1969, Folder 226, Powell Collection.

127. Stephen D. Schaffer, "Changing Party Politics in Mississippi," in Robert H. Swansborough and David M. Brodsky, eds., *The South's New Politics: Realignment and Dealignment* (Columbia: University of South Carolina Press, 1988), pp. 189–203.

128. Vindication was not as satisfying for Ramsay as it should have been. At the very moment when a faction loyal to the national Democratic party emerged in Mississippi, the national party no longer reflected the economic concerns of Roosevelt Democrats like Ramsay but the social concerns of middle-class activists. In addition to this disappointment, Ramsay had to suffer the condescension of those on his left. Loyalists who identified with changes occurring in the Democratic party increasingly dismissed Ramsay as a relic, courageous for his time but unable to keep up with it. Ramsay was belittled as one who had made his mark in the struggle for civil rights but had little to offer in the post-civil rights era. Ramsay, of course, returned such condescension with equally vigorous rejoinders, dismissing his left-wing critics as naive idealists who imagined they were in Berkeley and not Mississippi.

129. Al Kehrer, "Comment," in Reed, Hough, and Fink, eds., *Southern Workers and Their Unions*, pp. 138–39. I have taken some literary license with the quotes in Kehrer's text. For a description of the situation in the Pascagoula shipyards, see Oral History of Thomas Knight, pp. 265–70.

CONCLUSION

1. Robert A. Garson, *The Democratic Party and the Politics of Sectionalism, 1941–1948* (Baton Rouge: Louisiana State University Press, 1974), p. 234.

2. Key, *Southern Politics*, p. 340

3. Daniel Powell to Al Barkan, November 18, 1964, Folder 202, Powell Collection.

4. Barkan is quoted in the *Washington Post*, August 21, 1965.

5. Calvin Kytle, "A Long, Dark Night for Georgia?" *Harper's*, November 1948, pp. 55–64, presaged the coming of the Georgia Democratic Party Forum. Kytle wrote, "It is not unlikely that a few of the more aggressive representatives of labor, the Negroes, and the middle class city white folks might make the attempt" to challenge the Georgia Democratic party. "They probably will call themselves Independent Democrats . . . hoping to gain recognition of the national party. . . . At first they would try to work at the community level for basic election reforms; and when they had a following large enough . . . they would offer their own nominees for State office against the regular Democratic machine" (p. 64).

6. Greenberg, *Race and State in Capitalist Development*, pp. 329–330.

7. Claude Ramsay to Stanton Smith, December 14, 1964, 2131/4, Mississippi AFL-CIO Collection.

8. *Southern Courier*, August 28, 1965.

9. Jewish Labor Committee, "Report on Southern Survey," May 10, 1957, Box 1, Folder 2, Via Collection.

10. Emory Via to Ben Segal, May 20, 1957, Box 1, Folder 2, ibid. See also "South's Tension Seizes Labor," *Business Week*, April 14, 1956, pp. 47-50.

11. John E. Drotning, "Race Propaganda: The NLRB's Impact on Employer Subtlety and the Effect of This Propaganda on Voting," *Labor Law Journal* (March 1967): 181.

12. These figures are compiled from the table titled "Estimated Union Memberships" in Bartley, *Rise of Massive Resistance*, p. 311.

13. I compiled these figures from the 1953 and 1966 National Labor Relations Board, *Annual Reports* (Washington, D.C.: U.S. Government Printing Office).

14. Rudolph A. White, "Some Dimensions of Unionism in Mississippi," *Mississippi Business Review* (December 1968): pp. 9–16.

15. Bartley, *Rise of Massive Resistance*, p. 310.

16. "Negroes in South Push to Sign-Up," *Business Week*, November 13, 1965, pp. 59–60.

17. Jewish Labor Committee, "Report on Southern Survey," May 10, 1957, Box 1, Folder 2, Via Collection.

18. For a list of organizing drives that received support from civil rights organizations see E. T. Kehrer to Gene Kelley, July 18, 1969, Southern Area Civil Rights Department, AFL-CIO Collection, Southern Labor Archives, Georgia State University, Atlanta, Ga.

19. Greenberg, *Race and State in Capitalist Development*, p. 354.

20. Kornhauser, "Ideology and Interests," p. 57.

21. Good but conflicting analyses of southern politics since the civil rights movement include Richard Murray and Arnold Vedlitz, "Racial Voting Patterns in the South: An Analysis of Major Elections from 1960 to 1977 in Five Cities," *Annals of the American Academy* (September 1978): 29–39; Huckfeldt and Kohfeld, *Race and the Decline of Class in American Politics*; Bartley and Graham, *Southern Politics and the Second Reconstruction*; Alexander P. Lamis, *The Two Party South* (New York: Oxford University Press, 1984); Chandler Davidson, *Biracial Politics: Conflict and Coalition in the Metropolitan South* (Baton Rouge: Louisiana State University Press 1972); Davidson, *Race and Class in Texas Politics*; Edward G. Carmines and Harold Stanley, "Ideological Realignment in the Contemporary

South: Where Have All the Conservatives Gone?," in Robert P. Steed, Lawrence W. Moreland, and Tod A. Baker, eds., *The Disappearing South: Studies in Regional Change and Continuity* (Tuscaloosa: University of Alabama Press, 1990), pp. 21–33; Black and Black, *Politics and Society in the South*.

22. Huckfeldt and Kohfeld, *Race and the Decline of Class in American Politics*.

23. Thomas Byrne Edsall and Mary D. Edsall, *Chain Reaction: The Impact of Race, Rights, and Taxes on American Politics* (New York: Norton, 1991), p. 11.

24. Jonathon Reider, *Canarsie: The Jews and Italians of Brooklyn against Liberalism* (Cambridge: Harvard University Press, 1985).

25. Edsall and Edsall, *Chain Reaction*, p. 12.

26. The argument that race-specific policies are politically vulnerable and inappropriate and should be replaced by more universal programs that can appeal beyond blacks is found in William Julius Wilson, *The Truly Disadvantaged: The Inner City, the Underclass, and Public Policy* (Chicago: University of Chicago Press, 1987).

27. David J. Garrow, *Bearing the Cross: Martin Luther King, Jr., and the Southern Christian Leadership Conference* (New York: William Morrow, 1986). For an argument that blacks, not labor, are "the invisible mass movement" (to use Michael Harrington's phrase) for social democracy in the United States see my section of Calvin F. Exoo and Alan Draper, "Autonomous Cultures, Autonomous Institutions," in Calvin F. Exoo, ed., *Democracy Upside Down: Public Opinion and Cultural Hegemony in the United States* (New York: Praeger, 1987), pp. 208–24.

28. Gunnar Myrdal, *An American Dilemma: The Negro Problem and Modern Democracy* (New York: Harper & Row, 1944).

Bibliography

ARTICLES

Abramowitz, Jack. "The Negro in the Agrarian Revolt." *Agricultural History* (January 1950): 89–95.

Badger, Tony. "Segregation and the Southern Business Elite." *Journal of American Studies* (1989): 105–9.

Barkin, Solomon. "Operation Dixie: Two Points of View." *Labor History* (Summer 1990): 378–85.

——. "Southern Views of Unions." *Labor Today*, Fall 1962, pp. 31–36.

Barton, Bill. "Turmoil: Time Will Tell If Claude Ramsay's Labors Are Lost." *Mississippi Magazine*, Summer 1965, pp. 30–32.

Black, Earl, and Merle Black. "The Wallace Vote in Alabama: A Multiple Regression Analysis." *Journal of Politics* 35 (1973): 730–37.

Carmines, Edward G., and Harold Stanley. "Ideological Realignment in the Contemporary South: Where Have All the Conservatives Gone?" In Robert P. Steed, Lawrence W. Moreland, and Tod A. Baker, eds., *The Disappearing South: Studies in Regional Change and Continuity*, pp. 21–33. Tuscaloosa: University of Alabama Press, 1990.

Chasan, Will. "American Labor Attacks Its Own Segregation Problem." *Reporter*, May 1, 1958, pp. 27–30.

Cobb, James C. "Federal Farm Policy and Welfare Policy and the Civil Rights Movement in the Mississippi Delta." *Journal of American History* (December 1990): 912–36.

Colburn, Jerry. "Victor Bussie: Louisiana's Lord of Labor." *New Orleans Magazine*, August 1977, pp. 62–67.

Cook, Samuel Du Bois. "The Tragic Myth of Black Power." *New South*, Summer 1966, pp. 58–64.

Critchlow, Donald T. "Communist Unions and Racism: A Comparative Study of the Responses of the United Electrical Radio and Machine Workers and the National Maritime Union to the Black Question during World War II." *Labor History* 17 (Fall 1976): 230–44.

De Vyver, Frank T. "The Present Status of Labor Unions in the South, 1948." *Southern Economic Journal* 16 (July 1949): 1–22.

Dittmer, John. "The Politics of the Mississippi Movement." In Charles W. Eagles, ed., *The Civil Rights Movement in America*, pp. 65–93. Jackson: University Press of Mississippi, 1986.

Drotning, John E. "Race Propaganda: The NLRB's Impact on Employer Subtlety and the Effect of this Propaganda on Voting." *Labor Law Journal* (March 1967): 172–86.

Dwyer, Richard. "Workers' Education, Labor Education, Labor Studies: An Historical Delineation." *Review of Education Research* 47 (Winter 1977): 179–207.

Exoo, Calvin F., and Alan Draper. "Autonomous Cultures, Autonomous Institutions." In Calvin F. Exoo, ed., *Democracy Upside Down: Public Opinion and Cultural Hegemony in the United States*, pp.189–225. New York: Praeger, 1987.

Fairclough, Adam. "State of the Art: Historians and the Civil Rights Movement." *Journal of American Studies* 24 (1990): 387–98.

Feldman, Paul. "Young Democrats' Convention Considers New Role." *New America*, September 30, 1965.

Filiatreau, John. "The White Worker in the South." *Dissent*, Winter 1972, pp. 78–82.

Fleischman, Harry. "Equality and the Unions." *Religion and Labor* 4 (February 1961): 1–8.

——. "Is Labor Color Blind?" *Progressive*, November 1959, pp. 24–28.

——. "Labor and the Civil Rights Revolution: Trade Union Civil Rights for Negroes Proceed Slowly, but AFL-CIO Speeds Progress." *New Leader*, April 18, 1960, pp. 16–20.

Flug, Michael. "Organized Labor and the Civil Rights Movement of the 1960s: The Case of the Maryland Freedom Union." *Labor History* (Summer 1990): 322–46.

Flynt, Wayne. "A Vignette in Southern Labor Politics: The 1936 Mississippi Senatorial Primary." *Mississippi Quarterly* 26 (Winter 1972–73): 89–99.

Foner, Eric. "Politics and Prejudice: The Free Soil Party and the Negro, 1849–1852." *Journal of Negro History* (October 1965): 239–56.

Freyer, Tony A. "Politics and Law in the Little Rock Crisis, 1954–1957." *Arkansas Historical Quarterly* (Autumn 1981): 195–219.

Fuller, Helen. "Southerners and Schools." *New Republic*, January 12, 1959, pp. 9–12.

Golden, Harry. "Sit-ins." *Crisis*, March 1966, pp. 144–47.

Grob, Gerald N. "Organized Labor and the Negro Worker." *Labor History* (Spring 1961): 164–76.

Gross, James A. "Historians and the Literature of the Negro Worker." *Labor History* (Summer 1969): 536–46.

——. "The NAACP and the AFL-CIO: An Overview." *Negro History Bulletin* (December 1962): 111–12.

Guyot, Lawrence, and Mike Thelwell. "The Politics of Necessity and Survival in Mississippi." *Freedomways* (Second Quarter 1966): pp. 120–32.

——. "Toward Independent Political Power." *Freedomways* (Third Quarter 1966): 246–54.

Halpern, Rick. "Interracial Unionism in the Southwest: Fort Worth's Packinghouse Workers, 1937–1954." In Zieger, ed., *Organized Labor in the Twentieth Century South*, pp. 158–82. Knoxville: University of Tennessee Press, 1991.

Hathorn, Billy Burton. "Challenging the Status Quo: Rubel Lex Phillips and the Mississippi Republican Party, 1963–1967." *Journal of Mississippi History* 47:4 (1985): 240–64.

Hill, Herbert. "The AFL-CIO and the Black Worker: Twenty-five Years after the Merger." *Journal of Intergroup Relations* 10 (Spring 1982): 5–79.

——. "Myth-Making as Labor History: Herbert Gutman and the United Mine Workers of America." *International Journal of Politics, Culture and Society* 2 (Winter 1988): 132–200.

——. "Racism within Organized Labor: A Report of Five Years of the AFL-CIO, 1955–1960." *Journal of Negro Education* (Spring1961): 109–18.

Holloway, Harry. "Negro Political Strategy: Coalition or Independent Power Politics?" *Social Science Quarterly* (December 1968): 534–47.

Honey, Michael. "Industrial Unionism and Racial Justice in Memphis." In Robert H. Zieger, ed., *Organized Labor in the Twentieth Century South*, pp. 135–57. Knoxville: University of Tennessee Press, 1991.

——. "Labour Leadership and Civil Rights in the South: A Case Study of the CIO in Memphis, 1935–1955." *Studies in History and Politics* 6 (1986): 97–121.

——. "The Labor Movement and Racism in the South: A Historical Overview." In Marvin J. Berlowitz and Ronald S. Edari, eds., *Racism and the Denial of Human Rights: Beyond Ethnicity*, pp. 77–94. Minneapolis: MEP Publications, 1984.

——. "Labor, the Left, and Civil Rights in the South: Memphis during the CIO Era, 1937–1955." In Judith Joel and Gerald M. Erickson, eds., *Anti-Communism: The Politics of Manipulation*, pp. 57–85. Minneapolis: MEP Publications, 1987.

——. "Operation Dixie: Two Points of View." *Labor History* (Summer 1990): 373–78.

Huntley, Horace. "The Rise and Fall of Mine Mill in Alabama: The Status Quo against Interracial Unionism, 1933–1949." *Journal of the Birmingham Historical Society*, January 1979, pp. 5–13.

Irish, Marian D. "The Proletarian South." *Journal of Politics* 2 (August 1940): 231–58.

Jacobs, Paul. "The Negro Worker Asserts His Rights: A New Militancy Troubles an Old Alliance." *New Republic*, July 23, 1959, pp. 16–21.

Kehrer, Al. "Comment." In Merl E. Reed, Leslie S. Hough, and Gary M. Fink, eds., *Southern Workers and Their Unions, 1880–1975*, pp. 138–39. Westport, Conn.: Greenwood Press, 1981.

Killian, Lewis. "The Role of the White Liberal." *New South*, Winter 1967, pp. 63–67.

Kornhauser, William. "Ideology and Interests: The Determinants of Union Actions." *Journal of Social Issues* 9, no. 2 (1953): 49-60.

Korstad, Robert, and Nelson Lichtenstein. "Opportunities Found and Lost: Radicals and the Early Civil Rights Movement." *Journal of American History* (September 1988): 786–811.

Kytle, Calvin. "A Long, Dark Night for Georgia?" *Harper's*, November 1948, pp. 55–64.

Lawrence, Ken. "The Roots of Class Struggle in the South." *Radical America*, March–April 1975, pp. 15–37.

Levy, Peter B. "The New Left and Labor: The Early Years (1960–1963)." *Labor History* (Summer 1990): 294–321.

"Local Labor Supports WLBT." *Broadcasting*, August 24, 1964, pp. 66–67.

Lord, Guy Paul. "Mississippi Republicanism and the 1960 Presidential Election." *Journal of Mississippi History* 40: 1 (1978): 33–48.

Mabry, William Alexander. "Disfranchisement of the Negro in Mississippi." *Journal of Southern History* 4 (1938): 318–33.

Mandel, Bernard. "Anti-Slavery and the Southern Workers." *Negro History Bulletin* (February 1954): 99–105.

——. "Slavery and the Southern Workers." *Negro History Bulletin* (December 1953): 57–62.

Mann, Arthur. "Gompers and the Irony of Racism." *Antioch Review* (1953): 203–14.

Marshall, F. Ray. "Black Workers and the Unions." *Dissent*, Winter 1972, pp. 295–302.

——. "The Development of Organized Labor." *Monthly Labor Review*, March 1968, pp. 65–73.

——. "Impediments to Labor Union Organization in the South." *Atlantic Quarterly* 59 (1958): 409–18.

——. "Labor in the South." *Antioch Review* (Spring 1961): 80–95.

——. "The Negro and the AFL-CIO." In John H. Bracey, Jr., August Meier, and Elliot Rudwick, *Black Workers and Organized Labor*, pp. 199–227. Belmont, Calif.: Wadsworth, 1970.

——. "Some Factors Influencing the Growth of Unions in the South." In Gerald G. Somers, ed., *Proceedings of the Thirteenth Annual Meeting*, pp. 166–83. St. Louis: Industrial Relations Research Association, 1960.

——. "Union Racial Problems in the South." *Industrial Relations* (May 1962): 117–28.

——. "Unions and the Negro Community." *Industrial and Labor Relations Review* (January 1964): 179–202.

——. "Union Structure and Public Policy: The Control of Union Racial Practices." *Political Science Quarterly* 78 (September 1963): 444–58.

McCain, R. Ray. "Reactions to the United States Supreme Court Segregation Decision of 1954." *Georgia Historical Quarterly* 52 (December 1968): 371–87.

McElvaine, Robert S. "Claude Ramsay, Organized Labor, and the Civil Rights Movement in Mississippi, 1959–1966." In Merl E. Reed, Leslie S. Hough, and Gary M. Fink, eds., *Southern Workers and Their Unions, 1880–1975* pp. 109–37. Westport, Conn.: Greenwood Press, 1981.

McLaurin, Melton A. "The Racial Policies of the Knights of Labor and the Organization of Southern Black Workers." *Labor History* 17 (Spring 1976): 568–85.

McMillen, Neil R. "The Development of Civil Rights, 1956–1970." In Richard Aubrey McLemore, ed., *History of Mississippi*, 2:154–97. Jackson: University and College Press of Mississippi, 1973.

Meyers, Frederic. "The Knights of Labor in the South." *Southern Economic Journal* (April 1940): 479–87.

Mitchell, Broadus. "Labor Unions and Churches." *Christian Century*, November 13, 1946, pp. 1371–73.

Mitchell, George Sinclair. "The Negro in Southern Trade Unionism." *Southern Economic Journal* (January 1936): 26–33.

Morgan, Shubel. "The Negro and the Union: A Dialogue." *American Socialist*, July-August 1958, pp. 37–39.

Mosley, Donald C. "Holt Ross, the Second President of the Mississippi State Federation of Labor." *Journal of Mississippi History* 34 (August 1972): 237–46.

———. "The Labor Union Movement." In Richard Aubrey McLemore, ed., *A History of Mississippi*, 2:250–73. Jackson: University and College Press of Mississippi, 1973.

Muravchik, Emanuel. "Unions and Minority Discrimination." In J.B.S. Hardman and Maurice F. Neufeld, eds., *The House of Labor: Internal Operations of American Unions*, pp. 345–55. New York: Prentice Hall, 1951.

Murray, Hugh. "Change in the South" (Review Essay). *Journal of Ethnic Studies* 16 (1986): 119–36.

Murray, Richard and Arnold Vedlitz. "Racial Voting Patterns in the South: An Analysis of Major Elections from 1960 to 1977 in Five Cities." *Annals of the American Academy*, September 1978, pp. 29–39.

"Negroes in South Push to Sign-Up." *Business Week*, November 13, 1965, pp. 59–60.

Nelson, Bruce. "Class and Race in the Crescent City: The ILWU From San Francisco to New Orleans." In Steven Rosswurm, ed. *The CIO's Left-led Unions*, pp. 19–45. New Brunswick N.J.: Rutgers University Press, 1992.

Norrell, Robert J. "Caste in Steel: Jim Crow Careers in Birmingham, Alabama." *Journal of American History* (December 1986): 669–94.

———. "Labor at the Ballot Box: Alabama Politics from the New Deal to the Dixiecrat Movement." *Journal of Southern History* (May 1991): 201–34.

———. "Labor Trouble: George Wallace and Union Politics in Alabama." In Robert H. Zieger, ed., *Organized Labor in the Twentieth Century South*, pp. 250–72. Knoxville: University of Tennessee Press, 1991.

Olson, James S. "Organized Black Leadership and Industrial Unionism: The Racial Response, 1936–1945." *Labor History* (Summer 1969): 475–86.

Pincus, Walter. "Discriminating TV in Jackson, Mississippi." *New Republic*, June 5, 1965, pp. 7–8.

Pomper, Gerald. "The Southern Free Elector Plan." *Southwestern Social Science Quarterly* 45 (1964): 16–25.

Ray, Victor K. "The Role of the Labor Union." In Leland DuVall, ed., *Arkansas: Colony and State*, pp. 96–104. Little Rock: Rose Publishers, 1973.

Reed, Merl E. "Claude E. Ramsay." In Gary H. Fink, ed., *The Biographical Dictionary of American Labor*, pp. 476–77. Westport, Conn.: Greenwood Press, 1984.

Rehin, George. "Of Marshalls, Myrdals and Kings: Some Recent Books about the Second Reconstruction." *Journal of American Studies* 22 (1988): 87–103.

Rodriguez, Louis J. "Factors Influencing a Southern Central Labor Council: The Thibodaux Central Labor Council, a Case Study." *Louisiana Studies* (Spring 1969): 7–13.

Rony, Vera. "Bogalusa: The Economics of Tragedy." *Dissent*, May-June 1966, pp. 234–43.

Rose, Arnold. "The Influence of a Border City Union on the Race Attitudes of Its Members." *Journal of Social Issues* 9:2 (1953): 20–24.

Rosen, Sumner M. "The CIO Era, 1935–55." In John H. Bracey, August Meier, and Elliot Rudwick, *Black Workers and Organized Labor*, pp. 170–83. Belmont, Calif.: Wadsworth, 1970.

Ross, M. H. "Labor and the South." *Nation*, July 7, 1956, pp. 14–16.

Rustin, Bayard. "The Failure of Black Separatism." *Harper's*, January 1970, pp. 25–34.

Saunders, Robert. "Southern Populists and the Negro, 1893–1895." *Journal of Negro History* (July 1969): 240–60.

Schaffer, Stephen D. "Changing Party Politics in Mississippi." In Robert H. Swansborough and David M. Brodsky, eds., *The South's New Politics: Realignment and Dealignment*, pp. 189–203. Columbia: University of South Carolina Press, 1989.

Segal, Benjamin D. "Racism Stymies Unions in the South." *New Leader*, November 11, 1957, pp. 19–23.

Simpson, William. "The Birth of the Mississippi 'Loyalist Democrats.' " *Journal of Mississippi History*, February 1982: 27–44.

Skates, John Ray Jr. "Fred Sullens and the Growth of Organized Labor." *Southern Quarterly* (Summer 1972): 341–51.

"Southern Tension Seizes Labor." *Business Week*, April 14, 1956, pp. 47–48.

"Staff Training with a Southern Accent." *American Federationist*, September 1965, pp. 19–22.

Therborn, Goran. "The Role of Capital and the Rise of Democracy." *New Left Review*, May–June 1977, pp. 3–43.

Trewitt, Henry L. "Southern Unions and the Integration Issue." *Reporter*, October 4, 1956, pp. 25–28.

Vance, Rupert B. "When Southern Labor Comes of Age." *Monthly Labor Review*, March 1968, pp. 1–4.

Walton, Hanes, Jr. "The Negro in the Early Third Party Movements." *Negro Educational Review* 19 (April–July 1968): 73–82.

Watters, Pat. "Workers, White and Black, in Mississippi." *Dissent*, Winter 1972, pp. 70–77.

Wharton, Vernon L. "The Race Issue in the Overthrow of Reconstruction in Mississippi." *Phylon* (Fourth Quarter 1941): 369–77.

Wheeler, John H. "The Impact of Race Relations on Industrial Relations in the South." *Labor Law Journal* (July 1964): 474–81.

White, Rudolph A. "Some Dimensions of Unionism in Mississippi." *Mississippi Business Review* (December 1968): 9–16.

Widick, B. J., and Irving Howe. "The U.A.W. Fights Race Prejudice." *Commentary* 8 (September 1949): 235–44.

Worthman, Paul B. "Black Workers and Labor Unions in Birmingham, Alabama, 1897–1904." In John Bracey, Jr., August Meier, and Elliot Rudwick, eds., *Black Workers and Organized Labor*, pp. 44–71. Belmont, Calif.: Wadsworth, 1970.

Zander, James W. Vander. "The Klan Revival." *American Journal of Sociology* (March 1960): 456–62.

BOOKS

Alexander, Henry M. *The Little Rock Recall Election*. New Brunswick, N.J.: Eagleton Institute, 1960.

Anderson, Jervis. *A. Philip Randolph: A Biographical Portrait*. New York: Harcourt Brace Jovanovich, 1973.

Bartley, Numan V. *The Rise of Massive Resistance: Race and Politics in the South during the 1950s*. Baton Rouge: Louisiana State University Press, 1969.

Bartley, Numan V., and Hugh D. Graham. *Southern Politics and the Second Reconstruction*. Baltimore: Johns Hopkins Press, 1975.

Bass, Jack, and Walter DeVries. *The Transformation of Southern Politics: Social Change and Political Consequences since 1945*. New York: Basic Books, 1976.

Beifuss, Joan Turner. *At the River I Stand: Memphis, the 1968 Strike, and Martin Luther King*. Brooklyn, N.Y.: Carlson Publishing, 1989.

Berlowitz, Marvin, and Ronald S. Edari, eds. *Racism and the Denial of Human Rights: Beyond Ethnicity*. Minneapolis: MEP Publications, 1984.

Black, Earl, and Merle Black. *Politics and Society in the South*. Cambridge, Mass.: Harvard University Press, 1987.

Black, Merle, and John Shelton Reed, eds. *Perspectives on the American South: An Annual Review of Society, Politics and Culture*. Vol. 1. New York: Gordon and Breach Science Publishers, 1981.

Blossom, Virgil T. *It Has Happened Here*. New York: Harper & Row, 1959.

Bracey, John H., August Meier, and Elliot Rudwick, eds. *Black Workers and Organized Labor*. Belmont, Calif.: Wadsworth, 1970.

Branch, Taylor. *Parting the Waters: America in the King Years, 1954–1963*. New York: Simon & Schuster, 1988.

Campbell, Ernest Q., and Thomas F. Pettigrew. *Christians in Racial Crisis: A Study of Little Rock's Ministry*. Washington, D.C.: Public Affairs Press, 1959.

Carson, Clayborne. *In Struggle: SNCC and the Black Awakening of the 1960s*. Cambridge, Mass.: Harvard University Press, 1981.

Carter, Hodding III. *The South Strikes Back*. Westport, Conn.: Negro Universities Press, 1959.

Cayton, Horace R., and George S. Mitchell. *Black Workers and the New Unions*. Chapel Hill: University of North Carolina Press, 1939.

Davidson, Chandler. *Biracial Politics: Conflict and Coalition in the Metropolitan South*. Baton Rouge: Louisiana State University Press, 1972.

——. *Race and Class in Texas Politics*. Princeton: Princeton University Press, 1990.

Dawley, Alan. *Struggles for Justice: Social Responsibility and the Liberal State*. Cambridge, Mass.: Belknap Press of Harvard University Press, 1991.

Draper, Alan. *A Rope of Sand: The AFL-CIO Committee on Political Education, 1955-67*. New York: Praeger, 1989.

Eagles, Charles, ed. *The Civil Rights Movement in America*. Jackson: University Press of Mississippi, 1986.

Edsall, Thomas Byrne, and Mary D. Edsall. *Chain Reaction: The Impact of Race, Rights, and Taxes on American Politics*. New York: Norton, 1991.

Ely, James W., Jr. *The Crisis of Conservative Virginia: The Byrd Organization and the Politics of Massive Resistance*. Knoxville: University of Tennessee Press, 1976.

Exoo, Calvin F. *Democracy Upside Down: Public Opinion and Cultural Hegemony in the United States*. New York: Praeger, 1987.

Fink, Gary M., ed. *The Biographical Dictionary of American Labor*. Westport, Conn.: Greenwood Press, 1984.

——, ed. *AFL-CIO Executive Council Statements and Reports, 1955–75*. Westport, Conn.: Greenwood Press, 1977.

Foner, Philip. *Organized Labor and the Black Worker, 1619–1973*. New York: International Publishers, 1974.

Frady, Marshall. *Wallace*. New York: World, 1968.

Garrow, David J. *Bearing the Cross: Martin Luther King, Jr., and the Southern Christian Leadership Conference*. New York: William Morrow, 1986.

Garson, Robert A. *The Democratic Party and the Politics of Sectionalism, 1941–1948*. Baton Rouge: Louisiana State University Press, 1974.

Gates, Robbins L. *The Making of Massive Resistance: Virginia's Politics of Public School Desegregation, 1954–1956*. Chapel Hill: University of North Carolina Press, 1962.

Gentile, Thomas. *March on Washington: August 28, 1963*. Washington, D.C.: New Day Publications, 1983.

Goldfield, Michael. *The Decline of Organized Labor in the United States*. Chicago: University of Chicago Press, 1987.

Gould, William B. *Black Workers and White Unions: Job Discrimination in the United States*. Ithaca, N.Y.: Cornell University Press, 1977.

Goulden, Joseph. *Meany*. New York: Atheneum, 1972.

Green, George Norris. *The Establishment in Texas Politics: The Primitive Years, 1938–1957*. Norman: University of Oklahoma Press, 1984.

Greenberg, Stanley B. *Race and State in Capitalist Development: Comparative Perspectives*. New Haven: Yale University Press, 1980.

Griffith, Barbara S. *The Crisis of American Labor: Operation Dixie and the Defeat of the CIO*. Philadelphia: Temple University Press, 1988.

Harkey, Ira B., Jr. *The Smell of Burning Crosses*. Jacksonville, Ill.: Harris-Wolfe, 1967.

Hartz, Louis. *The Liberal Tradition in America: An Interpretation of American Political Thought since the Revolution*. New York: Harcourt, Brace, 1955.

Hill, Herbert. *Black Labor and the American Legal System: Race, Work and the Law*. Madison: University of Wisconsin Press, 1985.

Holloway, Harry. *The Politics of the Southern Negro*. New York: Random House, 1969.

Huckfeldt, R. Robert, and Carol Weitzel Kohfeld. *Race and the Decline of Class in American Politics*. Urbana: University of Illinois Press, 1989.

Jacobson, Julius, ed. *The Negro and the American Labor Movement*. Garden City, N.Y.: Anchor Books, 1968.

Jacoway, Elizabeth, and David R. Colburn, eds. *Southern Businessmen and Desegregation*. Baton Rouge: Louisiana State University Press, 1982.

Joel, Judith, and Gerald M. Erickson, eds. *Anti-Communism: The Politics of Manipulation*. Minneapolis: MEP Publishers, 1987.

Key, V. O. *Southern Politics in State and Nation*. New York: A. Knopf, 1949.

Kluger, Richard. *Simple Justice: The History of Brown vs. Board of Education and Black America's Struggle for Equality*. New York: Vintage Books, 1975.

Kovenock, David M., James W. Prothro, et al., eds. *Explaining the Vote: Presidential Choices in Individual States*. Chapel Hill: Institute for Research in Social Sciences, 1973.

Lamis, Alexander P. *The Two Party South*. New York: Oxford University Press, 1984.

Lewis, Anthony. *Portrait of a Decade: The Second American Revolution*. New York: Random House, 1964.

Lipset, Seymour Martin. *The First New Nation: The United States in Historical and Comparative Perspective*. New York: Norton, 1979.

Lord, Walter. *The Past That Would Not Die*. New York: Harper & Row, 1965.

Lubell, Samuel. *The Future of American Politics*. Garden City, N.Y.: Doubleday, 1956.

McLaurin, Melton Alonzo. *The Knights of Labor in the South*. Westport, Conn.: Greenwood Press, 1978.

McLemore, Richard Aubrey. *A History of Mississippi*, Vol. 2. Jackson: University and College Press of Mississippi, 1973.

McMillen, Neil R. *The Citizens' Councils: Organized Resistance to the Second Reconstruction, 1954–64*. Urbana: University of Illinois Press, 1971.

———. *Dark Journey: Black Mississippians in the Age of Jim Crow*. Urbana: University of Illinois Press, 1989.

Manis, Andrew. *Southern Civil Religions in Conflict*. Athens: University of Georgia Press, 1987.

Marshall, F. Ray. *Labor in the South*. Cambridge, Mass.: Harvard University Press, 1967.

———. *The Negro and Organized Labor*. New York: Wiley, 1965.

Mitchell, H. L. *Mean Things Happening in This Land: The Life and Times of H. L. Mitchell, Co-Founder of the Southern Tenant Farmers Union*. Montclair, N.J.: Allenheld, Osmun, 1979.

Muse, Benjamin. *Virginia's Massive Resistance*. Bloomington: Indiana University Press, 1961.

Myrdal, Gunnar. *An American Dilemma: The Negro Problem and Modern Democracy*. New York: Harper & Row, 1944.

Nunnelley, William A. *Bull Connor*. Tuscaloosa: University of Alabama Press, 1991.

Ogden, Frederic G. *The Poll Tax in the South*. University, Ala.: University of Alabama Press, 1958.

Patterson, James T. *Congressional Conservatism and the New Deal: The Growth of the Conservative Coalition*. Westport, Conn.: Greenwood Press, 1981.

Quadagno, Jill S. *The Transformation of Old Age Security: Class and Politics in the American Welfare State*. Chicago: University of Chicago Press, 1988.

Rachleff, Peter J. *Black Labor in the South: Richmond, Virginia, 1865–1890*. Philadelphia: Temple University Press, 1984.

Ranchino, Jim. *From Faubus to Bumpers: Arkansas Votes*. Arkadelphia: Action Research, 1972.

Reed, Merl E., Leslie S. Hough, and Gary M. Fink, eds. *Southern Workers and Their Unions, 1880–1975*. Westport, Conn.: Greenwood Press, 1981.

Reider, Jonathon. *Canarsie: The Jews and Italians of Brooklyn against Liberalism*. Cambridge, Mass.: Harvard University Press, 1985.

Reimers, David M. *White Protestantism and the Negro*. New York: Oxford University Press, 1965.

Robinson, Archie. *George Meany and His Times*. New York: Simon & Schuster, 1981.

Rosswurm, Steven. *The CIO's Left-Led Unions*. New Brunswick: Rutgers University Press, 1992.

Sarratt, Reed, ed. *The Ordeal of Desegregation: The First Decade*. New York: Harper & Row, 1966.

Silver, James W. *Mississippi: The Closed Society*. New York: Harcourt, Brace and World, 1964.

Smith, Frank E. *Congressman from Mississippi*. New York: Capricorn Books, 1964.

Somers, Gerald G., ed. *Proceedings of the Thirteenth Annual Meeting*. St. Louis: Industrial Relations Research Association, 1960.

Soukup, James R., Clifton McCleskey, and Harry Holloway. *Party and Factional Division in Texas*. Austin: University of Texas Press, 1964.

Steed, Robert P., Lawrence W. Moreland, and Tod A. Baker, eds. *The Disappearing South: Studies in Regional Change and Continuity*. Tuscaloosa: University of Alabama Press, 1990.

Swansborough, Robert H., and David M. Brodsky, eds. *The South's New Politics: Realignment and Dealignment*. Columbia: University of South Carolina Press, 1989.

Taft, Philip. *Organizing Dixie: Alabama Workers in the Industrial Era*. Westport, Conn.: Greenwood Press, 1981.

Walton, Hanes, Jr. *Black Political Parties: A Structural and Theoretical Analysis*. Philadelphia: Lippincott, 1971.

Watson, Denton L. *Lion in the Lobby: Clarence Mitchell, Jr.'s Struggle for the Passage of Civil Rights Laws*. New York: William Morrow, 1990.

Weisbrot, Robert. *Freedom Bound*. New York: Norton, 1990.

Wilhoit, Francis M. *Politics of Massive Resistance*. New York: Braziller, 1973.

Wilkinson, J. Harvie III. *From Brown to Bakke: The Supreme Court and School Integration, 1954–1978*. New York: Oxford University Press, 1979.

Wilson, William Julius. *The Truly Disadvantaged: The Inner City, the Underclass, and Public Policy*. Chicago: University of Chicago Press, 1987.

Zieger, Robert H. *American Workers, American Unions, 1920–1985*. Baltimore: Johns Hopkins University Press, 1986.

——, ed. *Organized Labor in the Twentieth Century South*. Knoxville: University of Tennessee Press, 1991.

UNPUBLISHED MANUSCRIPTS

Adedeji, Moses. "Crossing the Color Line: Three Decades of the United Packinghouse Workers of America's Crusade against Racism in the Trans-Mississippi West, 1936–1968." Ph.D. dissertation, North Texas State University, 1978.

Allred, William Clifton, Jr. "The Southern Regional Council, 1943–1961." M.A. thesis, Emory University, 1963.

Bailer, Lloyd. "The Negro in the Automobile Industry." Ph.D. dissertation, University of Michigan, 1943.

Beasley, Donna Sue. "A History of OCAW Local 4-228 Port Neches, Texas." M.A. thesis, Lamar State College of Technology, 1970.

Boyle, Kevin Gerard. "Politics and Principle: The United Automobile Workers and American Labor-Liberalism, 1948–1968." Ph.D. dissertation, University of Michigan, 1990.

Bracey, John H., Jr., and August Meier. "The NAACP and the Labor Movement, 1910–1964." N.d. In possession of the author.

Brooks, Gary H. "Inter- and Intra-Group Conflict in Black Politics: A Case Study of the Mississippi Freedom Democratic Party." M.A. thesis, Tulane University, 1970.

Colby, David C. "The Mississippi Freedom Democratic Party and the Democratization of the Democratic Party." Paper presented at 1990 American Political Science Association Convention, San Francisco.

Corley, Robert Gaines. "The Quest for Racial Harmony: Race Relations in Birmingham, Alabama, 1947–1963." Ph.D. dissertation, University of Virginia, 1979.

Dunston, Aingred Chislayne. "The Black Struggle for Equality in Winston-Salem, North Carolina, 1947–1977." Ph.D. dissertation, University of North Carolina, 1981.

Gross, James A. "The N.A.A.C.P., the A.F.L.-C.I.O. and the Negro Worker." Ph.D. dissertation, University of Wisconsin, 1962.

Haggerson, Stan P. "The Life and Times of Claude Ramsay, President of the Mississippi AFL-CIO, 1959–86." N.d. In possession of the author.

Honey, Michael. "Labor and Civil Rights in the South: The Industrial Labor Movement and Black Workers in Memphis, 1929–1945." Ph.D. dissertation, Northern Illinois University, 1987.

Kelley, Robin D. G. "Hammer 'n' Hoe: Black Radicalism and the Communist Party in Alabama, 1929–41." Ph.D. dissertation, University of California at Los Angeles, 1987.

Korstad, Robert Rogers. "Daybreak of Freedom: Tobacco Workers and the CIO, Winston-Salem, North Carolina, 1943–1950." Ph.D. dissertation, University of North Carolina, Chapel Hill, 1987.

Kundahl, George G. "Organized Labor in Alabama State Politics." Ph.D. dissertation, University of Alabama, 1967.

Lewis, Jan H. "Mississippi's Experiment in Biracial Politics, 1960–1973: A Challenge to White Supremacy." M.A. thesis, Mississippi State University, 1974.

McLemore, Leslie Burl. "The Mississippi Freedom Democratic Party: A Case Study of Grass Roots Politics." Ph.D. dissertation, University of Massachusetts, 1971.

Nelson, Bruce. "Mobile during World War II: Organized Labor and the Struggle for Black Equality in a 'City That's Been Taken by Storm.' " Paper presented at the Seventh Southern Labor Studies Conference, October 1991, Atlanta.

Payne, John Robert. "A Jesuit Search for Social Justice: The Public Career of Louis J. Twomey, S.J., 1947–1969." Ph.D. dissertation, University of Texas, 1976.

Regensburger, William Edward. "Ground into Our Blood: The Origins of Working Class Consciousness and Organization in Durably Unionized Southern Industries, 1930–1946." Ph.D. dissertation, University of California at Los Angeles, 1987.

Segal, Benjamin. Autobiography. In possession of Elizabeth Segal, Washington, D.C.

Smith, Dennis. "The Southern Worker." Columbia University, n.d. In possession of the author.

Symington, Marion. "Challenge to Mississippi." B.A., Honors thesis, Harvard University, 1969.

"Transcript of Comments by Barney Weeks." Southern Labor Archives, Georgia State University, Atlanta, Ga.

Zander, James Wilfred Vander. "The Southern White Resistance Movement to Integration." Ph.D. dissertation, University of North Carolina, 1957.

ARCHIVES

AFL-CIO Civil Rights Collection. George Meany Memorial Archives, Silver Spring, Md.

AFL-CIO COPE Research Department Collection. George Meany Memorial Archives, Silver Spring, Md.

Alabama AFL-CIO Files. Alabama AFL-CIO, Birmingham, Ala.

Arkansas AFL-CIO Files. Arkansas AFL-CIO, Little Rock, Ark.

Fund for the Republic Collection, Princeton University Library, Princeton, N.J.

Aaron Edd Henry Collection. Special Collections Department, Zenobia Coleman Library, Tougaloo College, Tougaloo, Miss.

Jewish Labor Committee Collection. Robert F. Wagner Labor Archives, New York University, New York, N.Y.

Louisiana AFL-CIO Files. Louisiana AFL-CIO, Baton Rouge, La.

George Meany Collection. George Meany Memorial Archives, Silver Spring, Md.

Mississippi AFL-CIO Collection. Southern Labor Archives, Georgia State University, Atlanta, Ga.

NAACP Collection. Library of Congress, Manuscripts Division, Washington, D.C.

National Institute of Labor Education Collection. Labor-Management Documentation Center, New York State School of Industrial and Labor Relations, Cornell University, Ithaca, N.Y.

North Carolina AFL-CIO Collection. Southern Labor Archives, Georgia State University, Atlanta, Ga.

Daniel Powell Collection. Southern Historical Collection, University of North Carolina Library, University of North Carolina, Chapel Hill, N.C.

A. Philip Randolph Collection. Library of Congress, Manuscripts Division, Washington, D.C.

Bayard Rustin Collection. Library of Congress, Manuscripts Division, Washington, D.C.

William Schnitzler Collection. George Meany Memorial Archives, Silver Spring, Md.

Benjamin Segal's Personal Papers, in possession of Elizabeth Segal, Washington, D.C.

Boris Shiskin Collection. George Meany Memorial Archives, Silver Spring, Md.

Southern Area Civil Rights Department, AFL-CIO Collection. Southern Labor Archives, Georgia State University, Atlanta, Ga.

Southern Regional Council Collection. Atlanta University Library Center, Atlanta University, Atlanta, Ga.

Southern Regional Council Collection. Birmingham Public Library, Birmingham, Ala.

Philip Taft Collection. Special Collections, Birmingham Public Library, Birmingham, Ala.

Texas AFL-CIO Collection. University of Texas at Arlington, Arlington, Texas.

Texas AFL-CIO COPE Collection. University of Texas at Arlington, Arlington, Texas.

L. J. Twomey, S.J. Collection. Special Collections and Archives of the Loyola University Library, Loyola University, New Orleans, La.

Emory Via Collection. Southern Labor Archives, Georgia State University, Atlanta, Ga.

Virginia State AFL-CIO Collection. Southern Labor Archives, Georgia State University, Atlanta, Ga.

Philip Weightman Collection. Robert F. Wagner Labor Archives, Tamiment Library, New York University, New York, N.Y.

NEWSPAPERS

AFL-CIO News
AFL-CIO News and Views
Arkansas Gazette
Arkansas Union Labor Bulletin
Atlanta Constitution
Atlanta Journal
Birmingham News
Birmingham Post
Birmingham Post-Herald
Birmingham World
Chattanooga Free Press
Chattanooga Times
Christian Science Monitor
Clarion-Ledger
Dallas Morning News
Dallas Times-Herald
Delta Democrat-Times
Durham Labor Journal
Hattiesburg American
Houston Post
I.U.D. Digest
Jackson Daily News
Jackson State Times
Journal of Labor
Labor Today
Labor World
Labor's Daily
Laurel Leader-Call
Memphis Commercial-Appeal
Mobile Press Register
New Orleans Times-Picayune
News Hi-Lites

New York Times
Pine Bluff Commercial
St. Louis Post-Dispatch
Southern Courier
Southern School News
Texas Observer
Tuscaloosa News
Union News
Washington Daily Times
Washington Post
Washington Star

ORAL HISTORY COLLECTIONS

Oral History of Ruben Farr. Historical Collection and Labor Archives, Patee Library, Pennsylvania State University, University Park, Pa.

Oral History of Thomas Knight. Oral History Program of the University of Southern Mississippi, Hattiesburg, Miss.

Oral History of Fannie Neal. Oral History Collection, Bentley Library, University of Michigan, Ann Arbor, Mich.

Oral History of Claude Ramsay. Oral History Program of the University of Southern Mississippi, Hattiesburg, Miss.

Oral History of Milton Webster. Oral History Collection, Columbia University, New York, N.Y.

CONVENTION PROCEEDINGS

AFL-CIO Convention Proceedings
Alabama State AFL-CIO Convention Proceedings
Alabama State AFL-CIO COPE Convention Proceedings
Arkansas State AFL-CIO Convention Proceedings
Louisiana State AFL-CIO Convention Proceedings
Mississippi State AFL-CIO Convention Proceedings
Virginia State AFL-CIO Convention Proceedings

INTERVIEWS

Earl Davis, March 22, 1988, Richmond, Va.
E. T. Kehrer, May 10, 1990, Atlanta, Ga.
Ed King, May 22, 1991, Jackson, Miss.
Tom Knight, May 21, 1991, Jackson, Miss.
Emanuel Muravchik, June 28, 1989, New York, N.Y.
Mae Helen Ramsay, May 22, 1991, Jackson, Miss.
Barney Weeks, January 7, 1987, Montgomery, Ala.

GOVERNMENT DOCUMENTS

National Labor Relations Board. *Annual Reports*, Washington, D.C.: U.S. Government Printing Office.

Hearings before the U.S. Commission on Civil Rights. Volumes 1 and 2. Jackson, Miss., 1965.

Index

Carpenters union, 22, 31
Carper, Julian, 48, 183n14
Carter, Hodding, III, 149, 150, 155
Central Arkansas Labor Council, 95–96, 97
Central Civic Forum (Portsmouth, VA), 106
Chaney, James, 143
Chattanooga, Tennessee, reaction to compliance with *Brown* decision in, 21–22
Chattanooga Free Press, 77
Christopher, Paul, 6
Chronicle (Pascagoula newspaper), 132–33, 141
Church in the South, the, 38, 59
Citizens Committee (Norfolk), 105–6
Citizens' Councils, 18, 27, 28, 30, 32, 75, 104; AFL-CIO condemnation of, 20–22, 29; in Arkansas, 51, 54, 59, 185n39; in Mississippi, 126, 133, 145; unions and, 19–27
Civil rights movement: black-labor coalition efforts in the South, 87–106; —, in Arkansas, 92–98; —, in Texas, 98–103; competing visions of union rank-and-file and union leadership, 15–16, 18–19; context in the South of, 13–14; in Mississippi, factional war between groups in, 148–53; political potential of, 167–69; realignment of party system in South; and, 86–106; —, in Arkansas, 92–98; —, black enfranchisement and, 14, 124, 168; —, in Texas, 98–103; results of, 171; sit-ins of 1960, 86–87; as social movement, 5; sources of opposition to, 164; unions' influence on members' attitude toward, 190n71
Clarion-Ledger (newspaper), 123, 139, 144
Clark, Robert, 122
Class, race and, 169–71, 176n39. *See also* Black-labor coalition efforts in the South
Cline, Ralph, 47, 48
Clinton, Tennessee, bombing of integrated high school in (1958), 63

Coleman, James, 133–34
Colmer, William, 128, 197n6
Committee for Voter Registration in Arkansas, 96
Committee to Retain Our Segregated Schools (CROSS) in Arkansas, 58
Committee to Stop This Outrageous Purge (STOP) in Arkansas, 57–58, 59
Communications Workers of America (CWA), 24, 114; Local 3060, 105; Local 3204, 28–29; Local 3507, 144; Local 3511, 144; Local 3902, 87, 110
Communist conspiracy, use of, 47, 184n21
Community Improvement Association, 147
Congress, the South's dominance of, 9, 13
Congress of Racial Equality (CORE), 7, 87, 130–31
Congress of Industrial Organizations (CIO), 12, 39, 64–65
Congress of Parents and Teachers, 50
Connally, John, 102, 103
Connor, Eugene "Bull," 23, 107, 111–12, 113
Continental Can Company, 23
Conventions, desegregation of union, 62–74
Coordinating Council of Greater New Orleans (CCGNO), 88–89
COPE, 26, 54–55, 87–90, 92, 96, 159; Alabama, 107–8; —, convention of 1964, 111–12; area conference in the South (1960), desegregation of, 73; Arkansas, 97; —, convention (1956), 51–52; black voter registration, funding of, 87–90; Little Rock area conference (1963), 135; Mississippi, convention of 1963, 133; screening committee, 134; Texas, 102; Virginia, 44, 105–6
Council of Federated Organizations (COFO), 137, 202n83
Council of Negro Organizations (Texas), 100
Council on Community Affairs (COCA), 96, 97

Woods, Henry, 51–52
Woodson, Robert, 156
Woodworkers union, 164
World War II, impact on veterans, 124,
    206n124

Yarborough, Donald, 102
Young, Charles, 152
Young, Sinway, 90, 105
Young, Whitney, Jr., 4

Young Democratic Clubs of America
    (YDCA), 148–49, 163
Young Democratic Clubs of Mississippi
    (YDCM), 148
Young Democrats of Alabama, 120
Young Democrats of Arkansas, 94–95
Young Democrats of Mississippi, 148–50,
    155

Zon, Mary, 119